MW01068131

International Legal Research in a Global Community

CAROLINA ACADEMIC PRESS
INTERNATIONAL LEGAL RESEARCH SERIES
Mark E. Wojcik, Series Editor

Anthony S. Winer, Mary Ann E. Archer, & Lyonette Louis-Jacques
International Law Legal Research

Paul Kossof
Chinese Legal Research

Heidi Frostestad Kuehl & Megan A. O'Brien
International Legal Research in a Global Community

International Legal Research in a Global Community

Heidi Frostestad Kuehl

Megan A. O'Brien

CAROLINA ACADEMIC PRESS

Durham, North Carolina

Copyright ©2018
Carolina Academic Press
All Rights Reserved

Library of Congress Cataloging-in-Publication Data

Names: Kuehl, Heidi Frostestad, author. | O'Brien, Megan A., author.
Title: International legal research in a global community / Heidi Frostestad
  Kuehl and Megan A. O'Brien.
Description: Durham, North Carolina : Carolina Academic Press, LLC, [2017] |
  Series: International legal research series | Includes bibliographical
  references and index.
Identifiers: LCCN 2017021290 | ISBN 9781611631999 (alk. paper)
Subjects: LCSH: Legal research.
Classification: LCC KZ1234 .K84 2017 | DDC 340.072--dc23
LC record available at https://lccn.loc.gov/2017021290

e-ISBN 978-1-5310-0834-5

CAROLINA ACADEMIC PRESS
700 Kent Street
Durham, North Carolina 27701
Telephone (919) 489-7486
Fax (919) 493-5668
www.cap-press.com

Printed in the United States of America

Contents

Series Note

Most lawyers and law students would benefit from a deeper understanding of international law and how to research it. International law is part of the law of the United States and, indeed, every other legal system in the world. Many cases depend upon rules of international law, even when lawyers do not initially realize that a treaty or a rule of customary international law controls their case. Outside of special seminar courses, the legal research and writing courses in most law schools devote little, if any, time to explaining how researchers should find and use international or comparative law. Bar associations, for the most part, offer few continuing legal education courses on how to research and use international or foreign law. Judges and their law clerks often do not have the resources or training to research international and foreign law, confronting international legal issues for the first time in briefs submitted by the parties. Scholars writing law review articles may lack the confidence to research how international or foreign law impact the subjects of their scholarship. And lawyers working in legislatures or administrative agencies may not realize that many problems confronting them have already been dealt with in foreign or international contexts. Although foreign statutes or international resolutions may not dictate a result in another country, it is at least useful to researchers and policymakers to know what other countries and international bodies have done.

This new book, *International Legal Research in a Global Community*, provides both substantive context and practical tips for legal researchers. The authors are Professors Heidi Frostestad Kuehl (Associate Professor of Law and Director of the David C. Shapiro Memorial Law Library at Northern Illinois University School of Law, and previously the Associate Director for Research and Reference Services and Foreign, Comparative, and International Law at Northwestern University School of Law's Pritzker Legal Research Center in Chicago) and Megan A. O'Brien (the Foreign, Comparative, and International Law Librarian and Adjunct Professor of Law at Marquette University School of Law, and a founding member of the International Legal Research Interest Group of the American Society of International Law). These professors have taught international legal research for many years and worked closely with individual researchers on issues of public and private international law. They have helped students competing in the Philip C. Jessup International Law Moot Court Competition and other international law competitions. And they have assisted lawyers whose cases involve some aspect of international law. Readers of this book are thus the direct beneficiaries of years of experience in researching international, foreign, and comparative law.

International Legal Research in a Global Community is a welcome addition to the International Legal Research Series published by Carolina Academic Press. Books in this series are intended to help attorneys, students, and policymakers find the source materials they need for specific research issues in international, foreign, and comparative law. This book serves that need by providing researchers with the substantive knowledge and practical tips that will enable them to research treaties, customary international law, and other sources of international law.

Mark E. Wojcik
Professor of Law
The John Marshall Law School—Chicago
Series Editor, International Legal Practice Series
Series Editor, International Legal Research Series

Preface—International Legal Research in a Global Community

We embarked on this project to build on existing international legal research texts. We have both taught international legal research over the years and have found students need a foundation in the law to understand why and how to carry out the research. This book offers that foundation as well as a revised approach to handling some of the sources of international law based on the development of the law as explained in the Restatement of the Law (Fourth) Foreign Relations Law of the United States (tentative drafts)[1] and in the 2016 Annual Report of the International Law Commission.[2] We hope the ideas and strategies offered within will prove useful to law students taking an advanced legal research course in international law, or other seminar courses that require writing a paper on issues related to public international law. As well, we trust that those law students involved with the Philip C. Jessup Moot Court Competition will find this book helpful. In addition, we hope that this book will be useful to lawyers practicing in the United States when confronted with an issue that implicates public international law. We have deliberately offered a U.S.-centric approach and recognize the difficulties of gaining true cultural competency in another jurisdiction.

As with any book that attempts to tackle a topic of this breadth, we struggled with the choice of what to include and what to forego. We decided to follow the structure of Article 38 of the Statute of the International Court of Justice

---

1. TENTATIVE DRAFT RESTATEMENT (FOURTH) OF THE FOREIGN RELATIONS LAW OF THE UNITED STATES, TREATIES, § 101 *et seq.* (Mar. 2016).

2. Int'l Law Comm'n, Annual Rep., Sixty-Eighth Session, U.N. Doc. A/71/10, at 99 (2016).

(ICJ)[3] and have provided a chapter for each of its enumerated sources. These sources include: international conventions, international custom, the general principles of law recognized by civilized nations, and, as a subsidiary means, judicial decisions and the teachings of the most highly qualified publicists.[4] Although this book is ordered according to the sources listed in Article 38 of the Statute of the ICJ, we acknowledge that this is not always the best order in which to tackle a research project. Often, it is more productive to consult secondary sources at the outset. For this reason, we invite researchers to consult the chapters in the order that is most useful for their particular research project.

Chapter 1 provides an overview of public international legal research. It includes a definition of public international law; an introduction to the Article 38 sources as well as *jus cogens* norms; the impact of U.N. General Assembly resolutions on the development of international law; and, an introduction to the concept of soft law. Chapter 2 provides in-depth coverage of treaty sources and research strategies for finding them. The U.S. treaty implementation process is explained in detail for the legal researcher. Chapter 2 also includes select research examples to highlight the research strategies in action. These examples illustrate the nuances related to the implementation of public international law at a national level. The third chapter goes further and delves into the difficult concept of researching and locating *travaux préparatoires*. The *travaux* are valuable for resolving any ambiguity in the text of a treaty and also for discerning *opinio juris* when dealing with a customary international law issue.

Chapters 4, 5, and 6 are meant to be read together. Chapter 4 covers customary international law concepts by providing a foundation at a level that is suitable for carrying out legal research. We recognize that there are multivolume sets that provide thorough coverage of customary international law. Admittedly, we have sanded down the rough edges of the substantive law. This was done so that researchers could focus on the legal research strategies. Chapter 4 furthers the existing body of literature on the legal research process because it incorporates strategies consistent with the development of the law articulated by the International Law Commission in its 2016 Annual Report. Chapter 5 covers general principles of law and highlights the difference between general principles of law used as a gap filler and general principles of law that serve as overarching principles governing public international law. Chapters 6 and 7 cover the subsidiary sources of law: the writings of highly

---

3. *See* STATUTE OF THE INTERNATIONAL COURT OF JUSTICE, ARTICLE 38, http://www.icj-cij.org/documents/?p1=4&p2=2#CHAPTER_II [https://perma.cc/FH86-NAXG].

4. *Id.*

qualified publicists and judicial decisions. The use of subsidiary sources as evidence of the law is generally a research approach that is unfamiliar to the U.S. legal researcher. These chapters work together and offer ways to help the researcher understand the unique manner in which these sources are used.

Chapters 8 through 10 comprehensively cover secondary sources, search strategies, and essential research planning. These chapters should be consulted first for those approaching an international legal research project for the first time.

Finally, we included a chapter on cultural competencies to help the legal researcher truly appreciate the challenges faced when tackling public international legal research projects. Chapter 11 might well have appeared at the front of the book as it is necessary for researchers to acknowledge the need to continually evolve their understanding of other cultures, or remain at a disadvantage. Placing it last was a way for us to bookend our effort to stress to the U.S. legal researcher the importance of situating oneself in the international community. By closing our book with a chapter that underscores that we live and work in a global community, we hope to encourage researchers to remain humble and appreciate the challenges of researching and working in worldwide legal systems.

Readers will find that we have included many research tips, strategies, charts, and checklists throughout the chapters. These are meant to help by providing a useful means for remembering complex concepts and sophisticated research strategies. Although international legal research may be overwhelming initially to researchers, we have attempted to distill the main international legal principles and the accompanying strategies for handling the sources of law into manageable portions.

We would like to thank our families, friends, and colleagues for their patience and ongoing support throughout the duration of this project. We would like to also thank the great international legal scholars in the U.S. and abroad who tremendously informed our work. Most especially, we would like to thank Mary Rumsey and Marci Hoffman, whose work and friendship have served as inspiration for this book. We would also like to thank Susan Goard, law librarian at the United Nations, who arranged for us to visit the Dag Hammarskjold Library and attend various training sessions. Special thanks to Susan Trimble at Carolina Academic Press, and Professor Mark Wojcik, of John Marshall Law School, the series editor for Carolina Academic Press' *International Legal Research Series*. Your support and attention to detail have been invaluable.

We would like to thank the David C. Shapiro Memorial Law Librarians and staff (especially Therese A. Clarke Arado who assumed additional duties while Heidi was writing this book and Cheryl Korth who provided proofreading assistance), colleagues on the faculty and in the extremely supportive administration at the Northern Illinois University (NIU) College of Law (especially former Dean Jennifer Rosato Perea, Current Interim Dean Mark Cordes, Associate Dean Marc Falkoff, Tita Kaus, and members of the NIU College of Law writing group who reviewed numerous drafts of this project—namely, Professors Laurel A. Rigertas, Dan S. McConkie, Jr., and Jeff A. Parness). Thanks also to research assistant, Zachary Bock, for thorough editing and research assistance. Heidi also wishes to thank the tremendous and wonderfully skilled law librarians at the Pritzker Legal Research Center who taught her so much about foreign and international law collections and how to be a well-rounded law librarian, especially Kathryn Hensiak Amato, Pegeen Bassett, Irene Berkey, Marcia Lehr, Jim McMasters, Maribel Nash, Audrey Chapuis, Eric Parker, Jamie Sommer, and Eloise Vondruska and the many terrific scholars at the Northwestern Pritzker School of Law who encouraged my research over the years.

We would also like to thank the entire faculty at Marquette University Law School, including Dean Kearney; Ryan Scoville, who read an early draft of the customary international law chapter; and Patricia Cervenka, the former Law Library Director of the Ray & Kay Eckstein Law Library. To the teaching librarians at Marquette Law School—Kathryn Amato, Leslie Behroozi, Deborah Darin, and Elana Olson—Megan wishes to say, my teaching, writing, and thinking is influenced and improved by our collective efforts. Thank you! Sincere thanks to the Marquette library staff whose patience and support were much appreciated. Thank you to law students, Paul A. Miller, for research support on Chapter 4, and Elisabeth Lambert for providing a valuable reader response. Library colleagues who provided helpful editorial support include Martin Kluge, Kayla Kasprzak, Leslie Behroozi, and Deborah Darin. Many thanks to you all.

We could not have completed this undertaking without the loving support and guidance of our families. We would like to thank the family of Heidi Frostestad Kuehl, especially her husband, Robert, and daughter, Grace. Thanks also to her loving parents, Eulyn and Franklin, brothers and family, Eric and Kathy, David and Emily, and supportive mother-in-law and father-in-law, Linda and John, and her uncle Ronald—who recently passed away prior to the publishing of this text but engaged in numerous conversations about the book.

We would also like to thank the family of Megan A. O'Brien, especially her husband, Mike, and her children, Michael Jr., Margaret, John, and Grace. We are grateful to the entire Kendall and O'Brien clans: Walter and Jacquelyn, Jude and Anne, Christopher and Jennifer, Sarah and Craig, Thomas and Sharon,

Jeff and Elaine, Tim and Ann, and Jimmy and Jackie. Special thanks to Megan's father and brother, Walter J. Kendall, III and Christopher C. Kendall, both lawyers, who provided valuable feedback on early drafts of this book. Heartfelt thanks to Sarah Kendall Hughes for unending support, as only a sister can provide.

Heidi Frostestad Kuehl, DeKalb, IL
Megan A. O'Brien, Milwaukee, WI

International Legal Research in a
Global Community

Chapter 1

Public International Legal Research

I. Introduction and Foundation Principles

Public international law has been characterized as a separate discipline with a distinct methodology from U.S law.[1] It follows that public international legal research would require a distinct research methodology. And yet, while the challenges of public international legal research are manifold, most of the legal research strategies that are familiar to the U.S. researcher translate well and can be utilized to research international law. Strategies for researching the sources of public international law that are less familiar to the U.S. researcher will be highlighted in this book, and an explanation of the law suitable to enable the researcher to handle the source of law will be provided.

There are a number of significant challenges that a U.S. legal researcher must account for when handling public international legal research. Some relate to the sources of law and the structure of the international system: There are considerable differences in the value and weight of authority ascribed to the sources of international law; two of the primary sources of law, treaties and custom, are equally positioned in the hierarchy; some of the primary

---

1. Oppenheim viewed international law as a science with a distinct 'method' for approaching legal problems. OPPENHEIM, *The Science of International Law: Its Tasks and Method*, 2 A.J.I.L. 313, 313 (1908). The method, in essence, is a framework for resolving concrete international law issues.

sources of law have no official publication and can only be demonstrated through the use of subsidiary sources of law. There is also no hierarchical structure for international tribunals, often no compulsory jurisdiction, and no formal recognition of the doctrine of stare decisis. Furthermore, the relation and implementation of international law in a national system must be considered.

Other significant challenges relate to the research materials themselves. Individual States collect and publish international law in accordance with their own legal system's language, requirements, and needs. Reliable translations of foreign law are needed in many instances. Abbreviations and citations may follow unfamiliar, foreign law citation manuals. International law sources, available across many jurisdictions, are without a centralized and unified international organizational arrangement, making research by subject and topic more challenging. Growth in the number of new States and intergovernmental organizations results in an ever-expanding body of legal materials—materials that may be found on the national, regional, supranational or international level.

Finally, there are challenges related to the on-going development of international law as a legal system and the complex nature of international relations in the modern era. Technologies related to the internet, transportation, security, and the world economy have contributed to the rapidity with which States communicate, interact, and influence each other. International law is purposefully dynamic, recognizing the tension between sovereign States' national interests and the need for international cooperation and coordination for matters of common concern. It provides a rules-based system within the normative structure of a global community.[2] The fact that a majority of the actors involved on the international stage are raised, educated, and practice law in legal systems that are not based on a common law legal tradition can present further challenges in understanding and interacting with others. Gaining legal and cultural competency in another system takes years of experience and is extraordinarily difficult without spending a considerable amount of time in that foreign jurisdiction.

And yet, despite these many and significant challenges that make public international legal research knotty, most of the research strategies used by U.S. legal researchers are equally effective for public international law sources. This book endeavors to offer the U.S. legal researcher an approach that will help to uncover areas where biases and blind spots exist in researching, understanding, and applying public international law as a result of living, being educated, and practicing law in the United States.

---

2. James Crawford, Brownlie's Principles of Public International Law, at 19 (8th ed. 2012) (hereinafter *Brownlie's Principles*).

II. Definition of Public International Law

Public international law has been defined as a body of rules governing the relations between and among States.[3] Historically, public international law has had its roots in matters related to wartime and the law of the sea.[4] More recently, it has grown to cover a variety of subject areas from contracts to the environment, human rights, labor, patents, and trademark, among others. As a consequence, the definition of international law has grown and expanded to include the law that governs relations not only between States but also among international organizations,[5] private entities[6] and even, at times, individuals.[7] Nevertheless, States are the principal actors on the international stage.

States are considered sovereign in the sense that they control what happens within their borders.[8] Sovereignty implies that States recognize and respect that they cannot compel another State to take a certain action within its own borders.[9] Generally, sovereignty may be equated to nationhood. The nations of the world, if based on membership in the United Nations, total 193.[10] Public international law governs the relations between and among these nations. Rec-

---

3. J.L. BRIERLY, THE LAW OF NATIONS: AN INTRODUCTION TO THE INTERNATIONAL LAW OF PEACE, Humphrey Waldock (7th ed. 2012).

4. For a concise explanation of the historical development of international law *see* Antonio Cassese, INTERNATIONAL LAW at 19–45 (2001) which traces the development of international law through four stages: (1) from 16th century to World War I; (2) from the establishment of the League of Nations to the end of World War II; (3) from the establishment of the United Nations to the end of the cold war (roughly 1989); and, (4) the present period.

5. VIENNA CONVENTION ON THE LAW OF TREATIES BETWEEN STATES AND INTERNATIONAL ORGANIZATIONS OR BETWEEN INTERNATIONAL ORGANIZATIONS, Mar. 21, 1986, 25 I.L.M. 543 (recognizes international organizations as having subject status to enter into treaties).

6. *See, e.g.,* DOCTORS WITHOUT BORDERS CHARTER, http://www.doctorswithoutborders.org/about-us/history-principles/charter, [https://perma.cc/7XV7-4C5G].

7. The Universal Declaration of Human Rights allows individuals to invoke its authority. UNIVERSAL DECLARATION OF HUMAN RIGHTS, G.A. Res. 217A (III), U.N. Doc. A/810 at 71 (1948), http://www.un.org/ga/search/view_doc.asp?symbol=A%2F810+&Submit=Search&Lang=E, [https://permacc/W9VY-J7M5].

8. JULIANE KOKOTT, States, Sovereign Equality, MAX PLANCK ENCYCLOPEDIA OF PUBLIC INTERNATIONAL LAW (2011).

9. *Id.*

10. *Compare* UNITED NATIONS, ABOUT THE UN, http://www.un.org/en/member-states/index.html, [https://perma.cc/UQN6-SAY3], *with* the U.S. DEPARTMENT OF STATE, INDEPENDENT STATES IN THE WORLD, http://www.state.gov/s/inr/rls/4250.htm, [https://perma.cc/L9HW-UJLS] (The U.S. Department of State recognizes 195 States.)

ognizing sovereignty at its core, nations must voluntarily participate in the system of public international law. They do this by participating in membership of international organizations, exercising international efforts or relations, and by entering into international conventions and treaties.[11]

Against this backdrop of relatively recent expansion, public international law must be distinguished from other fields of international law including foreign law, private international law, foreign relations law, supranational law, and transnational or global law.[12] Oftentimes, the term international law or global law is used loosely to encompass all or any of these fields of international law, but it is important for the legal researcher to be clear at the outset of the project which field will be researched because doing so informs the legal researcher's selection and use of the various sources of public international law.

III. Legal Personality: States, International Organizations, and Individuals

Identifying the players or actors involved in any international law dispute allows the legal researcher to more easily determine whether public international law, private international law, or foreign law governs. Where a controversy or dispute involves States as actors, public international law will likely govern. Where a dispute involves private individuals or other legally recognized personalities, such as corporations, private international law will typically apply.[13] Even so, the determination of whether public or private international law governs becomes a preliminary matter of inquiry itself for the legal researcher. Sometimes, identifying the actors involved will reveal both State and non-State actors.[14] For example, in the *Anglo-Iranian Oil Company*

---

11. OPPENHEIM'S INTERNATIONAL LAW, at 13–15 (Jennings & Watts, eds., 9th ed. 1996).

12. The definitions and contours of these fields has been treated elsewhere. *See generally* MARCI HOFFMAN & MARY RUMSEY, INTERNATIONAL AND FOREIGN LEGAL RESEARCH: A COURSEBOOK (2d ed. 2012); ANTHONY S. WINER & MARY ANN E. ARCHER, A BASIC COURSE IN PUBLIC INTERNATIONAL LAW RESEARCH (2005); J. PAUL LOMIO & HENRIK SPANG-HANSSEN, LEGAL RESEARCH METHODS IN THE U.S. AND EUROPE (2008).

13. As States may enter into law-making treaties to resolve conflicts of laws, private international law may implicate public international law. OPPENHEIM'S INTERNATIONAL LAW, *supra* note 11, at 7.

14. RESTATEMENT OF THE LAW (THIRD) THE FOREIGN RELATIONS LAW OF THE UNITED STATES, Pt II, *Persons in International Law*, introductory note (1987) (hereinafter RESTATEMENT (THIRD) FOREIGN RELATIONS).

case, the controversy involved a state, Iran, and a multinational corporation, the Anglo-Iranian Oil Company.[15] In these circumstances, the legal researcher must explore the issues involved to determine whether public or private international law governs.[16]

In addition to the 193 States recognized by the United Nations, other actors on the public international stage include intergovernmental organizations (IGOs) and non-governmental organizations (NGOs). IGOs are established through a treaty-making process where States agree to a charter or other founding documents that give the IGO an international legal personality. Typically, the founding members set forth the mission and function of the IGO in the charter. For example, the United Nations, an IGO, was established after World War II by the U.N. Charter to maintain international peace and security.[17] The International Labour Organization was created at the end of World War I as part of the Treaty of Versailles with an understanding that improving labor conditions would contribute to lasting peace.[18] There are many IGOs, each with differing functions, missions, and membership criteria.[19]

NGOs are usually non-profit organizations that are independent from direct governmental control. Nevertheless, many NGOs receive funding from various governments as well as from corporations and private individuals. Typically, an NGO will have a defined purpose and orientation that informs the types of activities in which it will engage. Examples of international NGOs include Amnesty International,[20] Doctors Without Borders,[21] and the International Committee of the Red Cross.[22]

---

15. Anglo-Iranian Oil Co. (U.K. v. Iran), Judgment, 1952 I.C.J. Rep. 53 (July 22).

16. Public international law governed and the United Kingdom brought the controversy before the ICJ on behalf of the Anglo-Iranian Oil Co., a British national. See 1952 I.C.J. 53, Application Instituting Proceedings at ¶ 9(f) (May 26, 1951).

17. See U.N. CHARTER, June 26, 1945, 59 Stat. 1031, T.S. 993, 3 Bevans 1153, *entered into force* Oct. 24, 1945.

18. See Preamble of the INTERNATIONAL LABOUR ORGANIZATION CONSTITUTION, http://www.ilo.org/dyn/normlex/en/f?p=1000:62:0::NO:62:P62_LIST_ENTRIE_ID:2453907:NO, [https://perma.cc/H3GG-UDBA].

19. THE YEARBOOK OF INTERNATIONAL ORGANIZATIONS compiles a list of 37,000 active IGOs and NGOs. See UNION OF INTERNATIONAL ASSOCIATIONS, OPEN YEARBOOK, http://www.uia.org/ybio/ [https://perma.cc/Q8NC-EM6K].

20. See AMNESTY INTERNATIONAL, https://www.amnesty.org/en/, [https://perma.cc/39SK-SVMZ].

21. See DOCTORS WITHOUT BORDERS CHARTER, *supra* note 6.

22. See INTERNATIONAL COMMITTEE OF THE RED CROSS, "Mandate and mission," https://www.icrc.org/en/who-we-are/mandate, [https://perma.cc/A7ZJ-7VY9].

Additional actors on the public international law stage include: the European Union, a supranational regional institution made up of 28 member States;[23] indigenous peoples; and, federal territorial units (where a State has conferred treaty making power).[24] These legal personalities may have certain rights and obligations under international law. At times, they may enter into treaties, obtain observer status at various conventions,[25] and participate in the development of customary international law to the extent that their actions and intent may be used to demonstrate additional evidence of custom.

Traditionally, individuals were not regarded as legal personalities under international law.[26] An individual had recourse under international law only through diplomatic protection as a national of a State.[27] In other words, an individual's State could make a claim on his or her behalf when injured by another State. Over time, individuals have been granted international legal rights[28] and can be held directly liable under international criminal law.[29] When dealing with human rights violations, a legal researcher must be particularly careful to determine whether public international law or foreign law governs because identifying the actors involved does not fit neatly into the rule of thumb, mentioned earlier, that where individuals seek redress, the controversy likely falls under private international law.

---

23. There are currently five state candidates for membership in the EU as well as two potential candidates. *See* EUROPEAN UNION, ABOUT THE EU, https://europa.eu/european-union/about-eu/countries_en, [https://perma.cc/G87G-X2QR]. The United Kingdom is preparing to leave the EU but currently retains full status. Id.

24. *See* THE OXFORD GUIDE TO TREATIES at 136–137 (Duncan B. Hollis, ed., 2012) for a discussion of how non-self-governing States enter into treaties.

25. The United Nations is considering whether to create a new category for indigenous peoples participation in the United Nations, recognizing that indigenous peoples are not NGOs. See Letter (Second draft dated May 16, 2016) from the President of the General Assembly to all Representatives and Permanent Observers of the U.N., http://www.un.org/pga/70/wp-content/uploads/sites/10/2015/08/16-May_Consultation-process-on-the-rights-of-indigenous-peoples-16-May-2016.pdf, [https://perma.cc/5ZQT-J3PV].

26. RESTATEMENT (THIRD) FOREIGN RELATIONS, *supra* note 14, at §101(1987). *See also,* OPPENHEIM'S INTERNATIONAL LAW, *supra* note 11, at 16.

27. Only states, not individuals, can appear before the International Court of Justice. STATUTE OF THE INTERNATIONAL COURT OF JUSTICE, June 26, 1945, art. 34, 59 Stat. 1031, http://www.icj-cij.org/documents/?p1=4&p2=2, [https://perma.cc/NY98-29PP].

28. *See, e.g.,* The Universal Declaration of Human Rights which allows individuals to invoke its authority. UNIVERSAL DECLARATION OF HUMAN RIGHTS, *supra* note 7, G.A. Res. 217A (III), U.N. Doc. A/810 at 71 (1948).

29. *See, e.g.,* Convention on the Prevention and Punishment of the Crime of Genocide, Dec. 9 1948, S. Exec. Doc. O, 81-1 (1949), 78 U.N.T.S. 277, which creates individual criminal responsibility for the crime of genocide.

IV. Sources of Public International Law

In the United States, all law has its genesis in one of the three branches of government. The law-making process is vertical, from the top down; Congress enacts statutes, agencies of the executive branch promulgate rules and regulations, and the judiciary issues opinions and decisions. On the international stage, the sources of law are generated from the bottom up, by the community of States or other recognized legal personalities who act. Those involved contribute to and experience horizontal rather than vertical law-making.[30]

There is no world constitution, no world legislature, and no hierarchical judicial authority in the sense that U.S. legal researchers understand them on the national level. And, while the United Nations is the largest international governmental organization, its resolutions and declarations are not binding,[31] and should not be likened to legislation. Jurisdiction is not compulsory at the International Court of Justice (ICJ), and decisions are only binding on the parties involved.[32] Moreover, the ICJ does not have an international enforcement mechanism. State compliance rests entirely on a State's willingness to conduct itself in accordance with the ICJ's decision or opinion. Additionally, there is nothing remotely close to an international executive organ. As such, the creation, development, and enforcement of law on the international stage is not akin to the creation, development, and enforcement of U.S. law. Grasping the concept of horizontal law-making is one of the challenges that U.S. legal researchers encounter as they prepare to conduct public international legal research.

Another fundamental difference between U.S. legal research and international legal research is the distinction between a source of law as binding authority and a source of law as a publication that represents or contains that binding authority. The U.S. legal researcher is accustomed to collapsing these two concepts into one, typically searching only for the official publication. For public international legal research, it is vital to keep the distinction between the two clear.[33] When handling public international legal research, source of

---

30. CRAWFORD, *Brownlie's Principles, supra* note 2, at 15–16.

31. Final Report of the Committee on Formation of Customary (General) International Law, INTERNATIONAL LAW ASSOCIATION LONDON CONFERENCE (2000), at 56 and footnote 147.

32. Statute of the ICJ, *supra* note 27, at art. 59, http://www.icj-cij.org/documents/?p1=4&p2=2#CHAPTER_II, [https://perma.cc/2KU7-VNXX].

33. CRAWFORD, *Brownlie's Principles, supra* note 2, at 20. Crawford recognizes that the distinction between the formal source and the publication or material that contains a manifestation of that source is difficult to maintain. Nevertheless, while the legal researcher must resort to using publications and materials that contain a representation of a particu-

law refers only to the method of creation of the legal authority: treaty, custom, and general principle.

A. Article 38 of the Statute of the International Court of Justice

Article 38(1) of the Statute of the ICJ sets forth:

> The Court, whose function is to decide in accordance with international law such disputes as are submitted to it, shall apply:
>> a. international conventions, whether general or particular, establishing rules expressly recognized by the contesting states;
>> b. international custom, as evidence of a general practice accepted as law;
>> c. the general principles of law recognized by civilized nations;
>> d. subject to the provisions of Article 59, judicial decisions and the teachings of the most highly qualified publicists of the various nations, as subsidiary means for the determination of rules of law.[34]

The language of Article 38(1) does not explicitly create a hierarchy of authority. However, for research purposes, it is generally best to proceed in the order listed as treaties tend to create a more specific legal obligation than customary international law or general principles and therefore will ordinarily prevail under the legal maxim *lex specialis derogat legi generali*.[35]

While later chapters are devoted to covering each of these sources of law in greater depth, it must be stressed at the outset for the U.S. legal researcher that subsidiary sources of law are not the equivalent of secondary resources. The concept that a subsidiary source of law may be used to show evidence of custom or general principles is initially confounding for the U.S. legal researcher. Because customary international law develops horizontally by the actions and understandings between and among States, no single publication manifests that law. Rather, subsidiary sources must be used to show evidence of that law, the custom. There is no equivalent on the U.S. domestic front.[36] This use of subsidiary sources of law is another of the fundamental differences between

---

lar law, it is essential to understand that the source of law is the method for creation of treaties, customary international law, and general principles.

34. STATUTE OF THE INTERNATIONAL COURT OF JUSTICE, *supra* note 27, at art. 38(1).

35. CRAWFORD, *Brownlie's Principles*, *supra* note 2, at 22.

36. Customary international law should not be likened to ancient custom as in English law. *See* CRAWFORD, *Brownlie's Principles*, *supra* note 2, at 23.

U.S. domestic research and public international legal research and it is discussed more fully in Chapters 4 through 6.

Because judicial decisions and the teachings of the most highly qualified publicists can be used in this dual capacity, it is best to consider and identify the intended use of them at the outset of the research project. The legal researcher must ask, "Am I consulting this resource to gather background information and understanding on an issue?" Or, "Am I consulting this resource to show evidence of a particular custom or general principle of law?" If the former, then the resource is considered a secondary source. If the latter, it may properly be characterized as a subsidiary source.

In short, subsidiary sources may contain a statement of the rule of law, but may only be used as evidence of that law, and not the law itself. The law itself is either a custom or a general principle. While some may argue this is a distinction without a difference, it benefits the legal researcher to bear this distinction in mind when researching because the use of secondary sources tends to occur earlier in the research process and for a different purpose than the use of subsidiary sources of law. As well, while every subsidiary source may fairly be characterized a secondary source, not every secondary source may be use as a subsidiary source.

B. *Jus Cogens*

Jus cogens is a Latin phrase generally interpreted in English to mean "compelling law." Article 53 of the Vienna Convention on the Law of Treaties (VCLT) recognizes *jus cogens* as a source of public international law that preempts the other five enumerated sources of law.[37] Additionally, according to Article 64 of the VCLT, the emergence of a new peremptory norm will prevail over a treaty in conflict.[38] Therefore, Article 38 of the Statute of the ICJ must be read together with Articles 53 and 64 of the VCLT to gather a complete understanding of the sources of public international law. In public international law, these compelling laws, or peremptory norms, are considered to be so important that states may not derogate from them via treaty or other international convention.[39] Neither the VCLT nor the United Nations has of-

---

37. Vienna Convention on the Law of Treaties, 1155 U.N.T.S. 331, Art. 53 (entered into force Jan. 27, 1980).

38. *Id.*, at Art. 64 (treaty becomes void and terminates).

39. Article 53 of the *Vienna Convention on the Law of Treaties* states that a treaty is void if it conflicts with a peremptory norm. Vienna Convention on the Law of Treaties, *supra* note 37. The United States has signed but not ratified this treaty but generally recog-

fered an authoritative list of *jus cogens*. However, the following examples are widely accepted: prohibition of genocide, prohibition of trade in slavery and the prohibition of the use of force except in self-defense.[40]

C. U.N. General Assembly Resolutions Passed Unanimously or Near Unanimously

The International Law Commission (ILC), which was established by the U.N. General Assembly to study and codify international law, recently concluded that resolutions of international organizations cannot themselves constitute international law or serve as conclusive evidence of a rule of customary international law.[41] Nevertheless, because the ILC acknowledged that such resolutions "do have value in providing evidence of existing or emerging law,"[42] most legal researchers include research into the actions of the various organs of the United Nations (beyond the ICJ). Because every State is recognized and has a vote in the U.N. General Assembly, finding General Assembly resolutions that passed unanimously or near-unanimously serves as an efficient launching point for the research process.

D. Soft Law

The concept of soft law presents another opportunity for further research. While there is little agreement on a precise definition of soft law, it is a concept used to capture the fact that rules have varying degrees of force.[43] Soft law plays a role in the development of international law because it may become binding when it is incorporated explicitly into international conventions or otherwise hardens into customary international law.[44]

---

nizes some of the clauses are customary international law. See U.S. Department of State, http://www.state.gov/s/l/treaty/faqs/70139.htm, [https://perma.cc/VVS8-NVYN] and RESTATEMENT (THIRD) FOREIGN RELATIONS, *supra* note 4, at § 101(1987).

40. CRAWFORD, *Brownlie's Principles, supra* note 2, at 595.

41. Int'l Law Comm'n, Annual Rep., Sixty-Eighth Session, U.N. Doc. A/71/10, at 106 (2016).

42. *Id.*

43. *See generally,* Daniel Thurer, *Soft Law,* MAX PLANCK ENCYCLOPEDIA OF PUBLIC INTERNATIONAL LAW (2009).

44. For example, the Universal Declaration of Human Rights has played a major role in the creation of "hard" law in that it served as a foundation for the International Covenant on Civil and Political Rights and the International Covenant on Economic, Social and Cultural Right. This is the process of 'hardening' into law. Id., at ¶ 11. Another example is the United Nations Environment Programme Guidelines that were subsequently incorporated

From a legal research perspective, soft law may be reflected in: (1) treaties not yet in force; (2) some provisions of international conventions (those that are advisory or aspirational in nature); (3) political declarations made by two or more states; that is, voluntarily observed standards;[45] (4) U.N. General Assembly resolutions, particularly when they are unanimous or near unanimous;[46] (4) in codes of conduct and codes of practice that govern international players;[47] (5) action plans; and (6) final acts of international conferences.[48] Each of these types of sources is discussed in greater detail in the following chapters.

Soft law is typically handled at the end of the research process and only after consulting the sources of law listed in Article 38 of the Statute of the ICJ and considering peremptory norms and General Assembly resolutions. The fact that there is disagreement over the use and value of soft law and, to an extent, General Assembly resolutions, is another of the fundamental differences between public international law and U.S. domestic law. It takes time for the U.S. legal researcher to fully grasp and appreciate that the use of certain sources of law and the weight of authority ascribed to them is not firmly settled. Naturally, such ambiguity allows for creative legal arguments. And certainly, from a research perspective, it presents additional opportunity for research.

V. Conclusion

For thorough and complete public international legal research, six sources of law must be consulted. Researchers should remember that these sources are categorized as either primary sources, subsidiary sources of law, or peremp-

---

into the 1991 ECE Convention on Environmental Impact Assessment in a Transboundary Context, UNEP/GC/DEC/14/25 (1987). See Maki Tanaka, *Lessons from the Protracted Mox Plant Dispute: A Proposed Protocol on Marine Environmental Impact Assessment to the United Nations Convention on the Law of the Sea*, 25 Mich. J. Int'l L. 337 (2004).

45. *See, e.g.*, Rio Declaration on Environment & Development, U.N. Doc. A/CONF.151/26 (vol. I); 31 I.L.M. 874 (1992).

46. *See* Declaration of Legal Principles Governing the Activities of States in the Exploration and Use of Outer Space, U.N. Doc A/RES/18/1962.

47. *See, e.g.*, International Atomic Energy Agency, *Guidelines on Reportable Events, Integrated Planning and Information Exchange in a Transboundary Release of Radioactive Materials*, IAEA/INFCirc/321 (1985).

48. *See, e.g.*, Organization of Security and Co-operation in Europe, The Final Act of the Conference on Security and Cooperation in Europe, Aug. 1, 1975, 14 I.L.M. 1292.

tory norms. The primary sources of public international law include (1) treaties, (2) custom, and (3) general principles. Subsidiary sources include (4) judicial decisions and the (5) writings of highly qualified publicists. Peremptory norms are (6) norms that are so fundamental to the international community that no derogation from them is permitted. In addition, legal researchers should consider the need for researching General Assembly resolutions and soft law, being ever-mindful of the continual development and refinement of the law as it relates to the use of these sources. The research effort should entail systematically working through each of these sources of law. It is best to prepare a research plan at the outset that explicitly describes the process for working with these sources of public international law. The following chapters are devoted to providing a legal research process for handling each of these sources of law, and research plans are covered in Chapter 10.

Chapter 2

Treaty Research and Treaty Implementation

I. Introduction

Article 38(1)(a) of the Statute of the International Court of Justice (ICJ) states that the Court shall apply "international conventions, whether general or particular, establishing rules expressly recognized by the contesting states" as a source of law in reaching decisions.[1] The phrase "international conventions" is often used interchangeably with the word treaty. The *Vienna Convention on the Law of Treaties* of 1969 (*VCLT*) sets forth that a treaty is an "international agreement concluded between States in written form and governed by international law...."[2]

This chapter explores this definition to offer a foundation in treaty law suitable for purposes of carrying out treaty research. It surveys various types of treaty collections. It next describes the treaty-making process so that researchers can confidently handle the research effort. The chapter then explores the need for implementing legislation for certain types of treaties in the United States.

---

1. International Court of Justice, Statute of the Court, Article 38, http://www.icj-cij. org/documents/?p1=4&p2=2#CHAPTER_II [https://perma.cc/7WL4-DN2D].

2. Vienna Convention on the Law of Treaties art. 2(1)(a), May 23, 1969, 1155 U.N.T.S. 331 (hereinafter *VCLT*). The *VCLT* was entered into force in January of 1980. One hundred and fourteen states have currently ratified the treaty. Although the United States has not ratified the treaty, it does recognize that many clauses are a codification of customary international law. RESTATEMENT (THIRD) OF THE FOREIGN RELATIONS LAW OF THE UNITED STATES, pt. III intro. note (AM. LAW INST. 1987).

Detailed examples using treaties that have U.S. implementing legislation are provided to demonstrate the nuances that arise when carrying out treaty research.

A. International Agreements

The phrase "international conventions," as used in Article 38(1)(a) of the Statute of the ICJ, is generally interpreted broadly.[3] It is meant to include not only international conventions but all other international agreements whether designated treaty, protocol, memorandum of understanding, memorandum of agreement, declaration, exchange of notes, accord, act, charter, or covenant, among other instruments.[4] While there are subtle distinctions among these designations,[5] they may fairly be lumped together for purposes of discussing treaty research. In fact, the designation of the document itself is less relevant to classifying it as an international convention than the other three elements of the definition.

It is important for the U.S. legal researcher to understand the breadth of this definition under public international law because treaties are defined more narrowly under U.S. law. Domestically, a treaty is an international agreement that has been subjected to the advice and consent process of the U.S. Senate. Authorized under Article II, Section 2 of the U.S. Constitution, the advice and consent process requires a two-thirds vote of those senators present to concur with ratification of a treaty.[6] U.S. legal researchers must be mindful of the far-reaching definition of treaties under public international law and proactively search beyond Article II treaties.

B. Between States

Treaties may be classified by the number of states involved. Bilateral treaties are concluded between two States whereas multilateral treaties are concluded

---

3. *See* U.N. Treaty Collection Glossary, https://treaties.un.org/Pages/Overview.aspx?path=overview/glossary/page1_en.xml [https://perma.cc/ARS3-AN2F].

4. *Id.*

5. *Id.*

6. U.S. Const. art. II, §2 (U.S. Constitution does not require 2/3rds of the full senate body). It should be noted that proposed amendments to treaties require a simple majority vote, not the 2/3 supermajority. *See* Valerie Heitshusen, CRS Rpt. 7-5700, *Senate Consideration of Treaties,* http://www.senate.gov/CRSpubs/2f870ad4-aadb-4302-ba39-3c375077 881d.pdf (Nov. 10, 2014) [https://perma.cc/FQM7-TCH8].

between three or more States. Over time, the term "States" has expanded to allow treaties to be concluded between "two or more parties possessing legal personality under international law."[7] As explored in Chapter 1, legal personality under public international law can sometimes include intergovernmental organizations (IGOs), nongovernmental organizations (NGOs), corporations, and individuals. While having legal personality under public international law affords some protections, not all legal personalities have the authority to enter into treaties. Only those IGOs that have been granted the authority in their founding documents, or in their constitutional documents, to negotiate and conclude treaties, may do so between States as well as themselves.[8]

The Vienna Convention on the Law of Treaties between States and International Organizations or between International Organizations[9] is an international agreement that is viewed as an extension of the *VCLT*. Article 1 of the Convention indicates it applies to treaties concluded between IGOs and States and between IGOs and other IGOs.[10] With thirty-one of the necessary thirty-five signatures required to enter into force, it serves as its own example of a treaty negotiated between and among States and IGOs.[11]

Taking note of the number of parties to a treaty allows the researcher to begin to assess where and how to find authentic copies of the treaty because each State party will have its official publication of the treaty instrument. It also allows the legal researcher to gauge the complexity of the process of researching the status of the treaty, which is discussed more fully below.

C. In Written Form

While historically there was no explicit requirement that treaties be reduced to writing, today customary international law, as codified in *VCLT*, requires

---

7. J.L. Brierly, The Law of Nations: An Introduction to the International Law of Peace 303 (Humphrey Waldock 6th ed. 1963).

8. For example, the E.U. has the capacity to conclude treaties under Articles 8 and 37 of the Treaty of the European Union and Articles 216–219 of the Treaty of the Functioning of the European Union. *See* EU Treaties, *European Union*, http://europa.eu/european-union/law/treaties_en [https://perma.cc/8559-TUKT].

9. Vienna Convention on the Law of Treaties between States and International Organizations or Between International Organizations, Mar. 21, 1986, 25 I.L.M. 543 (recognizes international organizations as having subject status to enter into treaties).

10. *Id.*, at Art. 1.

11. *Id.*

that treaties be concluded "in written form."[12] Sometimes, a treaty is comprised of more than one written document. Indeed, exchanges of letters, which are often at least two documents, satisfy the definition of treaty.[13]

D. Governed by International Law

With respect to the phrase "governed by international law,"[14] it is only where the parties involved *intend* to create international legal obligations that the documents may be considered treaties. Otherwise, the documents relate to foreign relations and policy. Researchers must distinguish treaties from unilateral declarations and political commitments. Although States may intend to honor them, declarations and political commitments occur without the intent to be bound.

Intent to be bound by international law may be determined by reviewing the terms of the treaty instrument itself. If a controversy exists related to intent to be bound by international law, the ICJ has demonstrated that it is willing to resort to exploring the circumstances surrounding the conclusion of the treaty.[15] Generally, the ICJ will not consider what States say afterwards when making a determination of intent to be bound by international law.[16] However, it will consider a State's actions, particularly those related to registration[17]

---

12. Vienna Convention on the Law of Treaties, 1155 U.N.T.S. 331, Art. 64 (entered into force Jan. 27, 1980).

13. *See,* TREATY HANDBOOK, UNITED NATIONS OFFICE OF LEGAL AFFAIRS E.12.V.1 (2012), https://treaties.un.org/doc/source/publications/THB/English.pdf [https://perma.cc/ NS8N-4JWM] (hereinafter *U.N. Treaty Handbook*).

14. Article 53 of the *Vienna Convention on the Law of Treaties* states that a treaty is void if it conflicts with a peremptory norm. Vienna Convention on the Law of Treaties, 1155 U.N.T.S. 331, Art. 53 (entered into force Jan. 27, 1980). The United States has signed but not ratified this treaty but generally recognizes some of the clauses are customary international law.

15. *See, e.g.,* Aegean Sea Continental Shelf (Greece v. Turk.), Judgment, 1978 I.C.J. Rep. 40 (Dec. 19) (court relied on a Brussels Communique, a joint communique issued by the Greek and Turkish Prime Ministers, and found there was no intent to be bound by international law). *See also* Chapter 3 on researching travaux préparatoires of treaties.

16. *Compare* Aegean Sea Continental Shelf (Greece v. Turkey), Judgment, 1978. I.C.J. Rep. 40 (Dec. 19) (ICJ found no intent to be bound) *with* Maritime Delimitation and Territorial Questions between Qatar and Bahrain (Qatar v. Bahr.), Judgment, 1995, I.C.J. Rep. 6 (Feb. 15) (ICJ found intent to be bound despite Bahrain Foreign Minister's protestations over an agreement to accept ICJ's jurisdiction).

17. *See, e.g.,* UN Glossary, *Treaty Registration,* https://treaties.un.org/pages/overview. aspx?path=overview/glossary/page1_en.xml#registration [https://perma.cc/5NSK-NY7P]. See also, Richard Caddell, *Treaties, Registration and Publication,* MAX PLANCK ENCYCLO-

or non-registration of the treaty document.[18] Although registration itself is not considered determinative of the existence of a treaty, it may be an indicia of intent (at least for the party registering the treaty). The converse also holds true. Simply because a treaty has not been registered does not mean that it is not a treaty. Some States take years to register a treaty.

II. Collections of Treaties

An understanding of the types of treaty collections will help the legal researcher decide where to begin the treaty research project. Treaty collections may be differentiated based on their scope and coverage. They may be general, historical, national, regional, or restricted to a particular subject area. Coverage may be complete, partial, or restricted by a distinguishing feature. Many collections may fairly be labeled a combination of any of these five types of collections, as explored below.

A. General Treaty Collections

General collections of treaties are just that: general. They are not restricted by the subject matter of the treaties included in the collection nor by a region or nation. As such, general treaty collections tend to be fairly large. Examples of general collections include the *United Nations Treaty Series* (1946–current),[19] the *League of Nations Treaty Series* (1920–1946),[20] and the *Consolidated Treaty Series* (1648–1920).[21]

The *United Nations Treaty Series* is currently comprised of 2,871 volumes. The *Series* offers a cumulative index for every fifty volumes.[22] Currently, Index

PEDIA OF PUBLIC INTERNATIONAL LAW (Rüdiger Wolfrum ed., 2008), http://opil.ouplaw. com/home/EPIL [https://perma.cc/79SM-HUTP] (hereinafter MPEPIL).

18. *See* ANTHONY AUST, MODERN TREATY LAW AND PRACTICE 34 (3d ed. 2013).

19. UNITED NATIONS TREATY SERIES, https://treaties.un.org/Pages/AdvanceSearch.aspx? tab=UNTS&clang=_en [https://perma.cc/4NZK-GY3F].

20. League of Nations Treaty Series, https://treaties.un.org/Pages/LONOnline.aspx? clang=_en [https://perma.cc/4ZYS-TR5B].

21. CLIVE PARRY, CONSOLIDATED TREATY SERIES (1989).

22. UNITED NATIONS TREATY SERIES CUMULATIVE INDEX, https://treaties.un.org/pages/ cumulativeindexes.aspx [https://perma.cc/FZJ7-AHRW].

Volume 54 covers *United Nations Treaty Series* volumes 2851–2900.[23] Researchers may view a chronological or alphabetical listing of treaties using the index.

B. Historical Treaty Collections

Historical collections generally span a designated period of time typically defined by world events. For instance, the *League of Nations Treaty Series* collects the treaties created between World War I and World War II.[24] This collection includes treaties between and among members of the League of Nations as well as those between members of the League of Nations and those not part of it. The series is arranged chronologically and contains indexes arranged chronologically and topically.

The *Consolidated Treaty Series* serves as the predecessor collection to the *League of Nations Treaty Series*. It collects treaties from 1648 to 1920, which spans the time frame from the close of the Thirty Years' War with the Peace of Westphalia treaties[25] to the start of the *League of Nations Treaty Series*. This treaty series is arranged chronologically and offers treaties in both English and French, where available. Where translations are not available, summaries are provided. The set includes an index and a guide that offers additional information including dates, titles, parties, place of signature, and other sources for locating the treaty document. This can be useful for the researcher who has some, but not all, of the detail required for purposes of finding or citing the treaty.

While the *League of Nations Treaty Series* and the *Consolidated Treaty Series* are generally consulted first when carrying out historical treaty research, legal researchers should also be aware of the Recueil des Principaux Traites d'Alliance, de Paix (five series between 1760–1943) by G.F. Martens, and the 1964 English translation comprising 129 volumes.[26] Bevans' *United States Treaties*

---

23. *Id.*

24. *See* UNITED NATIONS TREATY COLLECTION, *League of Nations Treaty Series Introduction,* https://treaties.un.org/Pages/Content.aspx?path=DB/LoNOnline/pageIntro_en.xml [https://perma.cc/K8VY-E3PF].

25. *See* Arnos S. Hershey, *History of International Law since the Peace of Westphalia,* 6(1) A.J.I.L. 30–69 (Jan. 1912). Modern public international law has its genesis in the Peace of Westphalia treaties which established a new system of order based on the sovereignty of states and a reluctance to interfere in the domestic business of other States. The treaties of Westphalia are considered to mark the beginning of the modern system of nation-states. *Id.*

26. G.F. MARTENS, MARTEN'S COLLECTION OF TREATIES (1964) is the English translation of G.F. MARTENS, RECUEIL DES PRINCIPAUX TRAITES D'ALLIANCE, DE PAIX (1795).

and Other International Agreements covers roughly the same time frame, from 1776–1949[27] and can be used as an alternative to these other options.

For treaties concluded prior to 1648, there is no single index or collection that may be consulted. Some chronological directories can be found at the beginning of certain national collections. For example, *Chronologisches Verzeichniss der bayerischen Staats-Verträge,* by Carl Maria von Aretin,[28] is an Austrian collection (sometimes classified under Bavaria), written in German, that includes not only the text of the treaties but a chronological directory of the treaties from 1503–1819. There are a handful of general collections for pre-1648 treaties including Dumont's *Corps Universel Diplomatique* which covers 800–1718 in eight volumes;[29] Leonard's *Recueil des Traitez de Paix;*[30] *The Martens' Treaty Series*[31] and Myer's *Manual of Collections of Treaties.*[32] These are considered "unofficial" sources according to *The Bluebook: A Uniform System of Citation.*[33]

Myer's *Manual of Collections of Treaties* is a bibliographic compilation of treaties offered in English and French and includes the text of treaties, as well as collections related to treaties.[34] It is arranged in four parts, with the first three devoted to treaty collections: general collections, collections by state from Abaqua Zoulou to Venezuela, and collections by subject matter. The last part covers International Administration.

For legal researchers who need to view and cite to the official source of the treaty, it must be remembered that, historically, many countries kept the original treaty documents, associated maps, and related papers in national archives. Prior to the 1450s and before the Gutenberg press, copies by hand were

---

27. Charles I. Bevans, *United States Treaties and Other International Agreements (1776–1949),* https://www.loc.gov/law/help/us-treaties/bevans.php [https://perma.cc/M24K-BWFS].

28. *See,* Karl Maria von Aretin, Chronologisches Verzeichniss der bayerischen Staats-Verträge, at 3–100, https://books.google.com/books?id=ILlAAAAAcAAJ&pg=PA401&source=gbs_toc_r&cad=4#v=onepage&q&f=false [https://perma.cc/WC3T-NHBK].

29. Jean Dumont, Corps Universel Diplomatique (1726), https://archive.org/details/corpsuniverseldi03dumo [https://perma.cc/63CN-JN7M].

30. Frederic Leonard, Recueil des Traitez de Paix (1693), https://books.google.com/books/ucm?vid=UCM5317967440&printsec=frontcover#v=onepage&q&f=false [https://perma.cc/K77D-9D8K].

31. *See* Martens, *supra* note 26.

32. Denys Peters Meyers, Manual of collections of treaties: and of collections relating to treaties (1922).

33. Harvard Law Review Association, The Bluebook, A Uniform System of Citation (20th ed., 2016).

34. Meyers, *supra* note 32.

carefully made for official use.[35] Collections of copies of older treaties are found, therefore, by researching national collections of the parties involved in the treaty.[36] Of course, the international legal researcher must have the ability to read not only in the vernacular but also in the anachronistic language and script of the original documents in order to use older treaty documents in these collections.

Publications that contain copies of these original treaties tend to be offered in chronological order which makes having a date or a date range essential when beginning the research process. Examples include the *Acta Regia*, a collection of English treaties that begins with the reign of Queen Elizabeth I (1558–1603) and ends with the death of King James I (1603–1625),[37] and Traités Publics de la Royale Maison de Savoie,[38] an eight volume collection of French treaties with coverage beginning in 1559.[39] For historical treaties related to the early Americas, *European Treaties bearing on the History of the United States and its Dependencies* covers 1445–1648.[40]

C. National Treaty Collections

National collections have grown in recent years, with an increasing number of governments placing their national treaty collections online. The official publication for the United States national treaty collection is *United States Treaties and Other International Agreements* (UST). It has been published by the Department of State since 1950.[41] In pamphlet format, the treaties are avail-

---

35. STEPHAN FUSSE, GUTENBERG AND THE IMPACT OF PRINTING (2005) (translated from German to English by Douglas Martin).

36. *See, e.g.*, UNITED KINGDOM NATIONAL ARCHIVES, *State Papers Foreign 1509–1782*, http://www.nationalarchives.gov.uk/help-with-your-research/research-guides/state-papers-foreign-1509-1782/ [https://perma.cc/FD68-MG7P].

37. M. RAPIN DE THOYRAS, ACTA REGIA (1558–1625). https://books.google.com/books?id=H7xXAAAAYAAJ&pg=PA3&lpg=PA3&dq=acta+regia+1558&source=bl&ots=DGgOKAICX7&sig=8JMVZ68JHdoyTgSEBgstd-odbi0&hl=en&sa=X&ved=0ahUKEwjCtNOBuffQAhVowlQKHcfmCnsQ6AEIIDAB#v=onepage&q=acta%20regia%201558&f=false [https://perma.cc/B464-8VBD].

38. TRAITÉS PUBLICS DE LA ROYALE MAISON DE SAVOIE, http://gallica.bnf.fr/ark:/12148/bpt6k93775c [https://perma.cc/BV62-L2VD].

39. *Id.*

40. EUROPEAN TREATIES BEARING ON THE HISTORY OF THE UNITED STATES AND ITS DEPENDENCIES (Frances Gardiner Davenport ed., Carnegie Inst. of Wash. 1917) (available on HeinOnline).

41. *United States Treaties and Other International Agreements*, U.S. DEP'T OF STATE (1950–1982). Prior to 1950 the publication of treaties was included in the *U.S. Statutes at Large*. GPO, STATUTES AT LARGE.

able in *Treaties and Other International Acts Series* (TIAS) since 1945.[42] As the slip format of publication, TIAS are available years before publication of UST. The U.S. Department of State is currently placing the TIAS online and offers those from 1996 forward.[43] While TIAS is the first official U.S. publication, prior to publication as TIAS, the text of treaties submitted to Congress in accordance with the Case Zablocki Act,[44] are available on the Department of State Treaty Affairs website.[45]

Finding other national collections involves consulting a legal research guide for that foreign jurisdiction to obtain the title to the official publication for that State's treaties.[46] A Worldcat[47] search will reveal which libraries hold the publications. Online, it involves identifying the Department of State or the relevant Foreign Ministry website to determine whether it offers a treaty collection listing or database.

D. Regional Treaty Collections

Regional treaty collections include treaties based on geographic region. Regional IGOs have websites that offer treaty collections. For example, the European Union,[48] the African Union,[49] and the Organization of American States[50] all have treaty collections. Some of these regional collections contain treaties that are also available in the general treaty collections. Researchers will find the *Treaty of Nice* in both the *Official Journal of the European Union* and the

---

42. *Id.*

43. *Texts of International Agreements to which the US is a Party (TIAS)*, U.S. Dep't of State, http://www.state.gov/s/l/treaty/tias/index.htm [https://perma.cc/6LNX-UB5X].

44. Case-Zablocki Act of 1972, 1 U.S.C. §§ 112a–112b (1972). It should be remembered that there are considerably more international agreements that are not submitted to Congress in accordance with the advice and consent process, as discussed earlier in the chapter and Chapter 1.

45. U.S. Department of State, *Treaty Affairs*, http://www.state.gov/s/l/treaty/tias/index. htm [https://perma.cc/VQE6-R8ZK]. *See also* U.S. Department of State, *Finding Agreements*, http://www.state.gov/s/l/treaty/text/index.htm [https://perma.cc/G8LB-LYFV].

46. *See, e.g.*, Law Library of Congress, Guide to Law Online—Nations of the World, https://www.loc.gov/law/help/guide/nations.php [https://perma.cc/FJN2-CPEH].

47. See http://www.worldcat.org/ [https://perma.cc/B3MF-HP66].

48. *EU Treaties*, E.U., http://europa.eu/european-union/law/treaties_en [https://perma. cc/8559-TUKT].

49. *OAU/AU Treaties, Conventions, Protocols & Charters*, O.A.U., http://www.au.int/en/ treaties [https://perma.cc/CYZ5-E7GD].

50. *Treaties and Agreements*, OAS, http://www.oas.org/en/topics/treaties_agreements. asp [https://perma.cc/CZ59-3VJX].

United Nations Treaty Series.[51] Similarly, the Organization of African Unity Convention for the Elimination of Mercenarism in Africa is available through the *Organization of African Unity/African Unity Treaties, Conventions, Protocols & Charters* collection as well as the *United Nations Treaty Series.*[52]

Additionally, the States that are parties to these regional treaties often offer the text of the treaty in their own national publications and/or databases. Experienced researchers are aware of their options for uncovering the text of the treaty and understand why one is preferable over another in any particular circumstance. Usually, this decision rests on citation requirements for a national or international tribunal, information related to updating the treaty, or simply whether it is readily available through a home institution's library.

E. Subject Treaty Collections

Subject collections of treaties tend to be related to commercial areas of law where users are willing to pay for translations and publications or international organizations that have the funding are willing to compile databases for their constituency. Examples of IGOs that offer subject treaty collections include the World Intellectual Property Organization's (WIPO) intellectual property treaty database and the International Labour Organization's collection of treaties related to labor laws offered through NATLEX.[53] Similarly, non-governmental organizations will sometimes compile and offer subject collections of treaties. For instance, the International Committee of the Red Cross offers a treaty collection related to International Humanitarian Law.[54] Finally, independent publishers are willing to publish treaty sets that they believe will return a profit. *Tax Treaties of All Nations*, originally published by Oceana, was recently purchased by Oxford University Press, both independent publishers.

---

51. *See, e.g.,* The Treaty of Nice, Feb. 26, 2001, 2001 O.J. (C 80) 1 and Treaty of Nice, Feb. 1, 2003, 2701 U.N.T.S. 3.

52. *See, e.g.,* Organization of African Unity Convention for the Elimination of Mercenarism in Africa, July 3, 1977, 1490 U.N.T.S. 89 and https://au.int/en/treaties/convention-elimination-mercenarism-africa [https://permacc.Z9DA-PMQE].

53. *See, e.g.,* International Labour Organization, NATLEX, http://www.ilo.org/dyn/natlex/natlex4.home?p_lang=en [https://perma.cc/5KFB-AGH6].

54. *Treaties, States Parties and Commentaries,* ICRC, https://ihl-databases.icrc.org/ihl [https://perma.cc/U3VS-E43R].

F. Combination Treaty Collections

While it is often productive for legal researchers to consider which type of collection may contain a particular treaty (subject, regional, national, historical, or general), it should be remembered that some collections may be fairly categorized as a combination of these types of collections.

An example of a national-historical collection is *Bevans' Treaties and Other International Agreements of the US, 1776–1949*.[55] This collection is classified as national because it contains only treaties to which the United States is a party. Similar to the other historical collections spanning significant historical events, this collection spans United States national events from the date of independence from England through the 1950s. An example of a historical-regional collection is the *European Treaty Series*, which is the predecessor to the *Council of Europe Treaty Series*. Regionally restricted to treaties involving the countries of Europe, the European Treaty Series contains treaties from 1949 through 2016.[56]

Understanding how the treaty collections are grouped helps the legal researcher to identify an appropriate collection or database in which to search for the treaty. Sometimes, the legal researcher will resort to checking more than one collection to obtain all the relevant pieces of information related to the research project.

III. Treaty Research Process

A. Find an Authoritative Text

Bearing in mind the types of collections described above, the international legal researcher must embark on a mission to find the official text and, at times, an authoritative translation of the text of a treaty, if it is not produced in English as an official language. Traditionally, this was handled by using an index. Today, with the strength of search engines with sophisticated algorithms and the availability of treaties online,[57] it is efficient to make a quick pass at locating the text of the treaty online before resorting to an index, whether in print or online.

---

55. Bevans, *supra* note 27.

56. *European Treaty Series*, Council of Europe, http://www.coe.int/en/web/conventions/full-list [https://perma.cc/N7DT-9TG2] (date range is based on 'open for signature" dates).

57. Often, States post current treaties in-force on the state department or foreign ministry website. *See, e.g.*, Ministry of Foreign Affairs, France, http://www.diplomatie.gouv.fr/

If the title to the treaty is known, a simple search including the title should reveal whether the text is immediately available online. Initially, researchers should not enclose the title in quotation marks and not include words such as *for* and *of* in the title. Excluding these words from the search query saves key strokes and has little to no impact on the results set when the legal researcher is using a general search engine, such as Google, due to the power of its relevancy ranking algorithm. For example, a legal researcher might search using the terms *convention, rights, persons,* and *disabilities* to obtain the Convention on the Rights of Persons with Disabilities. However, after the official title is discovered and verified it may then be used with quotations to narrow a results list within a particular treaty database (for instance on the depositary institution's website).

Carrying out an online search will often result in a list of websites that offer the text of the treaty. While ultimately the legal researcher should aim to find the text from the depositary institution website, perusing the text from a different website will usually yield important facts and details related to the treaty (such as entry into force dates, parties, and the designated depositary) to progress toward identifying and locating the depositary website. Specific strategies for finding and identifying the depositary institution are included in the next section.

Typically, the legal researcher needs a version of the treaty from the official source designated by a citation manual from within their jurisdiction. For the U.S. legal researcher, this is usually *The Bluebook, A Uniform System of Citation.*[58] Generally, this citation manual requires the researcher to cite to U.S. publications for treaties. It is for this reason that the U.S. legal researcher should determine at the outset, if possible, if the United States is a party to the agreement. If it is, then the agreement will be included in U.S. official publications. If it is not, then the legal researcher will adhere to the alternative options outlined in *The Bluebook.* As a default approach, the legal researcher should always set out to find the depositary institution website because that is where the most comprehensive information related to the current status of the treaty will be offered.

If an online search using the title to the treaty does not uncover the treaty text, the legal researcher must then consider whether a certain collection of treaties may contain the treaty document. This process requires two steps: de-

---

en/ [https://perma.cc/5FTJ-L95R]. Additionally, older treaties published within books which are out of copyright are generally available through Hathitrust. *See* Hathitrust Digital Library, https://www.hathitrust.org/ [https://perma.cc/77N6-HQMQ]. Many IGOs and NGOs offer the text of treaties online. *See, e.g.,* ICRC, International Humanitarian Law Database, https://ihl-databases.icrc.org/ihl [https://perma.cc/U3VS-E43R].

58. The Bluebook, *supra* note 33.

termining which website offers a database that may contain the treaty, and then navigating to that website to search within the treaty database to obtain the treaty text. Including "treaty" together with key words related to the region or subject matter plus "database" or "collection" or "series," when using a general search engine, will allow the legal researcher to obtain a results set that includes websites that offer a collection of treaties. For example, the search query *treaty database intellectual property* will offer a result set that includes the World Intellectual Property Organization's treaty database. Searching for the types of websites that may contain the information that is sought rather than searching for the document itself is sometimes more efficient and productive. Certainly, it is a useful tactic for the legal researcher to consider when initial attempts to find the information are unproductive.

i. Find Authoritative Texts and Subsequent and Related Treaty Actions

Legal researchers should remember that treaties are sometimes comprised of more than one document. Reading the text of the treaty itself or consulting secondary sources will reveal to the researcher whether more than one document must be uncovered. In Chapter 1 the term protocol was presented as satisfying the definition of treaty. Even so, documents designated "protocol" should alert the researcher of the need to find not only the protocol but also the underlying and related treaty document so that the two documents may be read together. The *United Nations Treaty Handbook* offers a succinct description of the various types of protocols and how they relate to the main treaty document.[59]

One strategy for finding related documents is to use the United Nations Multilateral Treaties Deposited with the Secretary-General (MTDSG) database which offers a listing of treaties by topic and includes all related treaty documents directly below the original treaty. The chapters of the MTDSG offer the main treaty document listed by number (1, 2, 3, …). Any subsequent actions related to that main treaty document are listed by a letter (a, b, c, …). For instance, the International Convention on the Elimination of All Forms of Discrimination is listed as document number 2 in chapter IV: Human Rights of the MTDSG. Directly below it, listed as 2A, is the Amendment to Article 8 of the International Convention on the Elimination of All Forms of Discrimination. Viewing the MTDSG chapters' page allows the legal researcher to gain confidence that all related treaties have been uncovered.

---

59. U.N. TREATY HANDBOOK, *supra* note 13, at 69.

There are two alternative strategies for finding subsequent or related treaty instruments. First, researchers may use a trusted research guide based on subject matter to uncover all treaties related to a particular subject area of public international law. For example, if a legal researcher was interested in international refugee law, a good research guide would offer a list of all relevant treaties related to refugees. For instance, the United Nations High Commissioner on Refugees publishes a Guide to Refugee Law.[60] This guide includes the following treaties that comprise the framework for Refugee Law: 1951 Convention relating to the Status of Refugees, 1967 Protocol Relating to the Status of Refugees, 1969 Organization of African Unity Convention Governing the Specific Aspects of Refugee Problems in Africa, the Cartagena Declaration, and the 1967 Declaration on Territorial Asylum (a United Nations General Assembly Resolution).[61]

Using a research guide from an IGO, an NGO, an academic institution, or another expert author to obtain the titles and dates related to treaty research is usually a productive first step in the treaty research process. The legal researcher would then use the information from the research guide to find an official text of the treaty instruments from the depositary. It is essential for the researcher to gather a sense of the treaty itself and subsequent actions related to that treaty as well as other treaties that operate in the same subject area to obtain a framework within which to operate.

The other strategy for finding related treaty actions is to use the United Nations Treaty Series indexes.[62] The chronological indexes set forth subsequent actions related to every treaty. For both bilateral and multilateral treaties, the subsequent actions are listed under the original treaty document entry. If the subsequent instrument (the one changing the status of the original instrument) appears for the first time in the most recent cumulative index, it will be reported under its date with a reference to the earlier index volume that contains the related original treaty. If there is more than one subsequent action in the most recent cumulative index volumes, the second or later action will appear under the earliest instrument listed in that same index volume.

For the researcher who is interested in all treaties on a related subject matter (as opposed to all treaties that are a subsequent action to an original treaty),

---

60. Kate Jastram & Marilyn Achiron, Refugee Protection: A Guide to International Refugee Law, UNHCR (2001), https://treaties.un.org/Pages/Overview.aspx?path=overview/glossary/page1_en.xml [https://perma.cc/QKT3-LJ5Z].

61. *Id.*

62. See *supra* note 22.

the alphabetical index must be consulted.[63] The legal researcher must find the treaty instrument by subject using this version of the index. Under the treaty instrument, the legal researcher will find *see* and *see also* references that will direct the researcher to other treaties identified as being in the same or closely related subject area.

By using both the chronological index and the alphabetical index for the United Nations Treaty Series, the legal researcher can be sure to carry out comprehensive research for treaties deposited at the United Nations. This same general approach should be utilized for treaties deposited elsewhere, though the practical steps may be slightly different depending on the availability of indexes and finding aids for other collections.

ii. Use Comprehensive Treaty Indexes to Find Authoritative Texts

While many treaty publications include an index and other finding aids within the volumes to cover that individual collection of treaties, there are also standalone treaty indexes that compile details related to treaties collected from across collections or publications. Rohn's *World Treaty Index* is the most comprehensive index. It is currently available online.[64] Mostecky's *Index to Multilateral Treaties: a Chronological List of Multipartite International Agreements from the Sixteenth Century through 1963*, which is based on Harvard Law School's treaty collection, is another valuable general index. Bowman & Harris' *Multilateral Treaties: Index and Current Status* is a comprehensive index that includes: treaty adoption date, entry into force date, duration, parties, and subject summary.[65] Additionally, the online *Flare Index to Treaties* offers multilateral treaties from 1353 to present and bilateral treaties from 1353–1815[66] and collected much of its original information from the print Bowman & Harris indexes. Gradually, it has expanded its database with selections from *International Legal Materials, Index to British Treaties*, Mostecky's *Index to Multilateral Treaties*, and the *Catalog of Treaties*.

---

63. *Id.*

64. *See World Treaty Index,* http://worldtreatyindex.com/ [https://perma.cc/FA3X-QDW4]. For additional information on the development of the *World Treaty Index* see GLENDA PEARSON, *Rohn's World Treaty Index: Its Past and Future,* 29 INT'L J. OF LEGAL INFO. 543 (2001).

65. M.J. BOWMAN AND D.J. HARRIS, eds., *Multilateral Treaties: Index and Current Status* (1984).

66. *See FLARE,* http://193.62.18.232/dbtw-wpd/textbase/treatysearch.htm [https://perma.cc/2EDE-QS2D].

The comprehensive national treaties index in the U.S. is *Treaties in Force* (TIF). This index is published by the Department of State and is available to download in PDF format from its website.[67] TIF is organized into a bilateral treaties section and a multilateral treaties section. The bilateral section lists the States with which the U.S. entered into an agreement, with subentries based on subject. The multilateral section is arranged by States and by subjects as main entries. TIF also includes entry into force date and depositary information.[68] There is a separate guide to the TIF offered by Kavass and Sprudzs.[69] This guide is available in print and through HeinOnline. It is particularly useful for researchers searching by topic because it offers a complete listing of all treaties by topic.

B. Identify the Depositary

The depositary should offer the most complete, authoritative and current information related to a particular treaty. Articles 76 through 79 of the *VCLT* set forth some of the formal duties of depositaries.[70] The depositary serves as the custodian of the treaty instrument itself and is responsible for its safekeeping. It issues certified copies and maintains records as to treaty status including parties, signatories, entry into force date, as well as reservations, understandings, and declarations. It also issues notifications, as required by the treaty.

Historically, States served as depositaries. For example, Switzerland serves as depositary for the Geneva Conventions.[71] Because The Hague sits in the Kingdom of the Netherlands, the Netherlands serves as depositary for over one hundred treaties.[72] Its database is available online and can be searched using an advanced search template.[73] Now, various IGOs have been designated de-

---

67. *Treaties in Force (TIF)*, Dep't of State, http://www.state.gov/s/l/treaty/tif/index.htm [https://perma.cc/K79W-XGPJ].

68. *Id.*

69. Kavass & Sprudzs, eds., *Guide to the United States Treaties in Force* (1982) (available on HeinOnline).

70. *VCLT, supra* note 2, arts. 76–79.

71. *See* Switzerland Federal Department of Foreign Affairs, https://www.eda.admin.ch/eda/en/home/foreign-policy/international-law/internationale-vertraege/depositary.html [https://perma.cc/P4S3-27WL].

72. *See* Government of Netherlands, *The administration of treaties,* https://www.government.nl/topics/treaties/contents/the-administration-of-treaties [https://perma.cc/VB3M-P8SZ].

73. Netherlands, Treaty Database, https://treatydatabase.overheid.nl/ [https://perma.cc/Y6M3-ETXV].

positaries, such as the United Nations and some of its specialized agencies (e.g., WIPO).[74]

While treaty documents may take many forms, the depositary information is generally included in the final clauses of a treaty document. The treaty provisions that provide for the depositary and its administrative functions are generally immediately applicable, even if the treaty has not entered into force.[75] In fact, many of the procedural matters related to the treaty will be included in the final provisions. It is imperative for the legal researcher to scan the entire text of the treaty and to pay close attention to the final provisions to find or verify the depositary information. A productive online research strategy when viewing a lengthy treaty document is to use the find function (control F on many computers) and search for the word "depositary," "depository," or "deposited" to locate these treaty provisions.

Because the depositary is the official custodian of the treaty, it is an efficient research strategy to find the depositary website as early as possible in the research process. While sometimes the depositary institution's databases and search mechanisms may be clunky, and it may be more effective to find the text of the treaty elsewhere, the legal researcher must eventually find the depositary institution to uncover all of the related treaty information in its most up-to-date format. Finding depositary information may occur during three distinct portions of the legal research process: while consulting the indexes; while searching online; or at the point in time the researcher is reading the final provisions of the text of the treaty. Certainly, after the legal researcher identifies the depositary, the other two points in the process may be used as a control strategy to confirm the information.

C. Check the Status of the Treaty

To check the status of a treaty, a researcher must find and compile three details related to the treaty: signatories and parties, entry into force date, and the reservations, understandings, and declarations (commonly called RUDs). Each of these details taken together has a bearing on the status of a treaty. Status is determined at a particular point in time, as these details may change over time as States continue to interact on the international stage. Researchers

---

74. The Vienna Convention on the Law Treaties allows for any state, organization or institution to be designated depositary. *See VCLT, supra* note 2, arts. 76–77.

75. *VCLT, supra* note 8, art. 24(4).

should always capture the date on which they checked the status of the treaty as part of the research process.

i. Identify Signatories and Parties to the Treaty

Determining the status of a treaty involves uncovering which States have signed, ratified, acceded to, or accepted the treaty. In the case of bilateral treaties, the legal researcher is dealing with only two parties. For multilateral treaties, the effort becomes considerably more complex as the number of States involved is greater and can change over time. An international legal researcher must have a strong grasp of the treaty-making process to handle this effort.

The treaty-making process is described in detail in the United Nations Office of Legal Affairs' *Treaty Handbook*.[76] This handbook offers a useful visual on the treaty timeline that is helpful for understanding the treaty-making process.[77] The *VCLT* governs the treaty-making process, including the rules for creating and administering the treaties.[78]

Multilateral treaties have a distinct but standard treaty-making process:

- treaty is negotiated at an international conference
- treaty is concluded when those involved settle on the text
- treaty text is signed by a State's representative; once signed, the State is considered a "signatory"
- domestic ratification process occurs at the national level (if the treaty is non-self-executing)
- State deposits the instrument of ratification with the designated depositary; once ratified, the State is considered a "party"
- reservations, declarations, and understandings may be included either during signing or at the point in time of filing the instrument of ratification
- treaty enters into force after the designated number of States have ratified it according to the treaty's terms
- States that did not originally sign the treaty while it was open for signature may later accede to the treaty ("accession")[79]

---

76. U.N. TREATY HANDBOOK, *supra* note 13.

77. *Id.* at 21.

78. *See VCLT, supra* note 2.

79. *See* UN Treaty Handbook, *supra* note 13, at 21; *See also* IAN BROWNLIE, PRINCIPLES OF PUBLIC INTERNATIONAL LAW 579–617 (6th ed., Oxford Univ. Press 2003); Malgosia Fitzmaurice, *Treaties*, MPEPIL, http://opil.ouplaw.com/home/EPIL [https://perma.cc/6KGP-8P9N].

Signature, ratification, acceptance, approval, and accession are all legal terms of art.[80] To fully grasp the status of any given treaty, the legal researcher must understand the treaty-making process and these definitions. In rather simplistic terms, any State that attends the convention and is involved in the negotiating process of the treaty may sign the treaty at the close of the convention and throughout the time that it is open for signature.[81] States that sign the treaty during this process become simple signatories to the treaty.

In general, signature indicates the intent to be bound. However, there are two types of signature: definitive signature and simple signature. Definitive signature indicates a treaty in simplified form.[82] This means that at the time of signature, the states involved indicate definitive intent to be bound. Often, States involved in the bilateral treaty-making process have the authority to sign definitively.

Simple signature indicates a State intends to be bound by the objects and purposes of the treaty until it formally ratifies the treaty or offers a clear indication of its intent to *not* be bound by it.[83] For example, a U.S. diplomat involved in treaty negotiations may have the authority to sign a treaty subject to ratification domestically. This is simple signature. Once domestic ratification is obtained, ratification of the treaty under public international law may occur. This involves definitive signature. For the U.S. legal researcher, it is vital to distinguish between domestic treaty ratification process and the public international law treaty ratification process.[84]

---

80. UN Treaty Collection Glossary, https://treaties.un.org/pages/Overview.aspx?path= overview/glossary/page1_en.xml [https://perma.cc/6LEY-AS3Z]. *See also*, Office of Legal Affairs, Treaty Section, *Treaty Handbook*, https://treaties.un.org/doc/source/publications/ THb/english.pdf [https://perma.cc/5GAE-7LHR].

81. *See id.* Typically, the treaty document itself will indicate the dates during which the treaty is open for signature.

82. These simplified form treaties have their roots in U.S. constitutional law related to executive agreements which do not have to go through the advice and consent process. Many European states modeled this practice during the Nineteenth and Twentieth centuries and it was eventually codified in the Vienna Convention on the Law of Treaties. *See VCLT, supra* note 8, art. 12.

83. *VCLT, supra* note 8, art. 18.

84. *See, e.g.,* Netherlands Ratification Procedure, https://www.government.nl/topics/ treaties/contents/the-difference-between-signing-and-ratification [https://perma.cc/Y6SM-QZA8] (requiring Parliamentary approval) versus the history of treaty approval or rejection in the United States via the Senate, http://www.senate.gov/artandhistory/history/common/briefing/Treaties.htm [https://perma.cc/KUL7-LK59] (noting the chronology of the ratification process in the United States).

ii. *Determine Entry into Force Date*

Bilateral treaties generally enter into force on the date that the parties agree, usually upon signature. Typically, a multilateral treaty will enter into force on a specified date or upon a specified number of States ratifying the treaty, or a combination of the two.[85] While some treaties have no explicit entry into force date,[86] most treaties include a description of the circumstances, or triggering event, according to which the treaty will enter into force.[87] Each State for which the treaty has entered into force is considered a party to the treaty regardless of whether that State was involved in the treaty-making process. The label "party" to a treaty is a legal term of art and should only be used for those States that have consented to be bound by it and for which the treaty has entered into force as it relates to them.[88] Under this process it is possible for some States to become bound to a treaty *after* its official entry into force date.[89]

The entry into force date allows the legal researcher to determine whether the signatories to the treaty are bound by it. It serves as the point in time at which the other parties to the treaty may enforce it against those parties who violate its terms (typically by sanctions but sometimes by incentives or rules, or as outlined in the treaty itself). Often, online treaty databases will contain the entry into force date as a separate metadata field.[90] Even if the entry into force date is readily available online, it is incumbent upon the international legal researcher to read the treaty itself paying particular attention to the final clauses to discover the entry into force triggering event. Conveniently, the depositary organization will sometimes offer this information in an index or other summary table format.

---

85. *See, e.g.,* UN Depositary Practice: I.L.M., 1996 p. 1097 paragraphs 244–245 ("The present Convention shall enter into force on the thirtieth day following the date of deposit of the thirty fifth instrument of ratification."), https://treaties.un.org/doc/source/publications/practice/summary_english.pdf [https://perma.cc/XU66-HWZN].

86. *See, e.g.,* Iraq-United Nations Memorandum of Understanding (MOU), May 20, 1996, 1926 U.N.T.S. 10.

87. *VCLT, supra* note 8, art. 24.

88. Many news outlets and lay people refer to States that have signed a treaty as a party to a treaty. The legal researcher should always verify this information by checking the entry into force date as it relates to the various signatories to the treaty.

89. *See, e.g.,* Berne Convention for the Protection of Literary and Artistic Works, opened for signature Sept. 9, 1886, 828 U.N.T.S. 221, S. Treaty Doc. No. 99-27, 99th Cong. (1986) (revised at Paris, July 24, 1979) and the research process example included, *infra*, on p. 41.

90. *See* Chapter 9 for an explanation of metadata fields.

iii. Find and Read the Reservations, Understandings and Declarations (RUDs)

When parties ratify or accede to a treaty, they may do so with a statement that relates to some of the other parties to or provisions of the treaty. Such statements may be labeled as reservations, understandings, or declarations. However labeled, if the statements serve to exclude or modify some legal effect of the treaty, they will be classified a reservation.[91]

A reservation is a unilateral statement by a party to the treaty at the time of signature, ratification, accession, acceptance or approval that, in essence, serves as a limitation on the legal commitment by the State as it relates to certain provisions of the treaty.[92] Certain treaties explicitly prohibit RUDs.[93] Once a reservation is filed, other parties to the treaty have up to twelve months to officially object unless the treaty itself provides a different time frame for lodging objections.[94] A researcher must take note of the chronology of the filing of RUDs to develop a complete picture of the status of a treaty in relation to other States and at any particular point in time. Because reservations may be withdrawn or modified at a later time,[95] unless the treaty text provides otherwise, the experienced legal researcher always gives an "as of" date when reporting status information.

Declarations[96] and understandings are also unilateral statements that are annexed to a treaty. They allow the parties to the treaty to interpret or explain a provision of the treaty. Interpretive declarations, unlike reservations, gener-

---

91. The depositary is responsible for determining whether understandings or declarations are technically reservations. See *VCLT*, at art. 2(1)(d).

92. Office of Legal Affairs, Treaty Section, *Treaty Handbook, supra* note 78.

93. *See, e.g.,* UNEP, HANDBOOK FOR THE MONTREAL PROTOCOL ON SUBSTANCES THAT DEPLETE THE OZONE LAYER, art. 18 (10th ed. 2016), https://perma.cc/3ZRW-7E5R.

94. *VCLT, supra* note 8, at art. 20(5). An example of many reservations and objections may be found in the Convention on the Elimination of all forms of Discrimination against Women. *See* Office of the UN High Commissioner on Human Rights, CEDAW Ratifications, http://ozone.unep.org/sites/ozone/files/Publications/Handbooks/MP-Handbook-2016-English.pdf [https://perma.cc/J8G3-AUL4]. Generally, human rights treaties will not have a provision related to reservations. *See, e.g.,* Ineta Ziemele and Lasma Liede, *Reservations to Human Rights Treaties: From Draft Guideline 3.1.12 to Guideline 3.1.5.6,* 24(4) E.J.I.L. 1135–1152 (2013), http://ejil.oxfordjournals.org/content/24/4/1135.full.pdf [https://perma.cc/F265-XTLK].

95. *VCLT, supra* note 2, arts. 22 & 23.

96. Declarations annexed to a treaty must be distinguished from declarations, a form of a treaty itself (e.g., the Tashkent Declaration) and from declarations that are statements that are aspirational and not meant to be binding (e.g., Universal Declaration of Human

ally have no impact on the legal effect of the treaty.[97] Certain treaties explicitly allow for optional or mandatory declarations. These types of declarations are binding on those States attaching them to their instruments of ratification. An example of a mandatory declaration can be found in the Optional Protocol to the Convention on the Rights of Child on the Involvement of Children in Armed Conflict.[98] These types of declarations can be found related to some human rights treaties.[99] Understandings are statements that allow a party ratifying or acceding to a treaty to set forth its understanding or interpretation of a particular treaty provision or relationship with another party. Argentina and the United States included understandings related to the International Covenant on Civil and Political Rights.[100]

Objections by other States may be made to reservations, understandings, and declarations.[101] Naturally, researchers must find and read the relevant States' RUDs as well as the subsequent objections lodged by other States to those RUDs, if any, to gather a complete understanding of the extent of the application of the treaty.

The RUDs are typically annexed to a treaty and can be found through the depositary collection. Domestically, for multilaterals that involve the U.S., the Senate report will be rich with detail related to RUDs. Those legal researchers who are familiar with foreign relations in a particular subject area may choose to check for RUDs earlier in the research process to gather a sense of the relationships between parties. Doing so earlier in the process sometimes allows the researcher to avoid carrying out unnecessary research, depending on the nature of the RUDs.

Rights or the Millennium Declaration). *See e.g.,* UN Depositary Practice: I.L.M., 1996 p. 1097, https://perma.cc/XU66-HWZN.

97. Office of Legal Affairs, Treaty Section, *Treaty Handbook, supra* note 78.

98. *See* Optional Protocol to the Convention on the Rights of Child on the Involvement of Children in Armed Conflict, Feb. 12, 2002, 2173 U.N.T.S. 236. The mandatory declaration requirement directs states to "deposit a binding declaration upon ratification … that sets forth the minimum age at which it will permit mandatory recruitment into its national armed forces." *Id.* at 237.

99. *See* Office of Legal Affairs, Treaty Section, *Treaty Handbook, supra* note 78, at 16.

100. *See* International Covenant on Civil and Political Rights, UN MTDSG, https://treaties.un.org/doc/source/publications/practice/summary_english.pdf [https://perma.cc/7Z3H-TTWV].

101. *See* Office of Legal Affairs, Treaty Section, *Treaty Handbook, supra* note 78, at 14.

IV. U.S. Treaty Implementation

Frequently, the U.S. legal researcher handling a treaty research project must also find the U.S. implementing legislation for the treaty or convention. This section offers background information on treaty implementation and describes the research process where the international convention is researched before the related U.S. domestic materials.

Over time, States have developed a monist or dualist approach when confronted with the implementation of treaties domestically.[102] Monists believe that international conventions take automatic effect in the State. Dualists believe that international conventions only take effect in the State as the State allows according to the limits of its constitutional law and sometimes only through additional, national, implementing legislation.[103] States may be partly monist and partly dualist.

Against this backdrop, and when handling treaty research, it is imperative to understand the difference between self-executing treaties and non-self-executing treaties. Generally, self-executing treaties have full force of law without the need for implementing legislation.[104] Under a dualist approach, implementing legislation is required to incorporate a non-self-executing treaty into legally enforceable domestic law. Once incorporated, courts will rely on and cite to the implementing legislation rather than the international agreement itself.[105]

According to Section 111 of the *Restatement (Third) of the Foreign Relations Law of the United States*, international agreements are non-self-executing if: the international agreement itself acknowledges the need for implementing

---

102. *See* JOHN P. GRANT & J. CRAIG BARKER, PARRY & GRANT ENCYCLOPAEDIC DICTIONARY OF INTERNATIONAL LAW 390 (3d ed., Oxford Univ. Press 2009) (stating that "monists believe that international and domestic law form one legal system and that international law is hierarchically superior ..."). *But cf.* GRANT, at 169 (defining dualism as "the theory according to which 'international law and the internal law of states are totally separate legal systems ... to the extent that in particular instances rules of international law may apply within a state they do so by virtue of their adoption by the internal law of the state'..."). *See also* Ryan Harrington, *Understanding 'Other' International Agreements,* https://papers.ssrn.com/sol3/papers.cfm?abstract_id=2593997 [https://perma.cc/PF79-UDBG] (2015) (describing the additional effects of other international agreements in the United States).

103. GRANT at 390.

104. *See* "Treaties as 'Law of the Land,'" 14 DIG. INT'L L. 298 (1970).

105. David Sloss, *Non-self-executing Treaties: Exposing a Constitutional Fallacy,* 36 U.C. DAVIS L. REV. 1 (Nov. 2002). *See also* T. Buergenthal, *Self-Executing and Non-Self-Executing Treaties in National and International Law,* 235 Rec. des Cours 303–400 (1992).

legislation;[106] the U.S. Senate may require it as part of the advice and consent process; or there is a constitutional basis for it.[107] Researchers should be cautioned to research and interpret whether a treaty is self-executing according to current judicial doctrine.[108] Historically, courts deemed certain treaties to be self-executing according to the terms of the treaties or international agreements.[109] After the *Medellin* case,[110] the U.S. Supreme Court has held that there is a presumption that treaties are non-self-executing in the U.S. and need domestic implementing legislation to have legal effect.[111]

The U.S. definition of treaty differs from the public international law definition of treaty. According to the U.S. Constitution, the president shall have "Power, by and with the Advice and Consent of the Senate, to make Treaties, provided two-thirds of the Senators present concur."[112] Such treaties are considered the "supreme law of the land" according to the Constitution and are hierarchically on par with statutes (at least if self-executing in nature).[113] These treaties are oftentimes referred to as Article II treaties. No matter the title of the instrument under international law, whether Protocol, Agreement, Convention, or Treaty, if it passes through the Senate advice and consent process, it is considered a treaty under U.S. domestic law.

After the conclusion of an international convention, the U.S. executive branch decides whether to subject any given agreement to the Senate advice

---

106. RESTATEMENT (THIRD) OF THE FOREIGN RELATIONS LAW OF THE UNITED STATES, § 111 (Am. Law Inst. 1987 & Supp. 2016). *See also* TENTATIVE DRAFT RESTATEMENT (FOURTH) OF THE FOREIGN RELATIONS LAW OF THE UNITED STATES, TREATIES, § 101 *et seq.* (Mar. 2016).

107. *Id.*

108. *See* Asante Technologies, Inc. v. PMC-Sierra, Inc., 164 F. Supp. 2d 1142 (2001); *see generally* Mark Cantora, *The CISG after Medellin v. Texas: Do U.S. Businesses Have It? Do They Want It?*, 8 J. OF INT'L BUS. & LAW 111 (Spring 2008).

109. Carlos Manuel Vásquez, *The Four Doctrines of Self-Executing Treaties,* 89 AM. J. INT'L L. 695–723 (1995).

110. Medellin v. Texas, 552 U.S. 491, 128 S.Ct. 1346, 1349 (2008). *But see* Case Concerning Avena and Other Mexican Nationals (Mex. V. U.S.), Judgment, 2004 I.C.J. 12, 47 I.L.M. 726 (Mar. 31) (revealing that the U.S. has international obligations not to defeat the purpose of the Vienna Convention on Consular Relations, and the U.S. breached its obligations under the Convention because it failed to duly inform detained Mexican nationals of their Consular authorities).

111. *See* Al-Bihani v. Obama, 619 F.3d 1, 16 (D.C. Cir. 2010). *See also* Rebecca Crootof, *Judicious Influence: Non-Self-Executing Treaties and the Charming Betsy Canon,* 120(7) Yale L. J. 1784 (May 2011).

112. U.S. CONST. art. II, §2, cl. 2.

113. U.S. CONST., art. VI, cl. 2.

and consent process.[114] The president sends the international agreement to the senate in a transmittal package that contains a letter of transmittal, letter of submittal form from the secretary of state, report of the secretary of state, and the English text of the treaty.[115] The *Senate Treaty Document* is then printed after the injunction of secrecy is removed, and this *Senate Treaty Document* is the first official form of the treaty document in the United States.[116] Most international agreements entered into by the U.S. are not Article II treaties.[117]

There are a number of non-Article II international agreements that are considered treaties under public international law. These types of agreements fall into three categories: congressional-executive agreements, presidential executive agreements, and executive agreements. There are many more executive agreements than there are Article II treaties under U.S. domestic law. Executive agreements may be internationally binding, but there may be a question domestically as to whether they are on par with statutes.[118]

A congressional-executive agreement requires a simple majority of a quorum of both houses rather than the two-thirds supermajority of the Senate required for an Article II treaty.[119] A presidential executive agreement does not require any action on the part of congress. Rather, the president uses his authority under the constitution to enter into an agreement without the formal consent of congress.[120] There are also executive agreements that are made pursuant to previously ratified treaties. These types of treaties are made under an

---

114. *See* Michael John Garcia, *International Law and Agreements: Their Effect Upon U.S. Law,* https://fas.org/sgp/crs/misc/RL32528.pdf [https://perma.cc/4AUF-ABLA].

115. *Id. See also* Congressional Research Service (LOC), *Treaties and Other International Agreements: The Role of the United States Senate,* Committee on Foreign Relations, United States Senate, S. PRT. 106-71 (Jan. 2001), https://www.gpo.gov/fdsys/pkg/CPRT-106SPRT 66922/pdf/CPRT-106SPRT66922.pdf [https://perma.cc/TE65-HVGD].

116. *Id.* at 338–343. Senate Treaty documents are available through the U.S. GPO and published in PDF format via Congress.gov, https://www.congress.gov/search?q={%22source %22:%22treaties%22} [https://perma.cc/KP4M-AZCE]; *see* Manley O. Hudson, *The "Injunction of Secrecy" with Respect to American Treaties,* 23(2) AM. J. INT'L LAW 329–335 (Apr. 1929) (discussing the historic Senate Rule 36 in the 1925 Senate Manual preserving the "injunction of secrecy" for transmission of American treaties).

117. Michael John Garcia, *International Law and Agreements: Their Effect Upon U.S. Law,* CONG. RESEARCH SERV., RL 32528 (2015), [https://perma.cc/4AUF-ABLA], at 22–37.

118. *Id.*

119. *Id.*

120. *See, e.g.,* Smith, Shedd & Murrill (CRS), *Why Certain Trade Agreements are Approved as Congressional-Executive Agreements Rather than Treaties,* https://fas.org/sgp/crs/misc/97-896.pdf [https://perma.cc/3RHY-LF8T] (April 2013).

extension of the original grant of authority, whether stemming from domestic enabling legislation or the advice and consent process.

Sometimes during the advice and consent process, the Senate requires implementing legislation for congressional-executive agreements. Without the implementing legislation, the U.S. will only be bound to the terms of the international agreement through the fundamental principle of *pacta sunt servanda* which means agreements must be honored based on the principle of good faith.[121] The rule of *pacta sunt servanda* is applied only when a treaty has entered into force according to the *VCLT*.[122] When a State has signed a treaty, but the treaty has not yet entered into force, then the State has an obligation according to Article 18 of the *VCLT* to not defeat "the object and purpose of the treaty" prior to its entry into force.[123]

One final caveat related to finding U.S. implementing legislation is in order. Implementing legislation can only be understood, and updated, by researching the judicial treatment of that legislation. Treaty researchers in the U.S. will need to read and understand sections 111–115 of the Restatement to gather a sense of how U.S. courts interpret the federal implementing legislation in light of international law, especially in circumstances where there is an inconsistency between the two. An in-depth explanation of U.S. case law research is beyond the scope of this book. However, it must be highlighted that in addition to regular case law research, and after the *Paquete Habana* case of 1900, customary international law norms have been considered to be U.S. law and applicable in U.S. courts.[124] Chapter 4 covers the research process for finding customary international law.

121. Karen Kaiser, MPEPIL, Treaties, Direct Applicability (Feb. 2013); *see also* Foster v. Neilson, 27 U.S. 253 (1829) (distinguishing between non-selfexecuting treaties and self-executing treaties for the first time in the U.S.); *see generally* Anthony Aust, MPEPIL, Pacta Sunt Servanda (Feb. 2007).

122. Anthony Aust, MPEPIL, Pacta Sunt Servanda (Feb. 2007).

123. *VCLT, supra* note 8, art. 18.

124. The Paquete Habana, 175 U.S. 677 (1900) (stating that the "rule of international law is one which prize courts, administering the law of nations, are bound to take judicial notice of, and to give effect to, in the absence of any treaty or other public act of their own government in relation to the matter.").

A. Sources for U.S. Treaty Implementation

Primary sources of law utilized for the research process related to U.S. treaty implementation include:

- *Treaties and other International Acts Series* (1945–present) or *United States Treaties and Other International Agreements* (1950–1982)[125]
- *Senate Treaty Documents* for Article II Treaties[126]
- Publications for congressional-executive and executive agreements at the Department of State Treaty Affairs[127]
- U.S. implementing legislation found in the U.S. Code (U.S.C./ U.S.C.A./U.S.C.S.)[128]
- Judicial interpretation of implementing legislation found in the case reporters including the Federal Supplement (F. Supp. 3d), the Federal Reporter (F. 3d.), and the United States Reports (U.S.)[129]

Secondary sources commonly used for treaty implementation research include the following. These and other secondary sources are covered in greater depth in Chapter 8.

- U.S. State Department's *Treaties in Force* (TIF)[130]
- *Restatement (Third) of Foreign Relations Law in the United States* and summaries of associated case law[131]

---

125. *See* HeinOnline's U.S. Treaties and Agreements Library, http://heinonline.org/HOL/ Index?index=ustreatieso&collection=ustreaties [https://perma.cc/R9HB-FNFZ] and U.S. Department of State, *Treaties*, http://www.state.gov/s/l/treaty/index.htm [https://perma.cc/ FGM7-55ST].

126. *See, e.g.,* Senate Treaty Documents, https://www.congress.gov/search?q={%22 source%22:%22treaties%22} [https://perma.cc/KP4M-AZCE] and "About Treaty Documents," Congress.gov, https://www.congress.gov/treaties/about [https://perma.cc/E27Q-X4BS].

127. Department of State, Treaty Affairs, http://www.state.gov/s/l/treaty/caseact/ [https:// perma.cc/77D7-3Z3A].

128. *See* Congress.gov, Treaty Documents, https://www.congress.gov/ [https://perma. cc/2Y7F-CFCB].

129. *See* U.S.C.A. (Thomson Reuters or on Westlaw) and U.S.C.S. (Lexis or on Lexis Advance) for judicial interpretation.

130. U.S. Department of State, *Treaties in Force,* http://www.state.gov/s/l/treaty/tif/ [https://perma.cc/PL73-QZ8N].

131. Restatement (Third) of the Foreign Relations Law of the United States, §301 *et seq.* (Am. Law Inst. 1987 & Supp. 2016). It should be noted that the Restatement of the Law Fourth, Foreign Relations Law of the United States may be completed in 2017.

- *Digest of U.S. Practice in International Law* (via the State Department).[132]
- Commentaries on international law and topical areas of international law.[133]
- Commentaries on international conventions written by prominent international law scholars[134] and by international organizations or nongovernmental organizations.[135]

B. Treaty Implementation Research Process through Selected Examples

The research process for determining the status of a treaty in the United States and its implementation may vary depending on the information available to the researcher at the outset of the project. Researchers must bear in mind that there is no single best way to approach treaty research. Rather, researchers have the greatest success when they harness finding aids and other research tools available to them and actively take note of references to U.S. implementation of the treaty. The following examples of the research process for multilateral conventions that required U.S. implementing legislation are offered to demonstrate the variations that occur when handling treaty research.

i. *Chemical Weapons Convention (1974 U.N.T.S. 45)*

The U.N. offers two treaty databases, the United Nations Treaties Series (UNTS) and the Multilateral Treaties Deposited with the Secretary General

---

TENTATIVE DRAFT RESTATEMENT (FOURTH) OF THE FOREIGN RELATIONS LAW OF THE UNITED STATES, TREATIES, https://www.ali.org/projects/show/foreign-relations-law-united-states/ [https://perma.cc/7BHV-YACJ].

132. 1989–2014 DIGEST OF UNITED STATES PRACTICE IN INTERNATIONAL LAW (this digest is also available on the Department of State's website: http://www.state.gov/s/l/c8183.htm [https://perma.cc/C8YY-5FLK]).

133. OXFORD COMMENTARIES ON INTERNATIONAL LAW, https://global.oup.com/academic/content/series/o/oxford-commentaries-on-international-law-ocils/?cc=us&lang=en& [https://perma.cc/S6BJ-QAFG].

134. *See, e.g.,* Olivier Corten and Pierre Klein, eds., THE VIENNA CONVENTIONS ON THE LAW OF TREATIES: A COMMENTARY (2011) and OXFORD COMMENTARIES ON INTERNATIONAL LAW, https://global.oup.com/academic/content/series/o/oxford-commentaries-on-international-law-ocils/?cc=us&lang=en& [https://perma.cc/S6BJ-QAFG].

135. *See, e.g., Commentary on the First Geneva Convention: Convention (I) for the Amelioration of the Condition of the Wounded and Sick in Armed Forces in the Field,* ICRC (2 ed. Mar. 22, 2016), https://ihl-databases.icrc.org/applic/ihl/ihl.nsf/INTRO/365?OpenDocument [https://perma.cc/2MQ3-LSGV].

(MTDSG). Researchers with a UNTS citation can proceed directly to the *United Nations Treaty Collection* to retrieve the text of the *Chemical Weapons Convention.*[136] While the UNTS contains more treaties than does the MTDSG, researchers who already know or suspect the U.N. serves as the depositary should search the MTDSG first so that they find all of the associated data related to the treaty. Search options for both the UNTS and MTDSG include: by "title" (use English title in UNTS), by participants, by full text, or through the advanced search feature (UNTS only).[137] When utilizing the advanced search feature of the UNTS, it is best to limit by phrase or "all these words" of the title to achieve a results list that contains the agreement. Failing to restrict to the title field will require the researcher to spend valuable time sorting through irrelevant results, including the subsequent accessions by countries to the agreement. For this example, a title search for chemical weapons achieves a results list that contains the relevant international convention: *Convention on the Prohibition of the Development, Production, Stockpiling and Use of Chemical Weapons and on their Destruction.*

Alternatively, for treaties to which the U.S. is a party, a legal researcher may elect to consult the Department of State's TIF. Browsing the multilateral treaty section by title of the treaty or by subject matter if the treaty title is unknown results in a TIAS citation and often a reference to the depositary for the treaty. Because TIF often refers researchers of multilateral treaties to the United Nations Treaty Collection website, it is often more efficient to simply start there because the depositary institution will offer the official text of the treaty and the most up-to-date information related to its status.

Next, the researcher scans the treaty to find or verify that the U.N. is the depositary for the treaty instrument. These types of provisions are usually included in the final clauses of the treaty document. After confirming that the U.N. is the depositary, the researcher can use the status information included in the MTDSG database to check for State ratifications. Here, the researcher finds that the Convention has 165 signatories and 192 parties. The U.S. signed in 1993 and ratified in 1997, with one statement/declaration.[138] It is at this point in the research process that the researcher will read the treaty closely and

---

136. Convention on the Prohibition of the Development, Production, Stockpiling and Use of Chemical Weapons and on Their Destruction (CWC), Jan. 13, 1993, 1974 U.N.T.S. 45.

137. *See* MTDSG, *United Nations Treaty Collection,* https://treaties.un.org/pages/ParticipationStatus.aspx [https://perma.cc/UVD3-CCWX].

138. *Id.; See also* UN Office for Disarmament Affairs, https://www.un.org/disarmament/wmd/chemical/ [https://perma.cc/T5RV-LMMP].

for complete understanding, after having scanned it earlier. Most researchers will consult secondary sources to help them understand the treaty provisions at the center of their research project.

In circumstances where the research project entails finding the U.S. implementing legislation, researchers must use domestic sources for federal statutory research (*U.S.C., U.S.C.A.,* or *U.S.C.S.*) and their associated finding aids, including the Popular Name Table and indexes. A Popular Name Table is available on Westlaw, Lexis, the Office of the Law Revision Council United States Code website,[139] and through print versions of the U.S. Code. Searching for Chemical Weapons Convention in the Popular Name Table directs the researcher to the "Chemical Weapons Convention Implementation Act of 1998" with the relevant U.S. statutory citation and implementation information: 22 U.S.C.A. §6701 *et seq.*

After the U.S. legislation is identified, it must be read carefully to determine whether the U.S. adopted all or portions of the treaty. After reading the text of the implementing legislation carefully, it is vital to consider case law interpretation of it. This can be handled using the "Notes of Decisions" in the annotated code. Researchers might also consider using secondary sources at this point in the process to find those that cite to and discuss the implementing legislation. Researchers without access to an annotated code can search a case law database using the citation to the implementing legislation to obtain a results list of all cases that have cited to the implementing legislation. Finally, if any ambiguity exists, the legal researcher must consider the possibility of compiling a legislative history for the relevant portions of the implementing legislation. As with all case law research, researchers should use a citator to update and understand the body of law.

ii. Paris Act Relating to the Berne Convention for the Protection of Literary and Artistic Property (1161 U.N.T.S. 3)

Finding the Paris Act related to the *Berne Convention* is a rather complex research project because the Berne Convention has been revised seven times since its initial drafting in 1886.[140] In addition, the United States was not an original party to the *Berne Convention* or the *Paris Act.* As such, researchers

---

139. Office of the Law Revision Council United States Code, http://uscode.house.gov/popularnames/popularnames.htm [https://perma.cc/9PE7-BA9H]. Researchers can use the pdf version and search using 'control F.'

140. *See, e.g.,* Berne Convention for the Protection of Literary and Artistic Works, WIPO (Sept. 28, 1979), http://www.wipo.int/treaties/en/text.jsp?file_id=283698 [https://perma.cc/SZ9V-Q3UW].

using the United Nations Treaty Collection website (as was demonstrated through the Chemical Weapons Convention example) easily become confused by the multiple versions of the *Berne Convention* and its subsequent and related treaty actions. Valuable research time would be required to read and understand the multiple versions of the Convention in an effort to find the Paris Act and determine whether the U.S. ratified it.

In circumstances where there is an IGO with subject area expertise it is often more efficient to use that website to find all relevant treaty information before verifying it at the depositary website. Carrying out a preliminary search to identify the IGO is an efficient strategy for finding the text of the treaty and all related status information. For example, the search *intellectual property international treaty collection* will provide a results list that reveals the IGO that administers the *Berne Convention* is the World Intellectual Property Organization (WIPO).[141] Evaluating the results list by scanning the URLs for an .int extension will often lead to the identification of the official IGO website.[142] Researchers should review the IGO Home or About page and then refer to the founding charter of the IGO to gather a sense of its charge, including its structure and duties.

Either through the initial online search or by using the WIPO's database, WIPOLex, researchers locate the Berne Convention landing page.[143] From this page, the Contracting Parties link offers a drop-down list that contains all the instruments (6 Acts and 1 Additional Protocol) related to the Berne Convention, including the Paris Act of 1971. After finding the authoritative text and the subsequent related treaty actions, the researcher can read the relevant treaty documents to identify the depositary.

When dealing with an IGO that administers treaties researchers must consider the treaty date against the founding date of the administering IGO. Treaties concluded after an IGO's founding date are deposited within it. Treaties concluded prior to an IGO's founding date are originally deposited elsewhere. IGOs that administer treaties originally deposited elsewhere generally serve in the same capacity as the original depositary.

In this example, by consulting secondary sources or the WIPO website, researchers find that the original Berne Convention existed long before the establishment of WIPO in 1967. Researchers will have likely noticed refer-

---

141. *See* WIPO-ADMINISTERED TREATIES, http://www.wipo.int/treaties/en/ [https://perma.cc/JGH6-MDW7]. WIPO administers 26 treaties.

142. A discussion of search techniques and evaluating result lists is included in Chapter 9.

143. *See* http://www.wipo.int/treaties/en/ip/berne/ [https://perma.cc/6ULN-6T54].

ences to the UN website and the UN treaty databases in their early searches. By exploring the UN treaty collections, the researcher finds that the Government of Switzerland was the original depositary for the Berne Convention. When WIPO was established to promote the protection of intellectual property, it was charged with administering all related treaties, including the Berne Convention.

Next, researchers verify the status of the original Berne convention as well as the Paris Act. Using this Contracting Parties list, the legal researcher determines that the United States acceded to the *Berne Convention* in 1988 and the accession entered into force according to the accession instrument in 1989 (the Berne Convention itself entered into force in 1984).[144] Using that same tool, the legal researcher determines that the United States also acceded to the Paris Act of 1971 in 1988 and it, too, entered into force in 1989 for the United States (the Paris Act itself entered into force in 1974).

By using WIPOLex, the legal researcher can uncover the 'details' page for the Berne Convention[145] to note that it supersedes the Paris Act. Using the link to the Paris Act's 'details' page,[146] the legal researcher confirms that the Paris Act was superseded by the Berne Convention and that the Paris Act itself superseded the Stockholm Act. Reading these pages together serves as a control strategy but never serves as a substitute for reading the documents.

Conveniently, the WIPOLex database also includes references to national laws and regulations of Member States. To find the U.S. domestic implementation of the *Berne Convention*, researchers select USA from the Member listing under WIPO/WTO/UN Members box.[147] Finding an entry is the most efficient way for researchers to determine that the United States has implemented the *Berne Convention*.[148] WIPOLex sets forth that implementation of the *Berne Convention* is part of the U.S. Copyright laws (17 U.S.C. § 101 *et seq.*).[149]

Next, researchers must verify this information by carrying out statutory research in the *U.S.C.*, *U.S.C.A.*, or *U.S.C.S.* starting with the indexes or Popu-

---

144. *See Accession by the United States of America*, WIPO, http://www.wipo.int/treaties/en/notifications/berne/treaty_berne_121.html [https://perma.cc/52XB-2HLC].

145. *See* http://www.wipo.int/wipolex/en/details.jsp?id=12214 [https://perma.cc/D64Y-QPKR].

146. *See* http://www.wipo.int/wipolex/en/details.jsp?id=12800 [https://perma.cc/7B7F-XXFP].

147. WIPO Lex, http://www.wipo.int/wipolex/en/ [https://perma.cc/X4BU-J8JR].

148. *See United States of America*, WIPO Lex, http://www.wipo.int/wipolex/en/profile.jsp?code=US [https://perma.cc/YUU9-Y3BS].

149. 17 U.S.C. § 101 *et seq. See also* WIPO Lex, http://www.wipo.int/wipolex/en/profile.jsp?code=US [https://perma.cc/YUU9-Y3BS].

lar Name Table. It is usually more efficient to locate the implementing legislation through the Popular Name Table of the federal code than to search for it full text. By looking for the *Berne Convention* in the Popular Name Table, researchers efficiently locate the *Berne Convention Implementation Act of 1988* and find that the copyright convention(s) are indeed codified at 17 U.S.C. §101 *et seq.* and that Section 4 of the *Berne Convention Implementation Act of 1988* (Pub. L. 100-568) is more specifically located at 17 U.S.C. §116.

Ultimately, researchers consult the text of the implementing legislation in U.S.C., the official version of the Code. Using the WIPO website and its database, WIPOLex, prior to carrying out traditional statutory research in the annotated U.S. Code is a particularly efficient strategy for finding the U.S. implementing legislation of world intellectual property laws. The same steps outlined in the prior example for working with U.S. legislation should be carried out here as well.

iii. *Kyoto Protocol to the United Nations Framework Convention on Climate Change (UNFCCC — UN Doc FCCC/CP/1997/7/ Add.1, Dec. 10, 1997; 37 ILM 22 (1998))*

Finding and understanding the Kyoto Protocol to the U.N. Framework Convention on Climate Change (UNFCCC) is a challenging research effort due not only to the number of the treaties involved but also due to the nature of the obligations under those treaties. The UNFCCC set no binding timetable or target levels for greenhouse gas emissions but was later revised by the Kyoto Protocol to require certain parties to reduce their emissions. The Kyoto Protocol itself was subsequently amended by the Doha Amendment. Later, in 2016, the Paris Agreement entered into force. It serves to build upon the UNFCCC by strengthening the response to the threat of climate change.

As with the prior example, it is recommended that researchers find the original document before searching for any associated acts, agreements, or protocols. Here, the official homepage for the United Nations Framework Convention on Climate Change[150] is easily found through a keyword search using the convention's title. The UNFCCC website is arranged with a static left menu bar that offers a link to the Convention, the Kyoto Protocol and the Paris Agreement under Key Steps. After selecting the Convention link, researchers arrive at a page that offers the text of the UNFCCC in its 6 official languages and another link for the status of the treaty.[151] Researchers will also note that

---

150. UNFCCC, http://unfccc.int/2860.php [https://perma.cc/U879-RFMN].

151. UNFCCC, http://unfccc.int/essential_background/convention/items/6036.php [https://perma.cc/LZ6A-ELTJ].

consolidated versions of the Convention are available. Consolidated versions of treaties suggest the existence of amendments and alert the researcher to search for them. By using the status link, the researcher finds that the U.S. ratified the treaty in 1992, and that it entered into force for the U.S. at the same time that it entered into force generally (Article 23 of the UNFCCC requires 90 days following the deposit of the fiftieth instrument of ratification).[152] A close reading of the UNFCCC reveals that it does not commit States to any limitations on greenhouse gas emissions. Rather, it merely includes aspirational goals for limiting the levels of greenhouse gas emissions.

Using the left menu bar, researchers next select the Kyoto Protocol to arrive at a page that offers the text of the protocol as well as a link to obtain the status of the Protocol.[153] This page reveals that the U.S. signed the Protocol but never ratified it.[154] The Kyoto Protocol entered into force generally in 2005. However, because the U.S. did not ratify the Kyoto Protocol, it may not be enforced against the U.S. Nevertheless, as discussed earlier in this chapter, because the U.S. signed the Protocol, it has a duty not to defeat the object and purpose of the protocol. Furthermore, because the U.S. did not ratify the Kyoto Protocol there will be no related domestic implementing legislation.

For thorough and complete research, despite the lack of U.S. ratification of the Kyoto Protocol, the Doha Amendment to the Kyoto Protocol must be explored using the same process described above. Additionally, researchers may choose to track domestic developments related to the Kyoto Protocol and the Doha Amendment. To monitor the U.S. status of the Kyoto Protocol, researchers should tap into current awareness updates through the Department of State's Treaty Affairs website or the Senate Treaties Approved and Received website.[155] For citation purposes, researchers would use the original text of the Convention, not the consolidated versions that have incorporated the Kyoto Protocol, unless specifically referencing them.

For this topical research effort, researchers may begin at the UNFCCC's website because it includes comprehensive background information, drafting

---

152. *See Status of Ratification of the* UNFCCC, http://unfccc.int/essential_background/convention/status_of_ratification/items/2631.php [https://perma.cc/CN34-A94J].

153. *See Kyoto Protocol*, UNFCCC, http://unfccc.int/kyoto_protocol/items/2830.php [https://perma.cc/P26T-G6NK].

154. *Status of Ratification of the Kyoto Protocol*, UNFCCC, http://unfccc.int/kyoto_protocol/status_of_ratification/items/2613.php [https://perma.cc/BDU5-NDFC].

155. *See Treaties*, U.S. Senate, http://www.senate.gov/legislative/treaties.htm [https://perma.cc/3KSF-AY5Q]; Department of State, TIAS, http://www.state.gov/s/l/treaty/tias/index.htm [https://perma.cc/VQE6-R8ZK] (revealing the most recent treaties released in *TIAS*).

history, full-text of the treaty and associated instruments, as well as the status of ratifications all in one location.[156] They must, however, verify using the depositary website. By reading Article 19 of the UNFCCC, researchers uncover that the U.N. is the depositary for the Convention.[157] As described earlier in the chapter, by using a browse strategy in the MTDSG database, researchers select the chapter entitled Environment to obtain a complete listing of all instruments related to the environment for which the UN serves as a depository. Scanning the list reveals the UNFCCC is the 7th listed instrument and it has four related instruments designated as 7a (Kyoto Protocol), 7b (Amendment to Annex B of Kyoto Protocol), 7c (Doha Amendment), and 7d (Paris Agreement). Researchers should select the Kyoto Protocol and examine the status table to verify that the U.S. signed but never ratified it.[158]

Researchers who checked the Popular Name Table and consulted the Treaties in Force index in search of the U.S. domestic implementing legislation for the UNFCCC, separate and apart from the Kyoto Protocol, would discover that none exists. Because the UNFCCC created only non-binding goals to limit greenhouse gas emissions, which are considered more political than legal in nature, there was no need for U.S. domestic implementing legislation.

V. Conclusion

Treaty research is generally carried out first when handling a public international legal research project. Because of the nature of customary international law, as discussed in Chapter 4, treaty research will likely be carried out again later in the research process. The steps for carrying out treaty research are not difficult so long as the legal researcher has a solid grasp of the treaty-making process and an understanding of where and how to find collections of treaty documents. Overall, it is advisable for the researcher to make it a practice to collect as much metadata as possible related to any particular treaty (signature dates, entry into force dates, parties, location of convention, etc.) as the research process unfolds in anticipation of the variety of finding aids and

---

156. *See* UNFCCC, http://unfccc.int/2860.php [https://perma.cc/U879-RFMN].

157. United Nations Framework Convention on Climate Change, May 9, 1992, S. Treaty Doc No. 102-38, 1771 U.N.T.S. 107, http://unfccc.int/resource/docs/convkp/conveng.pdf [https://perma.cc/W95D-2VNF].

158. *See* MTDSG, https://treaties.un.org/pages/ViewDetails.aspx?src=TREATY&mtdsg_no=XXVII-7-a&chapter=27&clang=_en [https://perma.cc/74EC-YCCU].

search options available for the various treaty collections. Such an approach serves to diminish the instances where a researcher must retrace steps.

For those projects that entail finding U.S. implementing legislation, researchers will resort to using national sources. Research strategies for moving between international law sources and national law sources, demonstrated through examples, illustrate the nuances that arise for various types of treaties, including those not yet implemented in the United States.

Chapter 3

The Use of *Travaux Préparatoires* for International Legal Research

I. Introduction

When treaties are vague on their face or the text of the treaty is not interpreted similarly by parties to a treaty, the Vienna Convention on the Law of Treaties allows for the use of the documents generated during negotiation of the treaty, and prior to its signing, for interpretation.[1] These documents are commonly referred to as "drafting documents," or "preparatory documents," also known as *travaux préparatoires*.[2] These preparatory documents can be

---

1. *See* Vienna Convention on the Law of Treaties, 155 U.N.T.S. 331, Article 32 (May 23, 1969), https://treaties.un.org/doc/Publication/UNTS/Volume%201155/volume-1155-I-18232-English.pdf [https://perma.cc/B2RQ-NXC3] which states that "recourse may be had to supplementary means of interpretation, including the preparatory work of the treaty and the circumstances of its conclusion, ... when the interpretation according to article 31: (a) leaves the meaning ambiguous or obscure; or (b) leads to a result which is manifestly absurd or unreasonable." For a description of the modern and traditional views of the use of travaux préparatoires for treaty interpretation, *see* Julian Davis Mortenson, *The Travaux of Travaux: Is the Vienna Convention Hostile to Drafting History?*, 107 AJIL 780 (2013).

2. According to *Black's Law Dictionary*, *travaux préparatoires* [French = "preparatory works"] are "materials used in preparing the ultimate form of an agreement or statute, and especially of an international treaty." *See Travaux Préparatoires*, BLACK's LAW DICTIONARY (9th ed. 2009). It is not premature to mention here that there is also a cross-reference to "legislative history" under the definition of *travaux préparatoires*. *See also* MARK E. VIL-

used to help the courts and States interpret ambiguous treaty language. International courts' dependence on *travaux préparatoires* is similar to U.S. courts relying on extra-statutory documentation produced during the legislative process to interpret vague or ambiguous statutory language.[3] While law-making, multilateral treaties are sometimes likened to a State's legislative process, there are substantial differences.[4] Nevertheless, the concepts and processes involved with compiling a U.S. legislative history and those involved with researching international *travaux préparatoires* are similar enough that likening them allows the U.S. legal researcher to more easily grasp the need for them as well as the legal research process involved.

This chapter begins by acknowledging U.S. courts use legislative histories to discern intent related to federal implementing legislation when it is ambiguous. This brief discussion of the use of legislative histories is included to form the basis of comparison. The chapter then explores U.S. courts' willingness to use *travaux préparatoires* where an international convention is ambiguous. An explanation of the resources and the types of documents a researcher can expect to encounter when handling the *travaux préparatoires* of a treaty is provided. Finally, a legal research process and strategies are offered for finding already-compiled travaux préparatoires as well as those not yet compiled.

LIGER, CUSTOMARY INTERNATIONAL LAW AND TREATIES: A MANUAL ON THE THEORY AND PRACTICE OF THE INTERRELATION OF SOURCES 231 (Kluwer 1997) (revealing that *travaux préparatoires* are preparatory materials comprising "all materials relevant to a treaty and generated prior to its conclusion, e.g., conference records, other observations of States, and the work of the drafting body" and "conventions prepared on the basis of drafts of the International Law Commission" will include materials such as the "reports of Special Rapporteurs, the debates, and votes within the Commission, and the final drafts and commentaries").

3. *See* VCLT, *supra* note 1, art. 32; *see also* RESTATEMENT (THIRD) OF THE FOREIGN RELATIONS LAW OF THE UNITED STATES, § 325 (AM. LAW INST. 1987 & Supp. 2016) (stating that "an international agreement is to be interpreted in good faith"). According to the Restatement, courts in the U.S. are "generally more willing than those of other states to look outside the instrument to determine its meaning." *See* RESTATEMENT (THIRD) OF THE FOREIGN RELATIONS LAW OF THE UNITED STATES, § 325 cmt. g (1987 & Supp. 2016). *See also* TENTATIVE DRAFT RESTATEMENT (FOURTH) OF THE FOREIGN RELATIONS LAW OF THE UNITED STATES, TREATIES, § 101 *et seq.* (Mar. 2016).

4. *See* Detlev F. Vagts, *Treaty Interpretation and the New American Ways of Law Reading*, 4 EJIL, 472, at 475–479 for an in-depth discussion of the treaty negotiation process.

II. U.S. Treaty Interpretation at the Federal Level & Legislative History Research

There are two schools of thought on the value of resorting to the use of a legislative history to resolve ambiguous statutory language in the United States, which may differ from other foreign jurisdictions of the world. Some U.S. judges are opposed, while others are more receptive.[5] When used, U.S. Courts will give a different weight to the various documents generated during the legislative process depending on when and how they were produced in the process. For example, using amendments to bills that require a vote by Congress can reveal collective intent more reliably than statements read into the record by individuals during debate. While both may reveal useful clues, the amendments are given greater weight by the courts.[6] In all instances, because the legislative process is not geared to capturing intent, courts must discern it.

Interpreting ambiguous U.S. treaties where there is implementing legislation involves research using the U.S. sources of law that would be used to compile a legislative history. A detailed discussion of the U.S. legislative history research process, including interpretive materials in treaty and statutory research, has been covered elsewhere and is not included here.[7] The sources involved include *Statutes at Large, Congressional Record, Congressional Reports*

---

5. *Compare* United States v. Stuart, 489 U.S. 353, 371–73 (1989) (Scalia, J., concurring) (stating a vigorous opposition to the use of extrinsic evidence to help interpret the plain language of a tax treaty and the intent of the treaty parties); *with* El Al Israel Airlines, Ltd. v. Tsui Yuan Tseng, 525 U.S. 155, 156 (1999) (holding that courts have "traditionally considered as aids to a treaty's interpretation its negotiating and drafting history *(travaux préparatoires)* and the post-ratification understanding of the contracting parties"). *See generally,* EDWARD SLAVKO YAMBRUSIC, TREATY INTERPRETATION: THEORY AND REALITY 19–27 (Univ. Press 1987) (revealing that it is United States practice to look at circumstances surrounding negotiation, negotiation history, and to follow the Restatement of Foreign Relations Law provisions for interpreting the purpose of the international agreement and ascertaining the intent of the parties); Kenneth W. Starr, *Observations About the Use of Legislative History,* 1987 DUKE L.J. 371–79 (1987); and Stephen Breyer, *On the Uses of Legislative History in Interpreting Statutes,* 65 S. CAL. L. REV. 845–74 (1992).

6. *See* Kenneth R. Dortzbach, *Legislative History: The Philosophies of Justices Scalia and Breyer and the Use of Legislative History by the Wisconsin State Courts,* 80 MARQ. L. REV. 161 (1996–1997).

7. For example, reputable legal research texts include sections on treaty research and federal legislative history within legal research texts. *See generally* STEVEN BARKAN, ROY MERSKY & DONALD DUNN, FUNDAMENTALS OF LEGAL RESEARCH 1 (9th ed., Foundation Press 2009); MORRIS L. COHEN, ROBERT C. BERRING & KENT C. OLSON, HOW TO FIND THE

and Hearings, C.I.S. Index, available statutory publications, *U.S.C.C.A.N.*, Pro-Quest Congressional, C.I.S. Masterfile on Microfiche or digitized now on Pro-Quest Congressional, available databases for legislative history research on Westlaw, Lexis, and CCH's Congressional Index.

III. U.S. Treaty Interpretation at the Federal Level & Use of *Travaux Préparatoires*

Similar to the debate related to the value of using a legislative history to resolve statutory language that is ambiguous,[8] the U.S. Supreme Court has been divided on the value of using *travaux préparatoires* to resolve treaty language that is vague or facially ambiguous.[9] Researchers should be careful to note that textualists like the late Justice Scalia and his counterparts are not likely to be receptive to the introduction of *travaux préparatoires* to resolve ambiguity. On some level, there is a stronger argument against its use given the manner in which treaties are negotiated and concluded as compared to the manner in which bills are debated and amended by Congress. Researchers must evaluate

---

LAW Ch. 7 & Ch. 15 (West 2001). We also recommend readings about the debate surrounding use of legislative histories and *travaux préparatoires* by courts. *See generally* Stephen Breyer, *On the Uses of Legislative History in Interpreting Statutes*, 65 S. CAL. L. REV. 845–874 (1992); Detlev F. Vagts, *Senate Materials and Treaty Interpretation: Some Research Hints for the Supreme Court*, 83 AM. J. INT'L. L. 546–550 (1989).

8. *See United States v. Stuart*, 489 U.S. 353, 371 (1989) (Scalia, J. concurring) (stating that the "plain language of a treaty (which is conclusive) does indeed effectuate the genuine intent ...")"; *see also* Merle H. Weiner, *Navigating the Road Between Uniformity and Progress: The Need for Purposive Analysis of the Hague Convention on the Civil Aspects of International Child Abduction*, 33(2) COLUM. HUM. RTS. L. REV. 275, 317–33 (2002) (articulating a treaty interpretation methodology from the Second Circuit); Michael S. Straubel, *Textualism, Contextualism, and the Scientific Method in Treaty Interpretation: How Do We Find the Shared Intent of the Parties?*, 40(2) WAYNE L. REV. 1191 (1994) (providing an overview of the Supreme Court's history when interpreting treaties).

9. *See, e.g.*, Air France v. Saks, 470 U.S. 392 (1985); Trans World Airlines v. Franklin Mint Corp., 466 U.S. 243 (1984); United States v. Jimenez-Nava, 243 F.3d 192 (5th Cir. 2001), *cert. denied*, 533 U.S. 962 (2001); United States v. Chaparro-Alcantara, 226 F.3d 616 (7th Cir. 2000); United States v. Lombera-Camorlinga, 206 F.3d 882 (9th Cir. 2000). *See also* Nial Fennelly, *Legal Interpretation at the European Court of Justice*, 20 FORDHAM INT'L L.J. 656 (1996) *with* Antonio F. Perez, *The Passive Virtues and the World Court: Pro-Dialogic Abstention by the International Court of Justice*, 18(3) MICH J. INT'L L. 399 (1997).

whether to make an argument based on *travaux préparatoires* in a similar manner to evaluating whether to make an argument based on legislative history. They must consider the forum, the bench, and the local rules. Researchers should check the federal jurisdictions where they are planning to introduce interpretive materials before spending significant time on this type of research.[10]

Given the process by which multilateral treaties are negotiated and concluded, finding and compiling the mass of preparatory documentation produced prior to the date of signing the treaty can be overwhelming.[11] Fortunately, portals provided by the European Union,[12] United Nations,[13] international trade organizations,[14] and individual nations or research institutions[15] include digitized and indexed *travaux préparatoires*. For example, Yale's law library[16] and the U.N. Audio-Visual archive[17] provide useful, already-compiled lists of preparatory documentation for international treaty research.

---

10. Researchers should check a court's website for court rules and information about filing. *E.g.*, United States Court of Appeals for the Seventh Circuit, http://www.ca7.uscourts.gov [https://perma.cc/B9R8-GJ3A]. They should also conduct a thorough search of case law within that jurisdiction to determine whether judges are inclined to accept arguments based on legislative history or introduction to *travaux préparatoires*.

11. *See, e.g., Air France v. Saks*, 470 U.S. 392 (1985). *See also* Peter C. Schanck, *The Only Game in Town: Contemporary Interpretive Theory, Statutory Construction, and Legislative Histories*, 82 Law Libr. J. 419 (1990).

12. *See, e.g., Treaties*, EUR-Lex, http://eur-lex.europa.eu/collection/eu-law/treaties.html [https://perma.cc/4LQL-UMBZ].

13. *See, Uphold International Law*, U.N., http://www.un.org/en/sections/what-we-do/uphold-international-law/index.html [https://perma.cc/KR97-LZU6].

14. *See, e.g., WTO Legal Texts*, WTO, https://www.wto.org/english/docs_e/legal_e/legal_e.htm [https://perma.cc/J647-DGL9] (containing the Uruguay Round Agreements and Negotiations and the Final Agreement Establishing the World Trade Organization and Multilateral Agreements on Trade in Goods (GATT)).

15. *See, e.g., African Studies*, Columbia Univ. Libraries, http://library.columbia.edu/locations/global/africa.html [https://perma.cc/9P2V-2SYG].

16. *See Collected Travaux Préparatoires*, Yale Univ., http://library.law.yale.edu/collected-travaux-préparatoires [https://perma.cc/2T8B-FHNF]; *see also* Jonathan Pratter, *UPDATE: À la Recherche des Travaux Préparatoires: An Approach to Researching the Drafting History of International Agreements*, GlobaLex (May 2015), http://www.nyulawglobal.org/globalex/Travaux_Préparatoires1.html [https://perma.cc/9B2D-TWR3].

17. *Audio Visual Library of International Law, Historic Archives*, U.N., http://legal.un.org/avl/historicarchives.html [https://perma.cc/N4R5-5TA3]; *Audio Visual Library of International Law, Treaty Documents*, U.N., http://legal.un.org/avl/treaties.html [https://perma.cc/JM4F-7QLW].

In addition, the University of Virginia School of Law recently created a database of *travaux préparatoires* for UN Human Rights treaties.[18]

Sometimes, U.S. Courts are interested in considering how foreign domestic courts have resolved ambiguity in the text of a treaty. In such circumstances, legal researchers can turn to the Oxford Reports on International Law in Domestic Courts, a subscription database. Alternatively, they can carry out foreign law research in the relevant jurisdictions, as described in greater detail in Chapter 11.

IV. The Legal Research Process

Presuming the legal researcher has already consulted a legal research guide that covers how to handle *travaux préparatoires*,[19] the first step in handling the research project is to isolate the vague or ambiguous language of the implementing legislation or the treaty text itself.[20] When working with the English language documents of U.S. legislation, the courts are called upon to consider words and language in English. When attempting to interpret the intent of the collective States involved in the treaty negotiating process the effort becomes exponentially more complex because the negotiating process "works back and forth across political frontiers and linguistic/cultural barriers. It implicates many people, some of whom are quite unaware of what other participants in

---

18. *See* University of Virginia School of Law, UN Human Rights Treaties—Travaux Préparatoires, http://hr-travaux.law.virginia.edu/ [https://perma.cc/JZ2U-EMG9].

19. *See, e.g.*, Marilyn Raisch, *Travaux and United Nations Treaties or Conventions: Using the Web Wisely*, 30 Int'l J. Legal Info 324–330 (2002); and Jonathan Pratter, *A la Recherche des Travaux Préparatoires: An Approach to Researching the Drafting History of International Agreements*, http://www.nyulawglobal.org/globalex/Travaux_Preparatoires1.html [https://perma.cc/8BFK-EP4H].

20. *See, e.g.*, *Volkswagenwerk Aktiengesellschaft v. Schlunk*, 486 U.S. 694, 701 (1988) (deciphering a portion of the Hague Convention on the Service Abroad of Judicial and Extrajudicial Documents in Civil or Commercial Matters and turning to the negotiating history of the Convention to determine whether service abroad must be determined by reference to the law of the forum state); *United States v. Duarte-Acero*, 208 F.3d 1282, 1285 (2000) (analyzing provisions of the International Covenant on Civil and Political Rights and even applying Bossuyt's *Guide to the Travaux Préparatoires of the International Covenant on Civil and Political Rights (1987)* to help with interpretation); and *Ancel Vincent Elcock v. United States*, 80 F.Supp.2d 70, 80 (2000) (interpreting provisions of an extradition treaty through use of travaux préparatoires and reference to the prominent works of M. Cherif Bassiouni (Prof. of Law at DePaul University) for help with this type of extradition agreement and construction).

the process have done by way of attaching meaning to the text."[21] One strategy that helps to control the size of the research project is to narrow to a specific word or phrase rather than consider entire sentences or paragraphs.

The next step involves finding the documents produced during the process of concluding the treaty and reading and understanding them in a meaningful way. Because many *travaux préparatoires* are now digitized and available through websites of international organizations or those international conferences that created the treaty,[22] a skilled legal researcher can locate one portal and have a complete index and chronology of events leading up to the signature of a treaty by a particular State.[23] Some already-compiled *travaux préparatoires* are available in print.[24] These can be found by searching a library catalog using the title to the treaty and the word "travaux."

In instances where a researcher does not have such a complete chronology or a comprehensive source for the documentation and its drafting history, finding the *travaux préparatoires* becomes more difficult. The researcher must uti-

---

21. *See* Vagts, *supra* note 4, at 480.

22. There are now helpful websites that provide digital access to the drafting histories of monumental conventions. *See, e.g.,* Pace Law School's *CISG (Convention on Contracts for the International Sale of Goods) Database—Legislative History of 1980 Vienna Diplomatic Conference,* http://www.cisg.law.pace.edu/cisg/conference.html [https://perma.cc/HRL4-4GMT] (containing digitized documents of the negotiations from the conference which led to the final draft of the Convention). *See also* Hague Conference on Private International Law's—*Proceedings of Diplomatic Sessions and Explanatory Reports,* https://www.hcch.net/en/publications-and-studies/publications2 [https://perma.cc/CMD2-4JEY] (digitizing preparatory documents of the Hague Conference for the researcher).

23. *See, e.g.,* World Intellectual Property Organization (WIPO), *Diplomatic Conference on Certain Copyright and Neighboring Rights Questions,* http://www.wipo.int/meetings/en/details.jsp?meeting_id=3010 [https://perma.cc/Q2G2-S5AF] and searching capability, http://www.wipo.int/meetings/en/archive.jsp [https://perma.cc/Q78A-KN2U] (containing a detailed chronology and digitization of meetings and negotiations surrounding the 1996 WIPO Copyright Treaties). Researchers can consult library catalogs and search for legislative histories or *travaux préparatoires* for certain treaty implementations, consult *International Legal Materials* for translations of international preparatory documentation, or search for scholarly journal articles that comprehensively discuss or compile *travaux préparatoires* for a convention or agreement. *See, e.g.,* David Weissbrodt & Mattias Hallendorff, *Travaux Préparatoires of the Fair Trial Provisions—Articles 8 to 11—of the Universal Declaration of Human Rights,* HUM. RTS. Q. 1061–1096 (1999) or Bernard D. Reams, Jr. and Jon S. Schultz, THE NORTH AMERICAN FREE TRADE AGREEMENT (NAFTA): DOCUMENTS AND MATERIALS INCLUDING A LEGISLATIVE HISTORY OF THE NORTH AMERICAN FREE TRADE AGREEMENT IMPLEMENTATION ACT: PUBLIC LAW 103–108 (Oceana 2003).

24. *See e.g.,* HIRAD ABTAHI, *The Genocide Convention: The Travaux Préparatoires* (2008). Researchers can search a library catalog by title using the phrase *travaux préparatoires.*

lize a piecemeal approach and strategize, initially, about which resources might have an English version of preparatory documentation, consult sophisticated databases of international organizations,[25] look for policy documents leading up to adoption of the treaty, and put together a chronology of events from references in a variety of secondary and primary international legal materials.[26] Oftentimes, a researcher might still come up "short" and consequently need to call an international organization, a foreign law library, or the individuals at the site of the treaty negotiation to solicit help from these specialists.[27]

One strategy that researchers might use involves exploring how other lawyers have made arguments based on *travaux préparatoires*. Researchers can examine the Memorials filed before the ICJ and other international courts and tribunals to gather a sense of how and when lawyers use *travaux préparatoires*. The Memorials will cite some of the documents comprising the *travaux préparatoires*. Researchers might also search across all ICJ opinions in a subscription database like Westlaw using variations on the way courts cite Article 32 of the VCLT to find all documents that reference it.

The crux of the effort involves reading and understanding the documents to discern intent. It is rare that researchers will find statements indicating collective intent. Rather, intent must be discerned through the examination of myriad documents. It involves the art of lawyering. Understanding how treaty

---

25. *See, e.g., Diplomatic Conference on Certain Copyright and Neighboring Rights Questions*, WIPO, http://www.wipo.int/meetings/en/details.jsp?meeting_id=3010 [https://perma.cc/RFZ6-CW4X], *Searching Meetings and Documents*, WIPO, http://www.wipo.int/meetings/en/archive.jsp [https://perma.cc/YJC6-9RB9] (containing a detailed chronology and digitization of meetings and negotiations surrounding the 1996 WIPO Copyright Treaties).

26. Researchers may consult library catalogs and search for legislative histories or *travaux préparatoires* for certain treaty implementations, consult *International Legal Materials* for translations of international preparatory documentation, or search for scholarly journal articles that comprehensively discuss or compile *travaux préparatoires* for a convention or agreement. *See, e.g.,* David Weissbrodt & Mattias Hallendorff, *Travaux Préparatoires of the Fair Trial Provisions—Articles 8 to 11—of the Universal Declaration of Human Rights*, Hum. Rts. Q. 1061–1096 (1999); Bernard D. Reams, Jr. & Jon S. Schultz, The North American Free Trade Agreement (NAFTA): Documents and Materials Including A Legislative History of the North American Free Trade Agreement Implementation Act: Public Law 103–108 (Oceana 2003).

27. The U.S. Department of State Country's Office's "Electronic Archive" is quite helpful for locating telephone numbers. *A–Z List of Country and Other Area Pages*, Dep't of State, http://www.state.gov/misc/list/index.htm [https://perma.cc/9V6D-5EQ6].

documents are negotiated, drafted, and concluded is essential to crafting an argument based on the collective intent of the parties to a treaty.

V. Conclusion

Arguably, one of the most difficult concepts for legal researchers is understanding how to use a federal legislative history to resolve ambiguous statutory language. Similarly, research related to the use of *travaux préparatoires* to resolve ambiguous treaty language is also difficult, particularly where an already-compiled travaux does not exist. In circumstances where the legal researcher's project involves a legislative history on U.S. implementing legislation, both the legislative history materials and the *travaux préparatoires* may be available and should be considered for thorough and complete research.

Chapter 4

Customary International Law

I. Introduction

Each U.S. source of law has its official publication. Legislatively-enacted law is published in the United States Code. Federal administrative rules and regulations are published in the U.S. Code of Federal Regulations. Case law is published in the various official reporters: United States Reports, Federal Reporter, and Federal Supplement. In contrast, U.S. legal researchers will find that there is no single publication for customary international law. Because customary international law must be determined through the use of other sources, researchers tend to be vexed by the imprecision of finding and demonstrating it. Attempting to carry out customary international law research before gathering a basic understanding of it as a source of law usually results in frustration and unnecessary effort.

This chapter offers a foundation in customary international law suitable for purposes of legal research. However, for more comprehensive treatment, legal researchers should consult United Nations materials,[1] treatises,[2] law review ar-

---

1. *See e.g.,* Michael Woods (Special Rapporteur), Int'l L Comm'n, '*Fourth report on identification of customary international law,* U.N. Doc. A/CN.4/695 (2016), http://legal.un.org/docs/?symbol=A/CN.4/695 [https://perma.cc/4MGS-NVZE] and A/CN.4/695+Add.1 (2016), http://legal.un.org/docs/?symbol=A/CN.4/695/Add.1 [https://perma.cc/C6U9-ZSCV]. The Addendum is a bibliography of customary international law writings, studies, articles, and textbooks.

2. *See* Re-examining Customary International Law (Brian Lepard ed., 2017); James Crawford, Brownlie's Principles of Public International Law, (8th ed. 2012) [hereinafter *Brownlie's Principles*]; D'Amato, A.A., The Concept of Custom in International Law (1971).

ticles,[3] and the opinions of international tribunals, particularly the International Court of Justice (ICJ).[4] Research strategies for determining rules of customary international law through the use of subsidiary sources and by demonstrating its two elements directly is explained in this chapter. A brief discussion of the challenges related to updating customary international law is also included.

II. Definition of Customary International Law

Article 38(1)(b) of the Statute of the ICJ directs the court to apply "international custom, as evidence of a general practice accepted as law" to resolve disputes.[5] A rule of customary international law is demonstrated by showing

---

3. *See, e.g.,* Frederick Schauer, *The Jurisprudence of Custom*, 48 Texas Int'l L. J., 523 (2013), http://www.tilj.org/content/journal/48/num3/Schauer523.pdf [https://perma.cc/7MSQ-7GK4]; Guzman, A.T., *Saving Customary International Law*, 27 Mich. J. Int'l Law, 115 (2005), http://scholarship.law.berkeley.edu/cgi/viewcontent.cgi?article=1631&context=facpubs [https://perma.cc/6Q4N-3F5H]; Anthea Elizabeth Roberts, *Traditional and Modern Approaches to Customary International Law: A Reconciliation*, 95 Am. J. Int'l L. 757 (2001).

4. *See, e.g.,* The ICJ's North Sea Continental Shelf cases which provide a definition and explanation of customary international law. North Sea Continental Shelf Cases (Federal Republic of Germany/Denmark; Federal Republic of Germany/Netherlands) 1969 I.C.J. 3, North Sea Continental Shelf Cases (Federal Republic of Germany/Denmark; Federal Republic of Germany/Netherlands) 1969 I.C.J. 3, http://www.icj-cij.org/docket/files/51/5535.pdf [https://perma.cc/JHZ2-UFES]. Almost 20 years earlier, in the *Fisheries Case*, the ICJ explored the state practice element. *See,* Fisheries Case, (U.K. v. Nor.), Judgement, 1951 I.C.J. 116, at 129–130 and 138–139, http://www.icj-cij.org/docket/files/5/1809.pdf [https://perma.cc/8MSV-W2NF]. Additionally, the *Nicaragua* case is often cited where a series of treaties are used to demonstrate, or show evidence of customary international law. *See* Military and Paramilitary Activities in and Against Nicaragua (Nicar. v. U.S.), Merits, 1986 I.C.J.14, http://www.icj-cij.org/docket/files/70/6503.pdf [https://perma.cc/C9BF-XPQX] (court relied on multilateral treaties to demonstrate custom)[hereinafter *Military and Paramilitary Activities Case*]. Historically, the Permanent Court of International Justice, the ICJ's predecessor, mentions customary international law in dictum in the Lotus Case, (Fr. v. Turk.), Judgement, 1927 P.C.I.J. 3, http://www.icj-cij.org/pcij/serie_A/A_10/30_Lotus_Arret.pdf [https://perma.cc/MM5D-VVCM]. The PCIJ refused to infer *opinio juris* based, in part, on the omission of action by States (States abstaining from instituting criminal proceedings in international courts does not demonstrate that States consider themselves obliged to prosecute such actions in state courts).

5. Statute of the International Court of Justice, June 26, 1945, art. 38, 59 Stat. 1031 [hereinafter *Statute of the ICJ*].

evidence of two elements: 'general practice' and 'accepted as law.' Similarly, the Restatement, Third, Foreign Relations Laws of the United States explains that customary international law can be broken down into two elements: (1) "general and consistent" state practice (2) followed out of a "sense of legal obligation."[6] Under both definitions, the first element is objective and the second is subjective.[7] The subjective element is referred to as *opinio juris sive necessitates*, or simply, *opinio juris*.

Unlike treaty law, which develops through a formal and structured process of States participating at a convention and concluding an agreement which is captured in the treaty document, customary international law develops in a more informal and decentralized manner. It arises organically, based on the activities and beliefs of States acting on the international stage over time. Customary law is unwritten and contains no formal enforcement mechanisms.[8]

The International Law Association's Committee on the Formation of Customary International Law explained that custom is nothing more than the ongoing process of States' claims and other States' responses as they interact.[9] Under this process, a State or a group of States may take an action or make a claim, whether explicit or implicit. Other States react or respond to the action or claim. These responses give rise to further responses, and so on. Eventually, over a period of time,[10] a set of obligations and a body of particular customs emerges. From these customs, a rule of customary international law can be articulated. The research effort involved in finding the documents that capture the variety of State interactions and motivations worldwide is complex and can be daunting.

To complicate matters, the interplay between a State's actions and its accompanying beliefs is comprised of objective and subjective elements and requires a sophisticated analysis. Sometimes, the ICJ infers *opinio juris* and other times it requires a positive demonstration of the subjective element.[11] Recently,

---

6. RESTATEMENT OF THE LAW (THIRD) THE FOREIGN RELATIONS LAW OF THE UNITED STATES, § 102(2) (1987) [hereinafter *Restatement (Third) Foreign Relations*].

7. *Id.*

8. Scholars, particularly the positivists, have noted that short of war, enforcement occurs by sanctions (or threat of sanctions) or fear of provoking general hostilities. See CRAWFORD, *Brownlie's Principles, supra* note 2, at 9.

9. INTERNATIONAL LAW ASSOCIATION, LONDON CONFERENCE: COMMITTEE ON FORMATION OF CUSTOMARY (GENERAL) INTERNATIONAL LAW, Final Rep., at 10 (2000), http://www.ila-hq.org/en/committees/index.cfm/cid/30, [https://perma.cc/T84J-7GGV].

10. *Id.* at 20. Typically, some amount of time will elapse; however, no precise amount of time is required.

11. CRAWFORD, *Brownlie's Principles, supra* note 2, at 26.

the International Law Commission (ILC) clarified that evidence for each of the two elements must be ascertained separately.[12] Even so, there is no explicit prohibition against using the evidence in support of the objective element as support for the subjective element as well.[13]

Researchers must also be mindful that there are traditional and modern views for how customary international law develops.[14] The traditional view emphasizes the importance of demonstrating state practice.[15] The modern view emphasizes demonstrating *opinio juris*.[16] Under the modern view, with its emphasis on *opinio juris*, an emerging custom can develop more rapidly into a rule of customary international law.[17] The research effort should focus on the resources that reveal patterns of behavior as States pursue their national interests and on the motivations accompanying those patterns of behavior.

Once a rule of customary international law emerges, it binds all States, whether or not they participated in its development.[18] There is not a comparable U.S. source of law to help the U.S. legal researcher understand this concept.

III. General State Practice

States act every day in a variety of ways that affect other States, often without implicating customary international law. These types of actions may be considered a practice. A practice is a group-held belief, without a sense of legal obligation, about how States should behave or act in a particular circumstance. There are practices and behaviors that are exercised out of respect, courtesy, friendship, ceremony, or comity between States that do not rise to the level of

---

12. *See*, Woods, *supra* note 1.

13. Int'l Law Comm'n, Annual Rep., Sixty-Eighth Session, U.N. Doc. A/71/10, at 99 (2016), http://www.un.org/ga/search/view_doc.asp?symbol=A/71/10 [https://perma.cc/KLK8-ARJ9] [hereinafter *Int'l Law Comm'n 2016 Annual Report*].

14. *See* Roberts, *supra* note 3, at 758. *See also*, Michael P. Scharf, *Accelerated Formation of Customary International Law*, 20.2 ILSA Journal of Int'l and Comp Law 305 (2014), http://scholarlycommons.law.case.edu/cgi/viewcontent.cgi?article=2166&context=faculty_publications [https://perma.cc/N5JE-6KZM].

15. *See* Roberts, *supra* note 3, at 758. For the traditional view, see North Sea Continental Shelf Cases (Federal Republic of Germany/Denmark; Federal Republic of Germany/Netherlands) 1969 I.C.J. 3. *See also*, Crawford, *Brownlie's Principles, supra* note 2, which traces the history of those who do not recognize the subjective or psychological element back to 1934.

16. *Id.*

17. Scharf, *supra* note 14.

18. *Restatement (Third) Foreign Relations, supra* note 6, § 102 (1987).

customary international law.[19] It is only where those practices are accompanied by a sense of legal obligation that they rise to the level of customary international law.

To handle the customary international law research effort, the legal researcher must consider both conduct and verbal actions.[20] While the verbal actions of official State actors or representatives are considered when assessing state practice, it is important to focus on State conduct against the backdrop of a stated policy. This necessarily entails a different type of research effort—one that may be less *legal* research and more political, historical, or social sciences research. There is a need to research more generally for the necessary context as a backdrop for interpreting and understanding a State's conduct and verbal actions.[21]

As a practical matter, it is challenging to determine the quantity of States that must be researched to demonstrate general and consistent state practice. It is well-settled that it is not necessary to demonstrate that *every* State engages in a particular practice.[22] At the other end of the spectrum, one commentator has suggested that only 3 or 4 States' practices, those with the largest navies, formed the basis for the law of the sea.[23] The ICJ has suggested that it is not necessarily the number of States but those States that are 'specially affected'[24] that forms the basis of a customary rule.

The legal researcher must assess which States to pursue for purposes of demonstrating a rule of customary international law. More than a simple quan-

---

19. Crawford, *Brownlie's Principles, supra* note 2, at 23–24 (offering the examples of ceremonial salutes at sea and exempting diplomatic vehicles from parking prohibitions as practices that do not rise to the level of custom because they do not reflect a legal obligation).

20. The Statute of the International Court of Justice: A Commentary, at 814–820 (Zimmerman, *et al.,* eds., 2d ed. 2012).

21. *Int'l Law Comm'n 2016 Annual Report, supra* note 13, at 85–86 (given that conduct "may be fraught with ambiguity" it must be evaluated within context).

22. *See, e.g., Restatement (Third) Foreign Relations, supra* note 6, at § 102 (practice must be extensive) and Int'l Law Ass'n London Conference, Final Rep., *supra* note 9, at 20 (practice must be widespread).

23. Oscar Schacter, *New Custom: Power, Opinio Juris and Contrary Practice,* Theory in International Law at the Threshold of the 21st Century, at 536–537 (Jerzy Makarczyk ed., 1996). *But see,* Bedjaoui, Mohammed, Toward a New International Economic Order 51–53 (1979), http://unesdoc.unesco.org/images/0003/000358/035806eo.pdf [https://perma.cc/SZ8P-6LCR] (custom related to freedom on the high seas was developed to protect wealthy States with large fleets and did not take into consideration those States along whose shores the wealthy States' fleets navigated)

24. North Sea Continental Shelf (Fed. Rep. of Germ/Den.; Fed. Rep. of Germ/Neth.), Judgment, 1969 I.C.J. 3.

titative analysis is required. The research objective is to find material, or evidence, that either supports or refutes that there is a settled practice that States believe to be legally binding. By beginning with specially-affected States, the legal researcher may sometimes avoid having to canvass or research a widespread number of States' practice. For example, if all of the specially-affected States conduct themselves in accordance with a particular practice, then it will not be necessary to carry out additional research into the remaining States' practices. Conversely, if some of the specially-affected States do not accept a particular practice, then an argument that a rule has matured into customary international law will likely be challenged.

Sometimes it is fairly easy to identify the specially-affected States. For example, if the researcher is considering a rule of customary international law related to outer space, those States with the ability to place objects in outer space might be considered the specially-affected States. Other times, it is more difficult to identify specially-affected States. The matter of which States can be labeled specially-affected may itself be a research project. Naturally, the subject matter of the rule of customary international law will inform the legal researcher's decisions on which States to pursue and which materials to use.

IV. Accepted as Law

The subjective element of the definition of customary international law is demonstrated by showing that a particular State practice is accompanied by a sense of legal obligation.[25] Acting out of a sense of legal obligation means that a State believes it is legally bound to act consistently with a particular practice and that failure to do so would, or should, result in international legal consequences.[26] A State must act out of more than a moral obligation, a politically expedient reason, or based on friendship, goodwill, or comity for its actions to rise to the level of evidence of a customary international law.[27] A State must act with the conviction that it is legally obligated for purposes of *opinio juris*. To satisfy the second element, the legal researcher must find materials that reveal a State's motivations for acting.

The challenge here is that the legal researcher must search for evidence of the mental state of a legally-constructed personality, a State. Due to the in-

---

25. See *Statute of the ICJ, supra* note 5 and *Restatement (Third) Foreign Relations, supra* note 6.

26. Crawford, *Brownlie's Principles, supra* note 2, at 17.

27. Crawford, *Brownlie's Principles, supra* note 2, at 23–24.

herent difficulty of discerning a State's motivations, this element of the definition is sometimes inferred from the statements and actions of those charged with representing the State in an official capacity.[28] Consequently, the same documents used to show state action may also be used to show *opinio juris*. Treaties,[29] General Assembly resolutions,[30] and the work of the ILC[31] have all been used to show evidence of *opinio juris*. An important distinction for the researcher to make is that these documents are used as evidence of States acting with the requisite sense of legal obligation, rather than to validate State action itself through the existence of the documents.

Despite the ability to rely on the same documents as evidence of state practice and *opinio juris*, the legal researcher is well-advised to carry out independent research for each element. Demonstrating *opinio juris* is complex. It requires understanding the interplay between documents, statements, and actions; it requires considering legal, political, and diplomatic events in chronological order to draw interpretations and conclusions as to a State's mental state. It most certainly engages the art of lawyering where the lawyer is called upon to stitch together a plausible explanation in support of a State's actions and beliefs based on such research. By taking each of the elements of the definition of customary international law in turn during the research process, the legal researcher can be sure to carry out thorough and complete research. Such an approach reinforces the need to handle and think about documents from various angles. The iterative nature of international legal research is particularly apparent when researching customary international law. Acknowledging this fact alone allows the legal researcher to gain confidence in their research effort despite that it may appear redundant or inefficient.

---

28. *See Restatement (Third) Foreign Relations, supra* note 6, § 102, cmt. c.

29. *See, e.g., The Diplomatic & Consular Staff in Tehran* case where the ICJ essentially codified the 1961 and 1963 Vienna Conventions on Diplomatic and Consular Relations. *Diplomatic & Consular Staff in Tehran*, (U.S.A. v. Iran), Judgement, 1980 I.C.J. 3 (1980).

30. *See, e.g., Military and Paramilitary Activities Case, supra* note 4, at 97–104, where the ICJ explored the attitude of the parties toward General Assembly Resolution 2625 (XXV), entitled "Declaration on Principles of International Law concerning Friendly Relations and Co-operation among States in accordance with the Charter of United Nations."

31. *See, e.g., Jurisdictional Immunities Case* (Germany v. Italy), Judgment, 2012 I.C.J. 99, at para. 56.

V. Actions in Contravention of Customary International Law

Once a rule of customary international law emerges, actions in contravention are considered breaches.[32] There are three exceptions to this general rule. First, States may subsequently ratify a treaty that is at odds with customary international law. It is generally accepted that treaty law will prevail over an inconsistent *existing* rule of customary international law according to the later-in-time rule.[33] The legal researcher should pay close attention to the timing of the emergence of the custom and the entry into force date for the treaty when determining which law governs a controversy.

Second, where a State can demonstrate opposition to a rule of customary international law developing over time, it may be considered a persistent objector and not governed by the rule.[34] A State must object to the formation of a custom at the outset, as it emerges, and must continue to act contrary to it consistently over time, to be considered a persistent objector.[35] A persistent objector circumstance does not negate a rule of customary international law. The legal researcher must take care to distinguish between a single persistent objector and circumstances where general state practice simply cannot be demonstrated.

The third exception to the general rule that customary international law governs all States involves circumstances where a local custom, as opposed to a general custom, exists between two or a limited number of States.[36] Unlike customary international law, local custom does not bind all States. Rather, it binds only those States within a geographical area that share a common practice as a matter of

---

32. *Military and Paramilitary Activities Case, supra* note 4.

33. *Restatement (Third) Foreign Relations, supra* note 6, § 115, cmt. j and rep. note 4. For an example of a treaty displaced by subsequent custom, *see* CRAWFORD, *Brownlie's Principles,* at 22–23 (citing *Air Transport Services Agreement* (1963), 38 ILR 182, 248–255).

34. It must be acknowledged that not all scholars agree on the topic of persistent objector. *See* JAMES A. GREEN, THE PERSISTENT OBJECTOR RULE IN INTERNATIONAL LAW (2016).

35. David A. Colson, *How Persistent Must the Persistent Objector Be?* 61 WASH. L. REV. 957 (1986).

36. *Restatement (Third) Foreign Relations, supra* note 6, at § 102(2), cmt. e. (citing the *Asylum Case,* (Columbia v. Peru), 1950 I.C.J. Rep. 266, 277).

right.[37] Local custom may be at odds with the emergence of a general rule of customary international law without defeating it.

The possibility of a local custom, a persistent objector, or a treaty that appears to be at odds with a legal researcher's argument that a particular norm rises to the level of a rule of customary international law, should not automatically preclude the legal researcher from demonstrating a rule of general customary international law. Mindful of these three exceptions, the legal researcher should not prematurely abandon a research effort in support of customary international law.

VI. *Jus Cogens*

There are certain customary international law norms that are so fundamental that there may be no derogation from them. These are peremptory norms and are commonly known by the Latin phrase, *jus cogens*. By definition, these peremptory norms prevail over regular customary international law norms. Only a subsequent peremptory norm of contrary effect may set aside established *jus cogens*.[38] Additionally, Article 53 of the Vienna Convention on the Law of Treaties (VCLT) directs that any treaty concluded in conflict with a peremptory norm is void *ab initio*.[39] Further, Article 64 of the VCLT directs that parties to a treaty provision in conflict with a *new* peremptory norm, are released from treaty obligation moving forward.[40] In short, *jus cogens* prevails over treaty law and regular customary international law norms.

Given the lack of clear guidelines or criteria for identifying peremptory norms, there is no authoritative list of *jus cogens*. Some scholars would expand any list of *jus cogens* drastically[41] while others would question the existence of *jus cogens* at all.[42] Nevertheless, the following list includes the least controversial examples, according to Brownlie:[43]

---

37. D'Amato, Anthony, *The Concept of Special Custom in International Law*, 63 Amer. J. Int'l L. 211 (1969), http://scholarlycommons.law.northwestern.edu/cgi/viewcontent.cgi?article=1115&context=facultyworkingpapers [https://perma.cc/43EP-AUEN].

38. CRAWFORD, *Brownlie's Principles, supra* note 2.

39. Vienna Convention on the Law of Treaties, art. 53, *opened for signature* May 23, 1969, 1155 U.N.T.S. 331.

40. Id., at art. 64.

41. *See, e.g.,* Parker and Neylon, *Jus Cogens: Compelling the Law of Human Rights*, 12 HASTINGS INT'L & COMP. L. REV. 411 (1989).

42. *See, e.g.,* KAROL WOLFKE, CUSTOM IN PRESENT INTERNATIONAL LAW, at 92 (1993).

43. CRAWFORD, *Brownlie's Principles, supra* note 2.

- Prohibition of the use of armed force except for self defense
- Prohibition of racial discrimination
- Prohibition of genocide
- Prohibition of crimes against humanity
- Prohibition of slavery
- Prohibition of piracy

The ILC acknowledged Brownlie's list and includes, in a footnote, the lists of *jus cogens* compiled by other scholars and those identified in ICJ opinions.[44]

VII. Sources & Legal Research Process for Customary International Law

Preliminarily, the researcher should determine whether the research project must show the formation of a *new* rule of customary international law or whether evidence is required of an existing and identified rule of customary international law. Because the "customary international law process is a continuing one [and] it does not stop when a rule has emerged"[45] both types of research efforts are complex, though the former usually is more complex than the latter, as explored below.

A. Subsidiary Means for the Determination of an Existing Rule of Customary International Law

From a research perspective, it is far easier to use subsidiary means for determining rules of customary international law than it is to carry out the extensive research needed to show general and consistent State practice, accompanied by a sense of legal obligation. Article 38(1)(d) provides the ICJ may use "... judicial decisions and the teachings of the most highly qualified publicists of the various nations, as subsidiary means for the determination of rules of law." Additionally, codification treaties that set forth a rule of customary international law have become significant, according to the ILC, because

---

44. *Fragmentation of International Law: Difficulties arising from the Diversification and Expansion of International Law.* REPORT OF THE STUDY GROUP OF THE INT'L L COMM'N, U.N. Doc A/CN.4/L.682 at 189, http://legal.un.org/ilc/documentation/english/a_cn4_l682.pdf [https://perma.cc/B3P3-UZDG].

45. *See,* M.H., Mendelson, *The Formation of Customary International Law,* 272 HAGUE ACADEMY OF INTERNATIONAL LAW, COLLECTED COURSES (1998), 155–410, at 175.

their stated purpose is to record and define rules of customary international law.[46] Although not technically considered a subsidiary means for the determination of a rule of customary international law, codification treaties are included in the discussion below because the ILC has recognized the significance of them for the identification of existing rules of customary international law.[47]

i. Research to Find Judicial Decisions to Show Evidence of Existing Customary International Law

Using judicial decisions as a subsidiary source is distinct from research related to world judicial decisions, a topic covered in Chapter 7. This section covers nuances where the legal researcher cites to a judgment of the ICJ, or other international tribunal, to show that the court has made a determination that a particular practice has emerged into a rule of customary international law.[48] It is only after an international tribunal accepts the arguments in the Memorials and holds that a particular State practice rises to the level of customary international law that the judgment itself can be used as a means for showing evidence of a rule of customary international law.

The use of judicial decisions in this manner, as a subsidiary source, should not be confused with using them to show state practice or *opinio juris*.[49] The authority to cite to judicial decisions as a subsidiary source falls under Article 38(1)(d) of the Statute of the ICJ; whereas the authority to cite to the filings underlying the judicial decisions as state practice falls under Article 38(1)(b). As a subsidiary means, judicial decisions are not themselves a source of law like treaties, custom or general principles. Rather, the judicial decisions are used as an auxiliary means to determine a rule of customary international law.

Using judicial decisions as a subsidiary source requires legal researchers to assess the quality of the court's reasoning paying particular attention to the evidence considered and the "reception of the decision by States and by other courts."[50] Additionally, researchers must consider the expertise of the members of the court, whether the decision was agreed to by a majority on the

---

46. *Int'l Law Comm'n 2016 Annual Report*, at 101–102, *supra* note 13.

47. *Id.*

48. It is long established that where the ICJ has been called upon to establish a rule of customary international law, the published documents of the case offer the "... fullest and most objective description of the formation of the custom in question." WOLFKE, CUSTOM IN PRESENT INTERNATIONAL LAW, *supra* note 42, at 84–85.

49. See *infra* at III and IV for a discussion of the research related to judicial decisions to show evidence of state practice.

50. *Int'l Law Comm'n 2016 Annual Report*, *supra* note 13, at 109.

court, and the conditions under which the court carries out its business.[51] Clearly, the research effort entails more than simply identifying judicial decisions that accept an argument based on a customary international law rule.

The phrase 'judicial decisions' in Article 38 has been interpreted to include the decisions and advisory opinions, including orders related to procedural matters, from the following courts:[52]

- International Court of Justice and its predecessor the Permanent Court of International Justice
- International Tribunal for the Law of the Sea
- International Criminal Court and other international criminal tribunals
- Regional human rights tribunals
- World Trade Organization Appellate Body
- Inter-State Arbitral Tribunals and other arbitral tribunals applying international law

While most of these international tribunals have websites, with access to their judgments and opinions, the work of the arbitral tribunals is more difficult to find and often the decisions are confidential.[53]

While the decisions of national courts are not explicitly rejected as a possibility for use as a subsidiary source of law, some caution must be exercised when using them. The ILC explained that national decisions often reflect a national perspective, may have been decided by judges with less international experience or expertise, and may lack the breadth of evidence that is usually at the disposal of an international tribunal in making a judgment.[54]

ii. Research to Find the Teachings of the Most Highly Qualified Publicists to Show Evidence of Existing Customary International Law

Generally, the same caveats that apply to judicial decisions do not apply to the teachings of the most highly qualified publicists because the efforts of these

---

51. *Id.*

52. *Id.* at 110.

53. See MARCI HOFFMAN & MARY RUMSEY, *International and Foreign Legal Research: A Coursebook* (2d ed. 2012), (Chapter 21 provides detailed explanation for finding arbitral awards and decisions).

54. *Int'l Law Comm'n 2016 Annual Report*, at 110, *supra* note 13. See also, Ryan M. Scoville, *Finding Customary International Law*, 101 Iowa L. Rev. 1893 (2016) (offering an in-depth analysis of how U.S. federal court judges find customary international law).

publicists, or authors, unless they act in official State capacity, cannot be used to show state practice or *opinio juris*. Other caveats do apply including the need to assess credibility, authority, and accuracy of the teaching, or writing, as well as the rigor of the study. These details and the research process and strategies for handling the teachings of the most highly qualified publicists is covered in greater depth in Chapter 6.

iii. Research to Find Codification Treaties to Show Evidence of Existing Customary International Law

Customary international law may be codified within a treaty. When this happens, both treaty law and customary international law form the basis of the law.[55] This might initially confuse the U.S. legal researcher. The ICJ explained that certain norms, when codified in a treaty, continue to exist and can be applied separately from treaty law, as customary international law.[56] When used in this vein, the legal researcher cites to the codification treaty to show evidence of an existing custom but relies on the custom itself, which governs all States, even those that have not ratified or acceded to the treaty. An example of a codified rule of customary international law is the rule that every state may act in self-defense against an armed attack. This rule of customary international law has been codified in the United Nations Charter, Article 51.[57]

Treaty research is covered in greater depth in Chapter 2. However, when using codification treaties to show evidence of customary international law, the U.S. legal researcher must be cautioned that it is rare for an entire treaty to be considered a codification of customary international law. For example, although many provisions of the Vienna Convention on the Law of Treaties are considered a codification of customary international law,[58] those provisions in *Part VIII* would not be considered a codification of customary international law as they relate to this treaty specifically. For this reason, the legal researcher should be careful to select and cite to only those individual provisions that codify a rule of customary international law.

---

55. North Sea Continental Shelf cases, 1969 I.C.J. (Apr. 26, 1968 and Feb. 20, 1969),

56. *Military and Paramilitary Activities Case, supra* note 4, at ¶ 175, where the ICJ explained, in dicta, that even if a treaty norm and a customary norm "have exactly the same content ..." the treaty would not deprive the customary norm of its separate applicability. *Id.*

57. U.N. Charter art. 51. https://treaties.un.org/doc/publication/ctc/uncharter.pdf [https://perma.cc/B6W7-SJVT].

58. *Restatement (Third) Foreign Relations, supra* note 6, § 102 (1987).

There are three research strategies that can be used to determine whether a treaty has codified customary international law. The first is to read the treaty language itself, including the preamble. The text of a provision may indicate an intent to codify customary international law.[59] Although the ILC warns against simply reading the text of the treaty,[60] for research purposes, finding a treaty with an express declaration of a rule of customary international law advances the research effort considerably because it offers a starting point for identifying which States to pursue for research purposes of demonstrating state practice and *opinio juris*.

The second strategy to determine whether a treaty sets forth a rule of customary international law is to examine the travaux préparatoires. Statements made by State delegates may show that the convention intended to codify a customary international law rule. Research related to travaux préparatoires is covered in Chapter 3.

The third research strategy is to use a commentary. A commentary is a particular type of scholarly writing that offers an explanation and discussion of a treaty, article-by-article.[61] Commentaries can be useful to the legal researcher for purposes of making a determination of whether any particular treaty provision is a codification of a rule of customary international law. Examples of commentaries include the Vienna Convention on the Law of Treaties: A Commentary[62] and The Charter of the United Nations: A Commentary.[63] There are others and they can be found by searching library catalogs with the title to the treaty and the word 'commentary.'

It should be stressed that these three strategies are *research* efforts connected to using a codification treaty to advance the effort to find evidence in support of a rule of customary international law. The researcher can use these strategies as a starting point but must always also research and find relevant state practice and *opinio juris* to offer in conjunction with the codification treaty. Given the structure and the language of Article 38 of the Statute of the ICJ, treaties cannot, in and of themselves, be used as a subsidiary means to deter-

---

59. *Int'l Law Comm'n 2016 Annual Report, supra* note 13, at 102–103.

60. *Id.*

61. Christian Djeffal, *Commentaries on the Law of Treaties: A review essay reflecting the genre of commentaries*, 24:4 Eur. J. Int'l L. 1223 (2013).

62. Vienna Convention on the Law of Treaties: A commentary (Olivier Corten and Pierre Klein, eds. 2011).

63. The Charter of the United Nations: A Commentary. (Simma Bruno, Hermann Mosler, Andreas Paulus, and Eleni Chaitidou eds. 3d ed., 2012).

mine a rule of customary international law, even in circumstances where it is a multilateral treaty ratified by a supermajority of States.

B. Updating Subsidiary Sources of Customary International Law

Where existing rules of customary international law are identified and accepted, the research effort becomes one of updating the rule. Development of customary international law does not stop upon a practice emerging as a rule. The objective when updating an identified rule is to demonstrate either that the custom has not changed since the point in time that it was articulated, acknowledged and accepted by the international community, or that it has changed and that a new rule has emerged.

While the U.S. legal researcher is generally accustomed to using a citator to update the law and some types of secondary sources; unfortunately, no citator exists for updating the rules of customary international law. Updating customary international law requires canvassing state practice and *opinio juris* since the date that the custom was identified and accepted. That research process is essentially the same process for demonstrating state practice and *opinio juris* in the first instance, as discussed below. Researchers should guard against merely updating the individual documents originally used to show evidence of the rule of customary international law. Certainly, that would be a first step. However, researchers must not fail to take a more comprehensive view to ensure that nothing is overlooked. Customary international law is dynamic and based on the ongoing interactions and motivations among States, including those that have occurred since the original determination that a rule emerged.

C. Finding Evidence of Rules of Customary International Law That Have Yet to Be Identified or Are New Rules

For the research project that entails supporting an argument for the emergence of a new rule of customary international law or for a rule that has yet to be identified in other sources, the legal researcher must research state practice and *opinio juris*. There is no single text or website that compiles state practice and *opinio juris*. A legal researcher must consult a multitude of diverse documents and websites to formulate the basis of the argument and to show evidence of State practice in support of the existence of a rule of customary international law. Indeed, the effort must be comprehensive and assessed as a whole.

The 2016 Annual Report of the ILC set forth the following forms of state practice: "diplomatic acts and correspondence; conduct in connection with resolutions adopted by an international organization or at an intergovernmental conference; conduct in connection with treaties; executive conduct, including operational conduct (on the ground); legislative and administrative acts; and decisions of national courts."[64] It recognized that its list was not exhaustive, should be interpreted broadly, and was not set forth in any particular order.[65] The ILC also set forth the following forms of evidence of *opinio juris*: "public statements made on behalf of States; official publications; government legal opinions; diplomatic correspondence; decisions of national courts; treaty provisions; and conduct in connection with resolutions adopted by an international organization or at an intergovernmental conference."[66]

Others have compiled the following types or categories of documents as state practice: "diplomatic correspondence, policy statements, press releases, the opinions of government legal advisers, official manuals on legal questions (e.g., manuals of military law), executive decisions and practices, orders to military forces (rules of engagement), comments by governments on ILC drafts and accompanying commentary, legislation, international and national judicial decisions, recitals in treaties and other international instruments (especially when in 'all states' form), an extensive pattern of treaties in the same terms, the practice of international organs, and resolutions relating to legal questions in U.N. organs, notably the General Assembly."[67]

Because the same documents may be used to demonstrate both state practice and *opinio juris*, an explanation for finding such materials will be taken together, below. Usually the norm under consideration will drive the researcher's choice of documents used to show evidence of state practice and *opinio juris*. While the focus is on U.S. resources and those available to the U.S. legal researcher, finding the same or similar types of documents in foreign jurisdictions takes no small amount of ingenuity, not to mention the ability to read and understand other languages. It is for this reason that the work of organizations comprised of international scholars and experts who have access to the documents and publications in their home jurisdictions is considered particularly valuable.

---

64. *Int'l Law Comm'n 2016 Annual Report, supra* note 13, at 77.
65. *Id.* at 92.
66. *Id.* at 99.
67. CRAWFORD, *Brownlie's Principles, supra* note 2, at 24 (citing UNCLOS, Arts 3, 17, 79, 87 as examples of 'all states' form).

i. *Treaties and Other Diplomatic Acts and Correspondence to Show State Practice and Opinio Juris*

Treaty research is covered in greater depth in Chapter 2 and codification treaties have been covered earlier in this chapter. The most common use of treaties to demonstrate state practice and *opinio juris* involves finding multilateral treaties that have been ratified by a majority of States. Researchers often use the Multilateral Treaties Deposited with the Secretary-General database[68] on the U.N. website although there are other collections maintained by individual States and other organizations.[69] Another strategy that legal researchers use is finding a series of treaties, concluded over time, that contain provisions that set forth a norm in the same or similar language. However, the ILC has warned against presuming such practice always reflects a rule of customary international law.[70] Under both approaches, the legal researcher must find and examine the state ratifications, as well as RUDs in an effort to demonstrate state practice and *opinio juris*. Additionally, documents produced in the process of negotiating and concluding a treaty may also be used to show state practice and *opinio juris*.[71] Research related to travaux préparatoires is discussed in Chapter 3.

Other diplomatic activity is generally collected in publications within a particular State jurisdiction. For example, in the U.S., the Foreign Relations of the United States set (FRUS) is published by the Government Publishing Office and available in print and online. FRUS contains papers from the "Presidential libraries, Departments of State and Defense, National Security Council, Central Intelligence Agency, Agency for International Development, and other foreign affairs agencies as well as the private papers of individuals involved in formulating U.S. foreign policy."[72] Researchers often use *Sources of*

---

68. United Nations Multilateral Treaties Deposited with the Secretary-General, https://treaties.un.org/pages/ParticipationStatus.aspx?clang=_en [https://perma.cc/U3MK-7NGR].

69. *See United Nations Audiovisual Library of International Law, Treaty Documents*, http://legal.un.org/avl/treaties.html [https://perma.cc/JM4F-7QLW] (use the tab for Collections maintained by States or the tab for Collections maintained by other entities).

70. *Int'l Law Comm'n 2016 Annual Report, supra* note 13, at 102.

71. ILC, A/71/10 at 104 (explaining that "statements by States in the course of the drafting process [of a treaty] that may disclose an intention to codify an existing rule of customary international law.").

72. Foreign Relations of the United States, U.S. Department of State, https://history.state.gov/historicaldocuments [https://perma.cc/2WJE-3Q4A]. *See also Id.*, Historical Description, Foreign Relations of the United States, https://history.state.gov/historicaldocuments/about-frus [https://perma.cc/25WA-U7QP].

State Practice in International Law[73] to find similar types of publications in other jurisdictions.

There are a number of other U.S. publications for diplomatic papers in print that can be found by searching catalogs using **United States — foreign relations** subject heading or key words including a combination of the following terms: American, United States, state papers, foreign policy. The Digest of United States Practice in International Law[74] is particularly useful. Published annually, it offers U.S. practices and views of both public and private international law.[75] Digests can be found using **Law reports, digests, etc. — Country** or by using a key word search in a catalog with Digests Country.

Generally, the diplomatic record for foreign States is quite restricted. Researchers should look for a national archives or ministry of foreign affairs website in a particular jurisdiction to ascertain what may be available online. The Office of the Historian offers a worldwide diplomatic archives index.[76] To find documents in print, use the subject heading: **State — foreign relations** or resort to key word searching within a library catalog, as above substituting American for the jurisdiction of interest. Ultimately, legal researchers may have to resort to requesting information and documents by placing an open records request in a particular jurisdiction, as these increasingly exist with efforts to encourage greater government transparency worldwide.[77]

ii. National Legislation

While foreign law research is covered generally in Chapter 11 in the context of cultural competencies and it is covered more fully elsewhere,[78] the strat-

---

73. RALPH F. GAEBLER & ALISON A. SHEA, eds, *Sources of State Practice in International Law* (2014).

74. *Digest of United States Practice in International Law*, https://www.state.gov/s/l/c8183.htm [https://perma.cc/3FCR-YDQD].

75. *Id.* Earlier volumes beginning in 1973 are available in print and through HeinOnline.

76. *See* Office of the Historian, https://history.state.gov/ [https://perma.cc/9PMJ-L99F].

77. Right2info.org/laws/constitutional-provisions-laws-and-regulations [https://perma.cc/XW32-UKAK].

78. *See* MARCI HOFFMAN & MARY RUMSEY, INTERNATIONAL AND FOREIGN LEGAL RESEARCH: A COURSEBOOK (2d ed. 2012); ANTHONY S. WINER & MARY ANN E. ARCHER, A BASIC COURSE IN PUBLIC INTERNATIONAL LAW RESEARCH (2005); J. PAUL LOMIO & HENRIK SPANG-HANSSEN, LEGAL RESEARCH METHODS IN THE U.S. AND EUROPE (2008).

egy for handling national legislation involves consulting a research guide for the relevant jurisdiction to obtain the titles to the publications that contain the national legislation and where such legislation is available in print and online. The *Foreign Law Guide*, an online subscription, is organized with subject headings that remain consistent across all jurisdictions and is a useful starting point.[79] Globalex is a reputable, free alternative.[80] Armed with the title to the publication that holds the national legislation, the legal researcher can determine whether the law is available online through the government website or only available in print. If print is required, researchers should search WorldCat[81] to obtain a listing of which libraries hold the title. Titles not held by a legal researcher's home institution may be requested through an interlibrary loan.

The use of government gazettes is another option for the legal researcher to find national legislation. The content of government gazettes varies among States and is generally offered in the vernacular. Government Gazettes Online[82] compiles a listing of most State's gazettes with links to where they are available online. While some of the links are outdated, the metadata available from this website can be used to carry out an independent search. To find gazettes in print within a library, carry out a subject heading search in the catalog using **gazettes—country**.

Failing that, yearbooks will sometimes contain summaries of national legislation, among other types of information. HeinOnline has a comprehensive collection of yearbooks, which have also been indexed in the *Index to Foreign Legal Periodicals*.[83] To find yearbooks in print within a library, carry out a subject heading search in the catalog using **international law—yearbooks**. Year-

---

79. *See* FOREIGN LAW GUIDE, (Hoffman ed., 2012), http://www.brill.com/publications/online-resources/foreign-law-guide [https://perma.cc/EF94-8VRM]. (available through HeinOnline).

80. Globalex Foreign Law Research, http://www.nyulawglobal.org/globalex/index.html# [https://perma.cc/VC4B-MYNE].

81. WorldCat, http://www.worldcat.org/ [https://perma.cc/9U4F-9NYH].

82. Government Gazettes Online, University of Michigan, http://www-personal.umich.edu/~graceyor/doctemp/gazettes/ [https://perma.cc/WG7F-5R95].

83. *See* HeinOnline, http://heinonline.org/ [https://perma.cc/8H5X-B3JR]. Choose the Foreign & International Law Resources database within HeinOnline for the yearbooks collection. The Index to Foreign Legal Periodicals is its own database within HeinOnline.

books may be found by employing a jurisdiction,[84] IGO,[85] or topic approach.[86] For a discussion on these approaches, see Chapter 9.

iii. National Decisions and State Filings in International Tribunals

Similar to using the work of a State's legislative organ to demonstrate state practice and *opinio juris*, the work of a State's judicial organ may also be used. Researching national decisions is a foreign law research project. The same approach employed for national legislation may be employed for national decisions: utilize a trusted research guide to identify the titles to the publications that contain the national decisions and then carry out a WorldCat search to find libraries that hold those publications. Decisions from all national court levels may be researched and considered.[87]

Using national decisions as evidence of state practice should be distinguished from using a State's filings in an international tribunal to show state action and *opinio juris*. The ICJ or other international tribunal is not a State organ (like the judicial, legislative or executive arms of national governments) and as such its opinions are not evidence of *a particular* State's practice. However, the Memorials submitted in support of a State's position that a particular norm should be considered customary international law, can be used to demonstrate that particular State's action and what it believes is customary international law.

Accordingly, a productive strategy for demonstrating what a State believes to be custom is to identify and find international tribunal opinions that consider issues that rest on customary international law. Once identified, the legal researcher can locate the Memorials filed by each State to find its assertions of state practice and *opinio juris* as well as the citations supplied in support of such assertions. In addition, the Memorial, itself, is evidence of state action and *opinio juris*.

---

84. *See*, POLISH YEARBOOK OF INTERNATIONAL LAW, http://www.inp.pan.pl/pyil/ [https://perma.cc/ZRE8-67MZ]. Researchers will notice an EN | PL option at the top right hand corner of the page. Researchers without facility in Polish should select the EN to work in English. The English translations may or may not be considered official. *See* Chapter 11, *infra*, on cultural competencies.

85. *See* YEARBOOK OF THE INTERNATIONAL LAW COMMISSION, http://legal.un.org/ilc/publications/yearbooks/ [https://perma.cc/S7RX-6BLA].

86. YEARBOOK OF CULTURAL PROPERTY LAW, http://www.culturalheritagelaw.org/yearbook [https://perma.cc/LE7G-P8JF].

87. *Int'l Law Comm'n 2016 Annual Report, supra* note 13, at 92.

iv. Conduct in Connection with Resolutions Adopted by an International Organization or at an Intergovernmental Conference

For purposes of demonstrating customary international law, researchers should identify States' conduct in connection with the adoption of a resolution by an international organization that includes representation of all States, such as United Nations. A U.N. General Assembly resolution, itself, does not contribute to the development of customary international law. Rather, it is the State's conduct, and in particular the State's conduct in relation to the resolution, that supports State practice accompanied by *opinio juris*. Even then, it should be remembered that the General Assembly is not a law-making body and its resolutions are considered recommendations according to the United Nations Charter.[88] Often, General Assembly resolutions are classified as either recommendations, declarations, or affirmations. The researcher should focus on the language of the resolution: those with firm obligations versus those that are merely aspirational or advisory in nature are more likely to be considered valuable as evidence of customary international law.[89]

Because a State's action of voting for adoption of a particular resolution supports the development of customary international law,[90] researchers often focus on those resolutions that are adopted unanimously or by a wide majority. These types of resolutions can be used to show evidence of general and consistent practice. To assess the voting record for General Assembly Resolutions during a particular session, legal researchers should use the Index to Proceedings of the General Assembly. This Index offers the work of the General Assembly by session year from its first session (1946) and is available online through the U.N. Dag Hammarskjold Library in pdf with links to the full-text resolutions from the 65th session forward.[91] There are two finding aids in the Index that the legal researcher will find particularly useful. The first is the List of Resolutions. The second is the Voting Chart for the resolutions adopted by

---

88. U.N. Charter, *supra* note 57, art. 10.

89. Michael P. Scharf, Customary International Law in Times of Fundamental Change: Recognizing Grotian Moments, at 54–55 (2013).

90. "... *opinio juris* may be deduced from, *inter alia*, the attitude of the Parties and of States towards certain General Assembly resolutions ..." *Military and Paramilitary Activities Case, supra* note 4, at para. 187–201.

91. *See Index to General Assembly Resolutions,* https://library.un.org/itp?field_organ_value=General+Assembly+-+regular+sessions [https://perma.cc/M8R8-5Q6M]. It is also available in print at various U.N. depository libraries.

roll-call or by recorded vote. Both of these finding aids are typically included at the end of the Index.

Scanning the List of Resolutions allows the legal researcher to uncover all resolutions passed unanimously or near-unanimously during any given session. The List offers a column that holds the vote summary which shows the raw number of 'yes,' 'no,' and 'abstain' votes. To obtain the full listing of how each State voted, the legal researcher must resort to the Voting Chart which lists each individual State alphabetically. Any corrections to the Voting Chart in the Index to Proceedings must be handled by consulting the verbatim records of the plenary meetings.

UNBISnet Voting Records Database[92] is the U.N. database that holds the voting summaries for U.N. General Assembly Resolutions adopted with and without a vote. Researchers can search by resolution symbol, key word, or date. There is no way to search by resolutions passed unanimously or near-unanimously (using a vote count range for yes votes, for instance). Nevertheless, if the legal researcher is interested in finding all resolutions related to a particular key word, a search using UNBISnet allows for a search across all session years rather than having to open individual pdfs for each session year. The results list conveniently offers the voting summaries as part of the snippet of information comprising the results. Researchers may select the 'link to' and English option to obtain the full text resolution, where available.

Using the Index to Proceedings of the General Assembly, which holds the same information as UNBISnet but is more cumbersome, is useful in three circumstances: (1) it can serve as a control strategy to ensure thorough and complete research; (2) it can be used where the UNBISnet is not functioning; or, (3) it can be consulted for purposes of citation. It should be remembered that not all General Assembly Resolutions are voted on. The UNBISnet allows researchers to refine their search to General Assembly Resolutions adopted with vote or without vote. Selecting the 'with vote' option allows the researcher to produce a more narrowly-tailored results set. The results set from UNBISnet provides a voting summary which details the number of member States voting yes or no, as well as abstentions, non-voting, and total voting members for any given resolution. For circumstances where the legal researcher is looking for a particular State's voting record to demonstrate that individual's State practice or *opinio juris*, simply select the U.N. resolution

---

92. United Nations Bibliographic Information Service, UNBISNet, http://unbisnet.un.org:8080/ipac20/ipac.jsp?profile=voting&menu=search&submenu=power#focus [https://perma.cc/E66P-89P5].

symbol to arrive at a page that list all States and provides the detailed voting for each State.

While the work of the ILC is often annexed to General Assembly Resolutions, its underlying efforts and output offer a valuable trove of documents and reports for the legal researcher attempting to show state practice or *opinio juris*. In particular, the ILC's surveys of state practice, and the oral and written comments received by it from States, should not be over-looked. The work of the ILC is available on its website as the Analytical Guide to the Work of the International Law Commission.[93] The Guide is organized by subject area and category or type of document produced by the ILC. Summaries of the work of the ILC can be used as a jumping off point because the summaries include links to the underlying work.[94] While many legal researchers incorporate General Assembly resolutions into their research effort when handling customary international law projects, the underlying work of the ILC should also be proactively searched.

v. Employing a Subject Matter Approach

Finding materials based on subject matter is handled in much the same manner the legal researcher handles all subject or topic searches. A complete explanation for the research process is offered in Chapters 9 and 10. The challenge on the international level is that there is no overarching organizational scheme that arranges the law by subject and topic that would allow the researcher to search across all jurisdictions at once. Rather, researchers must manually search individual jurisdictions or tap into a secondary source that has compiled such information. Subject heading searches in catalogs can be fruitful. Sometimes, there are NGOs that work in a particular subject area and these NGOs will offer collections of documents on their websites. Such options should not be overlooked as a basis for finding state action and *opinio juris*.

VIII. Conclusion

There is no single, clear path for finding and determining rules of customary international law because the documents used vary depending on the sub-

---

93. ANALYTICAL GUIDE TO THE ILC, http://legal.un.org/ilc/guide/gfra.shtml [https://perma.cc/7EWQ-B7H6].

94. SUMMARIES OF THE WORK OF THE INTERNATIONAL LAW COMMISSION, http://legal.un.org/ilc/summaries/summaries.shtml [https://perma.cc/AN8Q-QZCC].

ject matter of the custom. Additionally, it is particularly challenging to find and demonstrate multiple States' practice and *opinio juris* using the publications and documents from multiple foreign jurisdictions. Taking the time to understand customary international law as a source of law before starting the research process is vital. By following the strategies discussed within this chapter and by exercising no small amount of persistence and creativity, legal researchers should be able to handle the research challenges posed by customary international law as a source of law.

Chapter 5

General Principles
Accepted as Law

I. Background

Article 38(1)(c) of the Statute of the International Court of Justice (ICJ) lists "general principles of law recognized by civilized nations" as a source of international law that the court shall apply[1] to resolve international controversies. Subsection (1) is arranged such that general principles of law is listed after treaty and customary international law but before the subsidiary sources. Although general principles of law clearly are not subsidiary sources, some scholars consider them 'supplementary' to treaties and customary international law[2] while others stress that they "may give rise to rules of independent legal force...."[3]

Further, the language of Article 38(1)(c) refers to 'general principles of law,' not 'general principles of international law.' Apparently, this was by design and to allow the ICJ to develop and refine international law principles by drawing on the general principles of national jurisprudence.[4] International tribunals

---

1. STATUTE OF THE INTERNATIONAL COURT OF JUSTICE, June 26, 1945, art. 38(1)(c), 59 Stat. 1031, http://www.icj-cij.org/documents/?p1=4&p2=2 [https://perma.cc/NY98-29PP].

2. Restatement (Third) of the Foreign Relations Law of the U.S., Sec. 102, Comment 1.

3. OPPENHEIM'S INTERNATIONAL LAW, vol. 1, at 40 (Robert Jennings, ed., 9th ed. 2008).

4. See JAMES CRAWFORD, BROWNLIE'S PRINCIPLES OF PUBLIC INTERNATIONAL LAW, at 34 (8th ed. 2012) (hereinafter *Brownlie's Principles*), which discusses the effort of the Committee of Jurists that drafted the Statute of the ICJ. *See also*, THE STATUTE OF THE INTERNATIONAL COURT OF JUSTICE: A COMMENTARY, at 834–835 (Zimmerman, Tomuschat, Oellers-Frahm, and Tams eds., 2d ed 2012) (noting that interpreting 'general principles' to

generally, and arbitral tribunals particularly, have not reduced this source to a 'mechanical system of borrowing from domestic law' based on a consensus of State's national laws.[5] Rather, international tribunals adopt and adapt principles and legal reasoning from these national systems to create a body of rules compatible with the international legal system.[6] During this process, judges assess whether a particular principle is transposable to the international legal system.[7] This requires articulating the principle in a manner that transcends differences in details between the national laws and how they function.

Ordinarily, the use of general principles of law as a source arises where neither treaty nor international custom govern a matter.[8] It serves as a gap filler. Eventually, general principles of law can develop into customary international law.[9] The ICJ has rarely explicitly referred to Article 38(1)(c) in its judgments and opinions.[10] In the few instances where the ICJ resorts to general principles of law as a source of law, it does so without making the effort to demonstrate it, particularly in its advisory opinions.[11]

Over the years, the application and use of general principles of law arose more frequently in international criminal law.[12] In 1998, Article 21 of the Rome Statute of the International Criminal Court was drafted to explicitly state that the Court shall apply "general principles of law derived by the Court from national laws of legal systems of the world...."[13] Unlike the ambiguous language of Article 38 of the Statute of the ICJ, drafted in 1945, the ICC's statute made clear in 1998 that the general principles were to be derived from national laws.

---

be 'general *international* principles' would have them fall under Art. 38(1)(b) customary international law rather than Art. 38(1)(c), leaving this subsection superfluous).

5. CRAWFORD, *Brownlie's Principles*, *supra* note 4, at 34.

6. *Id.*

7. THE STATUTE OF THE INTERNATIONAL COURT OF JUSTICE: A COMMENTARY, at 840–841 (Zimmerman, Tomuschat, Oellers-Frahm, and Tams eds., 2d ed. 2012) (hereinafter *ICJ Statute Commentary*).

8. Giorgio Gaja, *General Principles of Law*, MAX PLANCK ENCYCLOPEDIA OF PUBLIC INTERNATIONAL LAW ¶ 24 (2013).

9. *Id.*, at 852–853 (offering *res judicata* as an example).

10. CRAWFORD, *Brownlie's Principles*, *supra* note 4, at 36. *See also*, *ICJ Statute Commentary*, *supra* note 7, at 833 (noting the court has only explicitly referred to Art. 38(1)(c) four times).

11. *ICJ Statute Commentary*, *supra* note 7, at 839.

12. ANTONIO CASSESE, INTERNATIONAL LAW, at 193 (2d ed. 2005).

13. ROME STATUTE OF THE INTERNATIONAL CRIMINAL COURT, 2187 U.N.T.S. 3, U.N.Doc. A/CONF.183/9, http://www.un.org/ga/search/view_doc.asp?symbol=A%2FCO NF.183%2F9&Submit=Search&Lang=E [https://perma.cc/5N6F-ZDY8] (emphasis added).

General principles of law have been used in matters related to evidence, procedure, and equitable doctrines such as estoppel, acquiescence or the obligation to make reparations.[14] They have also been used to recognize corporations as legal personalities.[15] Naturally, the use of general principles will not work in every instance where there is need for a gap filler. For example, in the *Right of Passage Case*,[16] even though Portugal argued it had a right of passage based on general principles of law and supported its argument based on the national laws of 64 States,[17] the ICJ declined to recognize the law of easements or servitudes, basing its decision on customary international law rather than general principles of law.

Some scholars recognize a difference between general principles of law under Article 38(1)(c) of the Statute of the ICJ and overarching fundamental principles of international law.[18] Overarching fundamental principles are legal standards that are constitutional in nature and generalized from treaty and customary international law.[19] They include: "sovereignty, recognition, consent, good faith, freedom of the seas, international responsibility, and self-defense."[20] The U.N. General Assembly Resolution, *Declaration on Principles of International Law concerning Friendly Relations and Co-operation among States in accordance with the Charter of the United Nations*, recognizes the following principles:[21]

---

14. CRAWFORD, *Brownlie's Principles*, *supra* note 4, at 36 (citing Factory at Chorzow, Merits, (1928) PCIJ Ser A No 17, 29). *See generally*, BIN CHENG, GENERAL PRINCIPLES OF LAW AS APPLIED BY INTERNATIONAL COURTS AND TRIBUNALS (1987).

15. Barcelona Traction case, Belgium v. Spain, Preliminary Objections, at 42–45 (1964) (see the third preliminary objection), available at http://www.icj-cij.org/docket/files/50/5341.pdf [https://perma.cc/7AUN-ECFJ].

16. Right of Passage over Indian Territory, Portugal v. India, Merits, at 41–45 (1960), http://www.icj-cij.org/docket/files/32/4521.pdf [https://perma.cc/TTG7-W7EH].

17. Right of Passage over Indian Territory, Portugal v. India, Reply of the Gov't of the Portuguese Republic at Annex 194 (1960) available at http://www.icj-cij.org/docket/files/32/9116.pdf [https://perma.cc/P4VP-YKQR]. *See generally*, FRANCIS T. FREEMAN JALET, *The Quest for the General Principles of Law Recognized by Civilized Nations*, 10 U.C.L.A. L. REV., 1041, 1081 (1962).

18. *See generally*, Rüdiger Wolfrum, GENERAL INTERNATIONAL LAW (PRINCIPLES, RULES, AND STANDARDS), MAX PLANCK ENCYCLOPEDIA OF PUBLIC INTERNATIONAL LAW (2010).

19. ANTONIO CASSESE, INTERNATIONAL LAW, at 46–48 (2d ed. 2005).

20. *See* PARRY & GRANT ENCYCLOPAEDIC DICTIONARY OF INTERNATIONAL LAW, at 479 (3d ed. 2009).

21. *Declaration on Principles of International Law concerning Friendly Relations and Co-operation among States in accordance with the Charter of the United Nations*, U.N. DOC. A/RES/25/2625, http://www.un.org/ga/search/view_doc.asp?symbol=A/RES/2625 [https://perma.cc/5MLY-Q83V] (XXV) (adopted without a vote).

1. The principle that States shall settle their international disputes by peaceful means in such a manner that international peace and security and justice are not endangered
2. The principle concerning the duty not to intervene in matters within the domestic jurisdiction of any State, in accordance with the Charter
3. The duty of States to co-operate with one another in accordance with the Charter
4. The principle of equal rights and self-determination of peoples
5. The principle of sovereign equality of States
6. The principle that States shall fulfil in good faith the obligations assumed by them in accordance with the Charter

While some scholars classify general principles of law as a source of law under Article 38(1)(c) of the Statute of the ICJ and fundamental principles of international law as customary international law under Article 38(1)(b), others characterize both as falling under Article 38(1)(c).[22] Given the vague language used by the ICJ in its opinions, there is considerable scholarly discussion about whether general principles of law may be derived only from a comparative study of national systems, from the international system itself, or both.[23] Fortunately, the International Law Commission of the U.N. has indicated in its 2016 annual report that it plans to study general principles of law next.[24]

II. Research Process

The research process differs for general principles of law and fundamental principles of law. The following description covers research related to a comparative study of national laws to derive a general principle of law. Those interested in researching fundamental principles of law should consult the chapters on treaty and customary international law for a research process.

Researching the general principles of law of a particular State begins as a foreign law research project. While researchers might endeavor to investigate the national law of all States to support an argument based on general principles, it is

---

22. See *supra* note 18.

23. *See* Michelle Biddulph and Dwight Newman, A Contextualized Account of General Principles of International Law, 26 Pace Int'l. L. Rev. 286, 298–301 (2014).

24. Int'l Law Comm'n, Annual Rep., Sixty-Eighth Session, U.N. Doc. A/ 71/ 10, at 378. (2016).

likely unnecessary,[25] although certainly not prohibited. Instead, rather than canvass all national systems, or even a substantial number of them, researchers can group them by the legal tradition upon which they rest. Identifying the general principles of civil law traditions, common law traditions, and mixed religious law traditions by researching "any (or some) of the [national] laws belonging to these various systems" is sufficient.[26] Legal traditions are discussed in greater depth in Chapter 11. Transposing what is uncovered among the national legal systems is handled by transmuting and adapting the comprehensive understanding of those principles and how they operate in their national legal systems into a single, coherent principle that functions in the international system.

General principles of law may be drawn from any of the primary sources of law at the national level and must be considered within the context of the functioning of the legal system. The doctrine of *res judicata* will be used as an example for demonstrating the complexities of transposing national principles to the international system.[27] For this research example, the doctrine as applied in the United States (common law tradition), Germany (civil law, Germanic tradition), and the United Arab Emirates (mixed civil-Muslim law tradition) will be offered.

The doctrine of *res judicata* has its origins in case law in the United States[28] and rests on the doctrine of estoppel.[29] In civil law traditions, such as Ger-

---

25. Zimmerman, *ICJ Statute Commentary*, supra note 7, at 837 (explaining that "such a requirement would, ..., be unrealistic: the material is hardly available to the parties or to the judges....").

26. *Id.* But see, Neha Jain, *Judicial Lawmaking and General Principles of Law in International Criminal Law*, 57 HARV. INT'L L. J. 111, 133–137 (2016)(discussing the problems of relying on comparative studies of 'legal families' and urging international courts to avoid a cursory survey of ostensibly representative national systems).

27. Although Article 60 of the Statute of the ICJ explicitly incorporates the doctrine of *res judicata* stating that its judgments are "final and without appeal...." see Statute of the ICJ, note 1 at art. 60, it is nevertheless useful for demonstrating the research process because it offers a clear example of a general principle of law recognized by civilized nations that has differences in scope and application across various legal systems. For a discussion of the doctrine as applied by the ICJ see ANDREAS KULICK, *Article 60 ICJ Statute, Interpretation Proceedings, and the Competing Concepts of Res Judicata*, 28 Leiden J. Int'l Law, 73-89 (2015), available at http://journals.cambridge.org/abstract_S0922156514000545.

28. *See, e.g.*, Migra v. Warren City School District Board of Education, 465 U.S. 75 (1984)(explaining that *res judicata* was eventually also codified in 28 U.S.C. 1738).

29. For a discussion of how U.S. doctrine of *res judicata* differs from other common law traditions see DE LY & SHEPPARD, *ILA Interim Report on Res Judicata and Arbitration*, 25 Arbitration Int'l 35 (2009).

many, where the law is generally codified, the doctrine is found in codes. In civil-Muslim traditions, such as the United Arab Emirates (U.A.E.), the Constitution, national legislation, and Shari'a law, particularly as it relates to the structure of the court system, are implicated.

The doctrine of *res judicata* in the United States serves to prevent the same parties from raising the same claim or same issue that has already been litigated and determined to be a final, in a subsequent action between them.[30] It has been extended to prevent a party from raising an issue that could have been raised in a prior proceeding between the same parties but was not. And, in certain circumstances, third parties may rely on the doctrine.[31]

Consulting the *Foreign Law Guide* for Germany provides that German laws are available online through the Federal Justice Ministry & Juris website.[32] Researchers able to search in the vernacular can use the official German website[33] to navigate to the Code of Civil Procedure. Researchers not proficient in the German language must find and use English translations.[34] Additionally, they should also consult the work of scholars writing in English to explain the doctrine.[35] For example, an entry-level treatise on German Civil Justice indicates that the doctrine of *res judicata* in Germany is not as broadly applicable as it is in the United States and that it applies only for dispositive issues and not necessarily the reasoning and findings behind them.[36]

Turning to the *Foreign Law Guide* for U.A.E., the researcher finds that there is a recommended article in English that describes the interaction between the civil and Shari'a courts.[37] Because the U.A.E. is a mixed tradition that rests on civil law, researchers will resort to the U.A.E. Codes. The *Foreign Law Guide*

---

30. Restatement (Second) of Judgments, §§ 17 and 27 (1982).

31. *Id.* at § 22.

32. Foreign Law Guide, *Germany—Compilations or Official Codes* (Country editor Jennifer Allison, 2016)(citing http://www.gesetze-im-internet.de/).

33. Google offers options to translate some foreign language websites. However, for purposes of determining the legal meaning of codes, laws and other jurisprudence, researchers should be cautious.

34. The official German website offers English translations and explicitly states that translations are provided for convenience only. See http://www.gesetze-im-internet.de/Teil-liste_translations.html.

35. *See* De Ly & Sheppard, ILA Interim Report, supra note 29, at 49 (citing German Code of Civil Procedure, Articles 322–327).

36. *See* Peter L. Murray & Rolf Sturner, German Civil Justice, at 355–66 (2004)(explaining German doctrine of *res judicata*).

37. Foreign Law Guide, *United Arab Emirates—Introductory Sources* (country editor Marci Hoffman) (citing B. Ali-Muhairi, the Development of the U.A.E. legal system and unification with the judicial system, 11 Arab L. Qtrly 116 (1996)).

explains that the Federal Code of Civil Procedure is codified as Law 11 of 1992.[38] The official U.A.E. government website offers an English translation of this law.[39] And, similar to the process for German law research, most U.S. researchers will resort to the work of scholars or reputable practitioners, writing in English, to learn about the application of the doctrine. Doing so here, the researcher discovers that its application in the U.A.E. is more restrictive than in the United States.[40]

Additionally, the mechanism by which the doctrine is raised varies between common law, civil law, and mixed religious systems. Whereas parties raise the matter of *res judicata* in common law systems, which are adversarial in nature; courts raise the matter in civil law systems, which are inquisitorial in nature.[41] And yet, perhaps somewhat surprisingly for the U.S. legal researcher, under the U.A.E. system which is a mixed civil-religious tradition, parties may raise the matter.[42] It is vital for researchers to carry out sufficient underlying research to understand the structure and nature of the various legal systems to be able to assess how the doctrine functions or operates in each of them.[43]

After considering the doctrine of *res judicata* as used in various legal systems,[44] international courts must adapt it when transposing it to the international legal system to articulate it as a single, coherent and useable general

---

38. *Id.*

39. Federal Law No. 10 of 1992, as amended by Federal Law No. 11 of 2014, http://ejustice.gov.ae/downloads/latest_laws2015/Federal_Law_10_2014_en.pdf [https://perma.cc/5M72-NP9X].

40. For a discussion of *res judicata* in the United Arab Emirates a mixed system of Muslim and customary law, see Meyer-Reumann & Partners, *Res Judicata* in Sharjah Rent Law, Lex Arabiae, (Apr. 2014), http://lexarabiae.meyer-reumann.com/res-judicata-in-sharjah-rent-law/ [https://perma.cc/94CR-GCS2] and Hadef & Partners, *Res Judicata*, the UAE Approach (Aug. 2015), http://www.hadefpartners.com/News/176/RES-JUDICATA-%E2%80%93-THE-UAE-APPROACH [https://perma.cc/254A-8YLC].

41. *Supra* note 37.

42. *Supra* Hadef & Partners, note 41.

43. For a discussion of the difficulties of comparing the English doctrine of *res judicata* and the French doctrine, see Kevin M. Clermont, *Res Judicata* as Requisite for Justice, 68 Rutgers Univ. L. Rev. (2016), http://scholarship.law.cornell.edu/cgi/viewcontent.cgi?article=2599&context=facpub [https://perma.cc/W6BU-8AAJ].

44. Page constraints limit the research examples to three jurisdictions and these suffice to offer a sense of the nuances related to the effort involved in gathering an understanding of the doctrine at the national level. Certainly, researchers would also consider the doctrine of *res judicata* as applied in additional legal systems including possibly another European civil law system based on Romanic legal tradition, a Latin American civil law system, and in various Asian legal systems.

principle of law. While theoretically international courts comprised of judges from various legal traditions, such as the ICJ, can guard against any one tradition being favored over another, an exploration of the case law of the ICJ on *res judicata* reveals just how difficult this is.[45]

An alternative approach for determining general principles of law is to use subsidiary sources. Article 38(1)(d) of the Statue of the ICJ indicates that subsidiary sources may be used to determine not only customary international law but also general principles of law. Researchers may use subsidiary sources to show evidence of general principles of law in much the same manner they use them to demonstrate custom, as explained in Chapter 4.

III. Conclusion

Under Article 38(1)(c) general principles of law as a source of law is a third means to develop new rules of international law, apart from treaties and custom. Researching general principles of law is largely a foreign law research project. Researchers should guard against simply searching for a statement of a general principle of law from within a particular national system. Instead, they must take a broader view and research to understand the legal system and how the general principle of law operates within that system. General principles of law from national systems should not be extracted wholesale. Rather, they must be considered together and transposed to the international system.

---

45. *See* discussion in ANDREAS KULICK, *Article 60 ICJ Statute*, supra note 27, at 84–89 (noting that case law falls into two categories: one related to the ICJ's application of *res judicata* on arbitral awards and another where the ICJ considers *res judicata* of its own judgments in contentious cases; and, concluding that a narrow application of the doctrine reconciles frictions that currently exist in the ICJ case law).

Chapter 6

Teachings of Highly Qualified Publicists as Subsidiary Sources

I. Introduction

Article 38(1)(d) sets forth that the ICJ shall apply "the teachings of the most highly qualified publicists of the various nations, as subsidiary means for the determination of rules of law."[1] Historically, it was only the writings of highly qualified publicists that contained a discussion of a particular custom and how it emerged that served as evidence of customary international law.[2] Today, the term "teachings" should be read broadly to include writings, lectures, and audio-visual materials.[3] The phrase "most highly qualified publicists of the various nations" has been interpreted to include individuals who are specialized

---

1. Statute of the International Court of Justice, June 26, 1945, Art. 38, 59 Stat. 1031.

2. James Crawford, Brownlie's Principles of Public International Law, at 3 (8th ed. 2012) (citing Vitoria, Gentili, Grotius, Pufendorf, Wolff, and Vattel as highly qualified publicists). The Supreme Court of the United States in the Paquete Habana case further explained it was the years of labor, research and experience that made these commentators highly qualified, "not for the speculations of their authors concerning what the law ought to be, but for trustworthy evidence of what the law really is." Paquete Habana, 175 U.S. 677, 700 (1900).

3. Int'l Law Comm'n, Annual Rep., Sixty-Eighth Session, U.N. Doc. A/71/10, at 111–112 (2016), http://www.un.org/ga/search/view_doc.asp?symbol=A/71/10, [https://perma.cc/DF4B-97FR] (hereinafter *Int'l Law Comm'n 2016 Annual Report*).

in the field of international law[4] and others so long as an assessment is made of the credentials of the writer as well as the methodology used to conclude that a particular norm is international custom.[5] The ILC acknowledges, though, that focus should be on eminent writers.[6]

The legal researcher must carry out supplemental research to assess an author's credentials and authority as well as the rigor, objectivity, and accuracy of the writing itself. The ILC stresses it is the quality of the writing and the rigor of the author's methodology rather than the author's reputation that matters most.[7] After making this preliminary assessment, the legal researcher must then evaluate whether the writer sets forth the law as it exists, rather than advocates for what it ought to be.[8] It is only where the writer sets forth what the law is that a legal researcher may rely on it as a subsidiary means for the determination of a rule of customary international law.[9]

The term 'publicist' has also been interpreted to encompass those organizations that are expert bodies in the area of international law. The ILC includes the Institut de Droit International and the International Law Association as examples, recognizing that others exist for the particular fields of international law.[10] The phrase "of the various nations" underscores the importance of considering the "… writings representative of the principal legal systems and regions of the world and in various languages."[11]

There is no official list of eminent scholars. And while the ICJ, and its predecessor the PCIJ, typically refrain from citing to individual scholars, both Oppenheim and Gidel have been cited.[12] The following short list of highly eminent scholars is offered for purposes of providing an example: Brierly,[13] Brownlie,[14]

---

4. *Id.*

5. *Id.*

6. *Id.*

7. *Id.*

8. See *supra* note 2.

9. *Id.*

10. *Int'l Law Comm'n 2016 Annual Report, supra* note 3, at 112.

11. *Id.*

12. Michael Wood, *Teachings of the Most Highly Qualified Scholars*, MAX PLANCK ENCYCLOPEDIA OF PUBLIC INTERNATIONAL LAW (2010) (the PCIJ and ICJ have cited to Oppenheim's International Law and Gidel).

13. J.L. BRIERLY, LAW OF NATIONS, AN INTRODUCTION TO THE INTERNATIONAL LAW OF PEACE (6th ed. 1963).

14. IAN BROWNLIE, PRINCIPLES OF PUBLIC INT'L LAW (1st–7th eds).

Crawford,[15] Oppenheim,[16] Shaw,[17] American Law Institute,[18] Institute of International Law,[19] International Law Association,[20] and the United Nations International Law Commission.[21] Certainly, there are others. Any writing from an author included in the list must be evaluated independently against the criteria set forth above.

One strategy for determining whether an author is considered a 'highly qualified publicist' is to examine the Memorials or documents filed before the ICJ and other international tribunals and national courts handling international law issues. This allows the researcher to discover which authors the experienced lawyers practicing before the international bar deem to be highly qualified.

The writings of eminent authors may be used as a subsidiary means for the determination of the rules of law. The ILC explains that the writings play an "auxiliary role" in that they bring value by "collecting and assessing State practice" as well as "in identifying divergences in State practice"[22] for purposes of determining a rule of customary international law. It is imperative that the researcher explore the author's methodology for concluding a norm rises to customary international law before using the source as a subsidiary source.

Subsidiary sources must be distinguished from the U.S. legal researcher's understanding of secondary sources. Secondary sources are considered persuasive authority and are not usually cited in court documents. U.S. legal researchers will typically resort to citing secondary sources in court documents only where no primary authority exists or in support of an argument that the law should be changed. In contrast, subsidiary sources of law are cited in court documents as an auxiliary means to determine rules of customary international law and general principles of law, both primary law sources. This is one

---

15. JAMES CRAWFORD, BROWNLIE'S PRINCIPLES OF PUBLIC INTERNATIONAL LAW (8th ed. 2012).

16. OPPENHEIM'S INT'L LAW (9th ed. 1992).

17. MALCOLM SHAW, INTERNATIONAL LAW (6th ed. 2011).

18. The American Law Institute publishes the RESTATEMENT OF THE LAW (THIRD) FOREIGN RELATIONS LAW OF THE UNITED STATES.

19. Materials of the Institut of Droit International are generally available at http://justitiaetpace.org/, [https://perma.cc/6TZR-HQCW]. See also, Peter Macalister-Smith, *Institut de Droit International*, MAX PLANCK ENCYCLOPEDIA OF PUBLIC INTERNATIONAL LAW (2011).

20. Reports of the ILA Conferences can be found in HeinOnline (contained in the International Law Association Reports Library).

21. Materials of the International Law Commission are generally available at http://legal.un.org/ilc/, [https://perma.cc/3XFZ-QJNK].

22. *Id.*

of the fundamental differences between secondary sources and subsidiary sources of law.

II. Sources for Teachings of Highly Qualified Publicists

The following sections explore how certain secondary sources can be used as subsidiary sources for some international legal research projects. Chapter 8 covers secondary sources generally.

A. Restatements of the Law

The Restatements of the Law are produced by the American Law Institute (ALI). The ALI Council, which consists of scholars, judges, and various practicing lawyers who work in private practice, for the government, and in law departments of businesses, produces the *Restatement (Third) of the Law, The Foreign Relations of the United States, (Restatement)*.[23] The *Restatement* is generally used as a subsidiary source to demonstrate customary international law by showing either U.S. practice or *opinio juris* on a particular matter. However, it should be remembered that the Restatement is put forth by the ALI which is a private organization and not affiliated with the United States government. The publication itself acknowledges that "[i]n a number of particulars the formulations in the Restatement are at variance with positions that have been taken by the United States Government."[24] The ALI is generally accepted to be a highly qualified publicist but researchers must nevertheless make an assessment of whether the stated rule is aspirational or accurately identifies the current state of U.S. practice.

---

23. Restatement of the Law (Third) the Foreign Relations Law of the United States at XI (1987). The third Restatement was originally intended to be a revision to the *Restatement (Second) of the Foreign Relations Law of the United States*, which was published in 1955. Given the lengthy revision process, it was designated "third" in an effort to indicate that it is in the generation of Restatements that have been issued since the publication of the generation of the second Restatements. The ALI is in the midst of updating the Third Restatement with a Fourth. *See*, American Law Institute, https://www.ali.org/projects/show/foreign-relations-law-united-states/ [https://perma.cc/4LCP-YH4S].

24. *Id.*

Restatements of the Law are divided into twenty-three legal subject areas and are arranged by chapters, subchapters, and sections.[25] Each section re-states a particular United States legal rule or principle. The rules of law are printed in bold font and are identified by a section number. Following the rule, legal researchers will find comments which often discuss examples, hypotheticals, and exceptions to the rule. Just prior to the rule, researchers will usually find an introductory note. In the *Restatement*, the introductory notes, rules, comments and reporters' notes consider not only U.S. legal resources, but also international law sources, including those that demonstrate customary international law.

The *Restatement* can be found in print by carrying out a title search in a law library's catalog or through worldcat. It is also available on Westlaw, Lexis and HeinOnline.

B. International Law Association Materials

The International Law Association (ILA) may be considered a highly qualified publicist.[26] The ILA consists of 3500 members and its work focuses on the "study, clarification and development of international law...."[27] In furtherance of its effort, the ILA establishes a number of committees to research and prepare reports on select areas of international law.[28] These reports can take various forms including: "a re-statement of the law; a draft treaty or convention; an elaboration of a code or rules or principles of international law; or a review of recent developments of law or practice."[29] The work of these committees is discussed and considered at biennial conferences.

Recent output of the International Law Association can be found on its website[30] and through HeinOnline.[31] An author search in a catalog using International Law Association will yield a list of documents and publications produced by the ILA.

---

25. *Id.*

26. *Int'l Law Comm'n 2016 Annual Report, supra* note 3, at 111–112.

27. See INTERNATIONAL LAW ASSOCIATION MISSION STATEMENT, http://www.ila-hq.org/en/about_us/, [https://perma.cc/YA73-9SKF].

28. For an index of current and former committees see http://www.ila-hq.org/en/committees/index.cfm, [https://perma.cc/XUA3-M66F].

29. *Id.*

30. International Law Association, http://www.ila-hq.org/, [https://perma.cc/S6UK-F6XY].

31. HeinOnline, www.heinonline.org [https://perma.cc/8H5X-B3JR] (contained within the Foreign and International Library).

C. Institut de Droit International Materials

The work of the Institut de Droit International (Institute of International Law) may be considered a highly qualified publicist.[32] The Statute of the Institute of International Law indicates that the Institute strives to "promote the progress of international law" and its codification.[33] It membership cannot exceed 132[34] and is comprised of three types of members: honorary members, members, and associates.[35]

The Institute's commission work,[36] declarations,[37] resolutions,[38] and reports[39] are available online. There is a subject index for the resolutions offered in English which allows for research by topic rather than citation.[40] The Institute's reports are contained in its yearbooks. The yearbooks from 2007 forward are available on its website.[41] Yearbooks prior to 2007 can be found by carrying out an author search in a catalog. As a control strategy, researchers can also search in the vernacular: Annuaire de l'Institute de Droit International.

D. International Law Commission Materials

Comprised of 34 elected members, the ILC is the General Assembly Committee charged with promoting "the progressive development of international

---

32. Institut de Droit International (Institute of International Law), http://justitiaet pace.org/historique.php, [https://perma.cc/8GF2-MX6Q].

33. STATUTE OF THE INTERNATIONAL INSTITUTE OF LAW, art. 1 (1873), http://justitiaet pace.org/status.php?lang=eng (English translation is not official), [https://perma.cc/8GF2-MX6Q].

34. *Id.*, at art. 3.

35. *Id.*

36. *See* International Institute of Law, http://justitiaetpace.org/commission.php, [https://perma.cc/M3L8-F778].

37. *See* International Institute of Law, *Declarations*, http://justitiaetpace.org/declarations.php, [https://perma.cc/558M-DA4M].

38. *See* International Institute of Law, *Resolutions*, (Resolutions available in English from 1957–. Earlier resolutions only available in French), http://justitiaetpace.org/resolutions.php, [https://perma.cc/6R55-MQMH].

39. *See* International Institute of Law, *Reports*, http://justitiaetpace.org/rapports.php, [https://perma.cc/TCL5-7KGR].

40. *See* International Institute of Law, *Subject Index to Resolutions*, http://justitiaetpace.org/resolutions.php, [https://perma.cc/6R55-MQMH].

41. See *supra* note 40.

law and its codification."[42] The ILC elects members from 5 regions based on a formula to ensure fair representation of the world.[43] Those serving on the ILC do so in an individual capacity and not as representative of their governments.

In connection with studying and making reports on the progressive development of international law, the ILC surveys state practice.[44] This is usually handled by special rapporteurs who are appointed by the ILC specifically for this task. The reports of the special rapporteurs are published in the ILC's Yearbook which are available on the ILC website[45] and through HeinOnline.[46] Researchers can also carry out a catalog search by title, *United Nation's Yearbook of the International Law Commission* to determine whether a print version is available in a library. Each Yearbook of the ILC is comprised of two volumes. Volume 1 contains summary records and volume 2 contains the report of the ILC to the General Assembly.

E. Law Reviews

Typically, U.S. law reviews are law school publications that are edited by law students with the oversight of an academic faculty advisor. Other than Canada, the vast majority of law reviews outside of the United States are peer-reviewed and not edited by students. In Canada, the law reviews are edited by students without the benefit of an academic or faculty advisor, but are generally peer-reviewed.

Law review articles cover a range of topics and are usually written by professors, lawyers, and judges. Notes and comments, which are also included in the law reviews, tend to be shorter in length and written by law students. The treatment of topics in law reviews is comprehensive and in-depth. Having conducted thorough research, the authors of U.S. law review articles offer many footnotes in support of their work. U.S. legal researchers tend to use law review articles as a secondary source for two purposes: (1) to gather a deeper understanding of a particular topic and (2) to use the citations included in the

---

42. Statute of the International Law Commission, U.N. Doc A/RES/174(II), art. 1 (1947), http://www.un.org/en/ga/search/view_doc.asp?symbol=A/RES/174(II), [https://perma.cc/3H7Z-TELM].

43. *Id.*

44. *See generally,* United Nations, The Work of the International Law Commission (8th ed 2012).

45. See http://legal.un.org/ilc/publications/yearbooks/, [https://perma.cc/S7RX-6BLA].

46. See www.heinonline.org [https://perma.cc/8H5X-B3JR] (contained in the Foreign and International Library).

footnotes to carry out further research. On the international law stage, articles and other materials written by eminent scholars and published in law reviews may be used as subsidiary sources of law.

i. Sources for Law Reviews

Historically, law reviews were available in print and through subscription databases including Westlaw, Lexis, and HeinOnline. Increasingly, law reviews offer their articles online, open access, and through a law school's institutional repository. These open-access journals are discoverable online via Google Scholar. Many legal researchers prefer to conduct their law journal research in Westlaw, Lexis, or HeinOnline to take advantage of the search functionality and the relevancy ranking algorithm.

ii. Searching for Law Review Articles Full Text

Many databases do not provide full coverage of law journals. For instance, Lexis and Westlaw law journals' coverage begins in the early 1980s, but it varies by title. From approximately the mid-1990s forward it is consistent. HeinOnline offers coverage back to the first volume for the publications included in its Law Journals database, but may not have the most recent issues. Researchers should be aware of these nuances and take them into consideration when generating a research plan that includes law journals research.

Most databases will contain a full listing of all journals included in the database. To determine whether a database contains a particular publication, the legal researcher must consult the List of Publications or the "information" link. The List of Publications is typically arranged alphabetically and is searchable. Consulting this list allows the legal researcher to determine whether the publication is included in the database while at the same time check the date range of the volumes included.

For example, suppose the legal researcher is interested in an article from the Leiden Journal of International Law. By checking the List of Publications included in HeinOnline Law Journal Library, the legal researcher discovers that the Leiden Journal of International Law is not included. Making this preliminary determination allows the researcher to avoid carrying out unnecessary searches in HeinOnline. The legal researcher would carry out this same strategy for other databases until finding that the Leiden Journal of International Law is offered through ProQuest.

Many journal databases allow the researcher to either restrict the list of journals searched to only those of a particular subject area, such as International Law, (pre-search filter) or to filter the search results to only those related to international law (post-search filter). While this is certainly useful for managing a results list, by restricting the search at the outset to only those classified as "international law," the legal researcher runs the risk of missing relevant information. For example, there may be an employment law article in a general subject law journal that discusses international employment law. Failure to search in general subject journals may result in the legal researcher overlooking something highly relevant. Indeed, there have been a number of law journals created in recent years to specifically cover international law. Prior to the existence of these relatively new outlets for publishing international law articles, articles that covered international topics were included in general subject area law reviews. For this reason, legal researchers should identify their objectives (especially if the research is historic in nature) before searching to avoid filtering a results list prematurely.

iii. Searching for Law Review Articles Using an Index

Even where the legal researcher has access to a full-text database, it is often productive to also consult an index. There are many more articles that have been indexed than are included in full-text databases. As such, carrying out an index search ensures thorough and complete research.

There are a handful of legal indices available to the researcher all of which offer varying, and sometimes overlapping, coverage. The Index to Legal Periodicals and Books (ILP) is offered through EBSCOhost and indexes over 1,025 English language titles (almost 300 of which are law reviews) from the United States as well as from Canada, Ireland, Great Britain, Australia and New Zealand.[47] The Current Law Index (CLI), published by Gale, indexes 900 titles.[48] The online version of CLI, Legal Trac, is available as an independent subscription,[49] and through Westlaw and Lexis. The Current Index to Legal Periodicals (CILP) is offered by the University of Washington in print and online,[50] as well as through Westlaw. CILP indexes over 650 legal publications by

---

47. *See* Index to Legal Periodicals and Books, https://www.ebscohost.com/academic/ index-to-legal-periodicals-and-books-full-text, [https://perma.cc/LSY9-3XZU] (database also includes 480 full-text periodicals dating back to 1981).

48. CURRENT LAW INDEX (2015).

49. LEGALTRAC, http://www.aallnet.org/mm/Publications/products/pub-legal-index, [https://perma.cc/SY3M-KW6Z].

50. CURRENT INDEX TO LEGAL PERIODICALS, https://lib.law.washington.edu/cilp/ cilp.html, [https://perma.cc/J9B5-CVFX].

104 subject headings, including international law.[51] CILP is typically available 4–6 weeks before the other indices if the researcher is in need of the most up-to-date information.[52]

The Index to Foreign Legal Periodicals (IFLP) is a print index that indexes over 500 legal journals, including a number of non-English language law journals.[53] It originally intended to index foreign legal periodicals that were not included in these other indices, but has grown to include some of them as a result of demand by international users of the index. It is available in print from 1960 and through HeinOnline in a searchable database from 1985 (and in pdf back to 1960).[54]

Whichever index a legal researcher uses, after identifying the titles to articles by subject in the index, resort must be made to a full-text database or to the print publications to obtain the text of the article. Searching full-text databases for the article may be achieved by using the advanced search feature and conducting a title and author search. Some platforms offer a citation look-up. When searching in print, the legal researcher must search the library catalog using the title to the publication rather than the title to the article. After the legal researcher determines the publication is available in the library, it may be obtained by proceeding to the proper location by call number. The relevant title and volume of the publication will contain the sought-after article.

iv. Updating Law Review Articles

Law review articles must be updated using a two-step process. First, articles published in law reviews included in Lexis and Westlaw may be run through the citator, Shepard's or KeyCite, respectively. Second, the citations from within the article itself may be run through a citator independently. The legal researcher does this to ensure that the law supporting the assertions in the article has not changed and to gather additional and more recent support.

F. Legal Treatises

A legal treatise is a book or a set of books that offer a narrative description of a particular legal topic. Some legal treatises contain a brief overview of a

---

51. *Id.*

52. *Id.*

53. INDEX TO FOREIGN LEGAL PERIODICALS, https://www.law.berkeley.edu/library/iflp/ , [https://perma.cc/9VQN-DPZS].

54. *Id.*

topic while others contain comprehensive coverage. While most legal treatises offer citations to primary law materials, some legal treatises will include appendices that reproduce the primary law so that the legal researcher has all relevant material on a topic in one publication. Treatises may be geared toward various audiences including students, practitioners, or academics. For example, West's Hornbook and Nutshell series are both geared toward law students while Lexis' Guide to International Legal Research is geared toward practitioners as well as law students.

i. Finding Legal Treatises

The legal researcher has a few options for locating relevant legal treatises. Legal treatises in print may be found by searching a catalog or by browsing the shelves of a print collection. Most libraries offer a subject listing that will direct the legal researcher to the shelves where materials on a particular topic are located. Similarly, if the legal researcher already has the call number for a relevant title, it is likely that there will be other titles of interest nearby on the shelves. As such, the legal researcher may proceed to that call number location and browse the nearby shelves.

Online, within subscription databases, the legal researcher may use a publications listing to determine whether the treatise of interest is included. If searching by topic, the legal researcher can use the post search filters to find relevant legal treatises.

ii. Updating Legal Treatises

Generally, legal treatises are not updated with pocket parts or supplementary pamphlets but, rather, by the issuance of a new edition. There are, however, some treatises that do contain pocket parts so the legal researcher must always make a point of checking when researching in print.

G. Finding Law Reviews and Treatises (Writings of Highly Qualified Publicists) in a Foreign Jurisdiction

While some foreign jurisdiction publications are included in U.S. indices and databases, the legal researcher can also employ the strategy of actively searching for equivalent types of sources in foreign jurisdictions. By consulting a research guide for a foreign jurisdiction, the legal researcher should be able to identify whether a parallel or similar resource exists and if so, its title. The strategies outlined above for each of the types of sources translate well to working with foreign law sources. While U.S. researchers might encounter slight nuances when working with the foreign publications, if they bear in mind the strategies for assessing scope and coverage of databases as explained in Chapters 9 and 10, employ appropriate search syntax in full-text databases, consider currency, utilize the finding aids, and understand that not all foreign jurisdictions are based on a common law tradition, they should be able to achieve success with slight adaptations.

For example, a U.S. researcher carrying out law journal research in U.K. materials, would consult The Legal Journals Index which contains U.K. legal articles from 1986,[55] similar to using ILP or CLI for U.S. journals. Alternatively, the legal researcher might utilize JustCite which indexes over fifty-six legal journals from the U.K. as well as Ireland.[56] JustCite is a subscription database that offers vendor-neutral citation (and links) for articles dating from 2005. While the titles to the indices and their availability may be different, the research strategies employed are similar.

Legal researchers should not expect to find an equivalent to every U.S. publication in each foreign jurisdiction. The converse is that there may be certain types of publications and research tools available in a foreign jurisdiction for which there is no U.S. equivalent. For these reasons, it is imperative to consult a trusted research guide for the relevant foreign jurisdictions. Researchers who encounter an unfamiliar type of resource should explore the arrangement of the source, its finding aids, and how it relates to other resources from that jurisdiction before using it.

III. Conclusion

When citing to legal treatises or law reviews written by eminent scholars or materials of the ALI, ILC, ILA, or the Institut de Droit, as a subsidiary source of law it is vital to assess the author's credibility and authority as well as the rigor of the methodology used for concluding a norm rises to customary international law. The use of the teachings of highly qualified publicists as a subsidiary means to determine rules of customary international law is one of the most challenging concepts for U.S. legal researchers to grasp as there is no

---

55. The U.K. Legal Journals Index is available online through Westlaw U.K., it is no longer offered in print.

56. Over time, JustCite has increased its offerings for commonwealth countries including Australia, Singapore, Canada, Bermuda and Jamaica. JustCite also includes some United States journals. See JUSTCITE, https://www.justcite.com/, [https://perma.cc/5CZ9-C22Z].

equivalent in the national system. U.S. researchers must guard against viewing subsidiary sources as nothing more than an exalted secondary source. The purpose for which subsidiary sources are used is significantly different than the purpose for which secondary sources are used. A solid understanding of subsidiary sources and how they are used will always inform the researcher's selection of the various secondary sources that sometimes serve in this fashion. While all subsidiary sources may also be used as secondary sources, the reverse is not always true.

Chapter 7

World Judicial Decisions

I. Introduction

Using judicial decisions as a subsidiary means for the determination of the rules of international law is covered in Chapter 4. This chapter is broader in scope. Following a discussion of the research challenges that arise due to the growth in number of international courts and a lack of overarching structure among them, this chapter touches on matters that impact the research effort including: the weight of authority ascribed to judicial decisions, the doctrine of *stare decisis*, compulsory jurisdiction, and enforcement of judgments. Against this backdrop, a general research process for handling international judicial decisions is explained. This chapter explores a variety of types of courts and tribunals: courts of general jurisdiction, ad hoc tribunals, supranational courts, specialty courts and regional tribunals, to demonstrate the differences in the finding aids and materials available for research.

II. Growth in the Number of International Courts and Tribunals

A substantial challenge U.S. legal researchers confront when considering world judicial decisions is accounting for the increasing number of courts, tribunals, and specialized quasi-judicial bodies in existence.[1] There is no world

---

1. Roger P Alford, *The Proliferation of International Courts and Tribunals: International Adjudication in Ascendance*, 94 Am. Soc'y Int'l L. Proc.160 (2000).

constitutional document or overarching rules and procedures that govern the relationship among international courts.[2] While the decentralized growth of judicial courts and tribunals contributes to a diverse, autonomous, and self-governing international judicial system, it poses challenges for the legal researcher.

U.S. legal researchers are trained to find judicial decisions as primary authority from within a three-tiered system of inter-related courts: trial, appellate, and courts of last resort. While the International Court of Justice (ICJ) is the principal judicial organ of the United Nations, there is no International Supreme Court. Rather, and due in part to the horizontal nature of the development of international law, a decentralized variety of courts coexist. As such, legal researchers must sometimes account for the incongruities and conflicts that can arise as these judicial bodies operate independently.[3] Indeed, certain research projects involve the preliminary matter of understanding the options available in a system where courts have overlapping or concurrent jurisdictional authority.

A brief survey of several types of international courts and tribunals provides the necessary backdrop for carrying out international judicial decisions research. The ICJ is considered a court of general jurisdiction, which is able to decide a wide variety of subject matter controversies.[4] The International Criminal Court[5] (ICC) and the International Law of the Sea[6] (ITLOS) were originally established by U.N. multilateral conventions but are now independent. Established through the U.N. Security Council, the International Criminal Tribunal for Yugoslavia[7] (ICTY) and International Criminal Tribu-

---

2. *See generally,* Jonathan I. Charnay, *The Impact on the International Legal System of the Growth of International Courts and Tribunals,* 31 NYU J Int'l L. & Pol. 697 (1999), http://www.pict-pcti.org/publications/PICT_articles/JILP/Charney.pdf [https://perma.cc/3FD6-8JFR].

3. *Id. But see,* BRUNO SIMMA, *Universality of International Law from the Perspective of a Practitioner,* 20 (2) Eur J Int'l Law 265–297 (2009), https://academic.oup.com/ejil/article-lookup/doi/10.1093/ejil/chp028 [https://perma.cc/8UQ2-ZL6X].

4. *See* STATUTE OF THE INTERNATIONAL COURT OF JUSTICE, http://www.icj-cij.org/documents/?p1=4&p2=2 [https://perma.cc/7WL4-DN2D].

5. *See* ROME STATUTE OF THE INTERNATIONAL CRIMINAL COURT, https://www.icc-cpi.int/nr/rdonlyres/ea9aeff7-5752-4f84-be94-0a655eb30e16/0/rome_statute_english.pdf [https://perma.cc/NDB2-PUZV].

6. *See* STATUTE OF THE INTERNATIONAL LAW OF THE SEA, Art. 21, https://www.itlos.org/fileadmin/itlos/documents/basic_texts/statute_en.pdf [https://perma.cc/9L8L-GVAT].

7. *See* STATUTE OF THE INTERNATIONAL CRIMINAL TRIBUNAL FOR THE FORMER YUGOSLAVIA, ICTY, http://www.icty.org/en/documents/statute-tribunal [https://perma.cc/QZ3E-R3RF].

nal for Rwanda[8] (ICTR) are ad hoc criminal tribunals, created to handle war crimes and genocide that took place in those States and their surrounding regions. Some ad hoc tribunals are hybrid in nature. For example, the government for Sierra Leone and the United Nations together established the independent Special Court for Sierra Leone (SCSL) to handle humanitarian violations from that region.[9] There are also subject matter tribunals such as the dispute settlement forums of the World Trade Organization[10] (WTO) which deal with trade issues at the global level. Regional tribunals can be found in the Americas, Africa, and Europe. Examples include the Inter-American Court of Human Rights,[11] the African Court on Human and People's Rights,[12] and the Court of Justice of the EU.[13]

Clearly, without any hierarchical structure or relationship among these types of courts (general jurisdiction, ad hoc, subject matter, and regional) certain controversies might fall within the purview of several of them, leaving a State with a handful of options for dispute settlement. Determining where to file a controversy is itself a complicated research inquiry. Researchers must: analyze the court's statute or founding documentation to assess the scope of the court's jurisdiction;[14] review statement(s) of jurisdiction that may exist between the parties, including through governing treaties or contractual terms; consider a court's procedural and evidentiary rules; and, explore the body of work by the particular courts under consideration as well as the body of work of the judges who currently sit those courts, in an effort to evaluate how a court will likely decide. As well, researchers must consider whether a court has a professional code of conduct that governs the parties during its proceedings and, if not,

---

8. ICTR, http://unictr.unmict.org [https://perma.cc/N7SR-HJLE].

9. *See* http://www.rscsl.org/ which is the official website for the Residual Special Court for Sierra Leone after the close of the SCSL in 2013.

10. *See* World Trade Organization Dispute Settlement, https://www.wto.org/english/tratop_e/dispu_e/find_dispu_cases_e.htm [https://perma.cc/PFW2-FYFY].

11. *See* Inter-American Court of Human Rights, http://www.corteidh.or.cr/index.php/en [https://perma.cc/X6WW-BMD9].

12. African Court on Human and Peoples Rights, http://www.african-court.org/en/ [https://perma.cc/FJS7-E8TZ].

13. Court of Justice of the European Union, https://europa.eu/european-union/about-eu/institutions-bodies/court-justice_en [https://perma.cc/DYP3-WXBD].

14. *See* STATUTE OF THE INTERNATIONAL COURT OF JUSTICE, *supra* note 4; *see also* ROME STATUTE OF THE INTERNATIONAL CRIMINAL COURT, https://www.icc-cpi.int/nr/rdonlyres/ea9aeff7-5752-4f84-be94-0a655eb30e16/0/rome_statute_english.pdf [https://perma.cc/NDB2-PUZV].

the impact of the individual parties' obligations under their respective professional codes of conduct, as discussed in Chapter Eleven.

III. Weight of Authority of Judicial Decisions & The Doctrine of *Stare Decisis*

Another challenge U.S. legal researchers face arises from the fact that judicial decisions are not a primary source of law under Article 38(1) of the Statute of the ICJ and international courts and tribunals typically do not recognize the doctrine of *stare decisis*.[15] Article 59 of the Statute of the ICJ provides that the decisions of the ICJ have "no binding force except between the parties and in respect of that particular case."[16] Without binding force beyond the parties involved, judicial decisions are relegated to persuasive authority. Nevertheless, international law judges do go to great lengths to avoid contradicting earlier decisions.[17]

These differences in the international legal system require the U.S. legal researcher to adjust their thinking when handling judicial decisions. They must refrain from the urge to search across the entire body of a court's work. Indeed, researchers will rarely find databases or websites that offer full-text searching across the entire output of a single court or tribunal, let alone across multiple of them. Instead, the strategies used are more akin to those used for secondary sources. International courts' websites will generally provide lists of judicial decisions based on date or title—either by party name or some other short and memorable designation based on the subject matter of the controversy. Browsing lists of cases by year with a known citation is often the most efficient approach. And, citations to judicial decisions will usually be found through the use of secondary sources.

---

15. STATUTE OF THE INTERNATIONAL COURT OF JUSTICE, Art. 38(1), http://www.icj-cij.org/documents/?p1=4&p2=2#CHAPTER_II [https://perma.cc/7Wl4-DN2D]; see also GILBERT GUILLAUME, *The Use of Precedent by international Judges and Arbitrators*, 2(1) J. Int'l Dispute Settlement, 5 (2011).

16. *See* STATUTE OF THE INTERNATIONAL COURT OF JUSTICE, *supra* note 15, at Art. 59.

17. BRUNO SIMMA, *Fragmentation in a Positive Light*, 25 Mich. J Int'l L 845, at 846 (2003–2004).

IV. Compulsory Jurisdiction and Enforcement of Judgments

Other distinguishing features of the international legal system that U.S. legal researchers must take into consideration include whether jurisdiction is compulsory and whether there is an enforcement mechanism. For example, while all 193 members have ratified the Charter of the United Nations and the annexed Statute of the ICJ, the jurisdiction of the ICJ is not compulsory and there is no enforcement mechanism.[18] A State must submit to the jurisdiction of the ICJ and agree to abide by its judgment. In contrast, the jurisdiction of the ICC is compulsory for ratifying States according to its founding document, the Rome Statute, but there are no repercussions for parties who refuse to cooperate in circumstances where there is otherwise no excuse or immunity.[19] While the United States, Russia and China have not ratified it, 124 other States have.[20] More complex issues related to the lack of compulsory jurisdiction and the difficulties involved with enforcing judgments arise when the research project entails selecting a court to decide a particular controversy.

V. Research Process for Finding World Judicial Decisions Generally

Most projects related to world judicial decisions require researchers to identify a relevant international court or tribunal, understand its purview, and find relevant decisions. The updating process for international judicial decisions is handled differently than it is in jurisdictions that adhere to the doctrine of *stare decisis*. U.S. legal researchers might be surprised to find that many international judicial decisions cannot be evaluated using a citator.

---

18. STATUTE OF THE ICJ, art. 36, http://www.icj-cij.org/jurisdiction/?p1=5&p2=1&p3=3 [https://perma.cc/65YG-53UU]. However, 72 States have deposited declarations recognizing compulsory jurisdiction among and between all other States that have accepted the same obligation. Id.

19. STATUTE OF THE ICC, arts. 11–13.

20. *See* MTDSG for Rome Statute, https://treaties.un.org/Pages/ShowMTDSGDetails.aspx?src=UNTSONLINE&tabid=2&mtdsg_no=XVIII-10&chapter=18&lang=en [https://perma.cc/ZA74-FERB].

There are a handful of research guides covering various international courts and tribunals generally that may be used in preparation for the research effort.[21] Referring to such guides will help the legal researcher to gather a sense of the workings of a court, including its jurisdiction. Researchers should also find and read the documents that create the court and establish its authority, sometimes referred to as a court's basic documents[22] or core legal texts.[23]

Additionally, consulting secondary sources at the outset of a research project provides the legal researcher with the necessary background and context related to the international court or tribunal as well as the issue at the center of the research project. While using secondary sources in this manner, the legal researcher will encounter citations to judicial decisions. Collecting these citations to judicial decisions is essential. Books, encyclopedias, journal articles, American Law Report annotations, and yearbooks are particularly productive starting points and are discussed in depth in Chapter Eight. It is worth highlighting that hard-to-find judicial decisions can sometimes be found in the *International Legal Materials* journal.[24] It reproduces, in English, the full text of some judicial decisions and is worth searching if no earlier searches have been successful.

Armed with the citation information gathered from secondary sources, the legal researcher can locate either the court's website or a subscription database that contains the text of the decision or opinion. Finding a court's official website involves the straightforward effort of searching online using the court or international tribunal's name and scanning the results list to find the official website. Those researchers using a subscription database must first determine whether the database contains the opinions and decisions of the international court of interest by utilizing a 'list of publications included' or other tool that offers a complete listing of what is included in a database.

---

21. *See, e.g.,* GlobaLex, http://www.nyulawglobal.org/globalex/UN_Criminal_Tribunals_Research_Guide.html [https://perma.cc/J9MK-57UU] and Georgetown, http://guides.ll.georgetown.edu/c.php?g=365747&p=2471255 [https://perma.cc/89NH-C6BP].

22. *See, e.g.,* http://www.icj-cij.org/documents/index.php?p1=4 [https://perma.cc/TT7C-ERTN].

23. *See, e.g.,* https://www.icc-cpi.int/resource-library#coreICCtexts [https://perma.cc/DDA8-279D].

24. *International Legal Materials (I.L.M.),* https://www.asil.org/resources/international-legal-materials [https://perma.cc/67ED-GA89], or *I.L.M.* in print or searchable on Westlaw and Lexis.

Absent a citation, the legal researcher can use a court's digest or index of case law, where one exists. For example, the World Court Digest serves as a finding aid for the opinions of the ICJ by summarizing the ICJ Reports by topic.[25] Each court or tribunal website might index or digest according to its own set of keywords and legal concepts. Keywords that work for one court may not work for another. A heightened level of persistence and creativity is required for legal research across world judicial decisions.

Although many international courts and tribunals now offer their opinions online, and some archive them along with related information,[26] there are also a handful of subscription databases that include some portion of the available international legal decisions worldwide, including: Westlaw, Lexis, Oxford Law Reports, and HeinOnline. Given the manner in which international judicial decisions are used, researchers typically turn to these subscription databases to exploit full-text search capability and the ability to carry out terms and connectors searches. This may be useful for lengthy international judicial decisions or searching across the body of work from a particular court or tribunal. The chart at the end of this chapter offers the coverage and availability of international judicial decisions by various databases and subscriptions.[27]

U.S. legal researchers, operating in a legal system that rests on a common law tradition, spend considerable time updating case law research by using citators, either Lexis' Shepard's or Westlaw's KeyCite. This effort is handled differently on the international level. The lack of overarching structure among international courts and tribunals and the absence of the doctrine of *stare decisis*, diminishes the need for using a citator to update a case. Nevertheless, the citators in Westlaw and Lexis are available for some of the documents contained in those subscription databases. Additionally, there are some less robust citators within various other subscription databases, including Oxford Reports Online[28] and World Legal Information Institution (WorldLII).[29]

---

25. World Court Digest (1986–2000); http://www.mpil.de/en/pub/publications/archive/wcd.cfm?fuseaction_wcd=aktdat&aktdat=100000000006.cfm [https://perma.cc/WDL4-QDK8].

26. *See, e.g.,* CURIA, http://curia.europa.eu/jcms/jcms/Jo2_7045/en/ [https://perma.cc/V4N4-X4XQ]; *Cases,* ICJ, http://www.icj-cij.org/docket/index.php?p1=3 [https://perma.cc/AZ47-7VC8].

27. *See, infra,* Appendix I, of this Chapter.

28. *See, e.g.,* Oxford Law Citator, http://citator.ouplaw.com/about [https://perma.cc/5MJA-CAB8].

29. WorldLII is a comprehensive portal for international, regional, and national decisions.See WorldLII, http://www.worldlii.org [https://perma.cc/9G53-9Q9B].

VI. Selected Examples of Resources for World Judicial Decisions

The following examples are provided to demonstrate the types of resources available and the strategies that may be employed related to judicial decisions from the various types of courts: courts of general jurisdiction, ad hoc tribunals, supranational courts, specialty courts and regional tribunals. The Project on International Courts and Tribunals (PICT) provides a historical synopsis chart that shows international courts and tribunals categorized by the type of court. It also offers information on basic documents, judicial biographies, and other links.[30]

A. International Court of Justice and Permanent Court of International Justice

The Permanent Court of International Justice (PCIJ) and the ICJ were established following World War I and World War II, respectively, to resolve international disputes and controversies.[31] Their founding documents, the Statute of the PCIJ and Statute of the ICJ,[32] indicate these courts were established to have general jurisdiction to hear all manner of controversies.

The reports of the ICJ (1946–present) and the PCIJ (1920–1945) are published in the *Report of Judgments, Advisory Opinions, and Orders*. Some academic law libraries hold these judgments in print because they are the official publication according to *The Bluebook: A Uniform System of Citation*.[33] However, most researchers rely on the versions available online to carry out their research including the judgments, pleadings, and other related documents on the ICJ's website.[34] Because the ICJ judgments on the court's website are not full-text searchable, when necessary, legal researchers will use Westlaw or Lexis for this purpose.

---

30. *See International Criminal Court (ICC)*, PICT, http://www.pict-pcti.org/courts/ICC.html [https://perma.cc/2M5X-655R]. Although this site has not been maintained since 2003, it serves as a useful starting point because a good number of courts continue to function. Researchers must independently verify any information gleaned from the PICT chart and website.

31. *See* Shabtai Rosenne, *Permanent Court of International Justice*, MPEPIL (Oct. 2006).

32. *Id.*

33. The Bluebook: A Uniform Manual for Citation (20th ed. 2015).

34. *See, e.g., List of Cases referred to the Court since 1946*, ICJ, http://www.icj-cij.org/docket/index.php?p1=3&p2=2 [https://perma.cc/5476-QPWC].

The United Nations Dag Hammarskjold Library offers a research guide that describes the arrangement of ICJ opinions on the court's website and includes references to major treatises and other secondary sources.[35] The Peace Palace Library also offers a useful research guide that covers the ICJ.[36] Many law schools in the U.S.[37] and abroad[38] offer research guides related to the work of the ICJ and researchers are encouraged to find them by searching online using a query that contains the words: international court of justice ICJ research guide.

Legal researchers can search across the body of work by the ICJ by subject matter using the online version of *The World Court Digest*, which is published by the Max Planck Institute for Comparative Public Law and International Law.[39] U.S. legal researchers are generally familiar with the value of consulting a digest to find all case law on a particular topic, accustomed as they are to using West's Topic and Key Number System.[40] While *The World Court Digest* is not as robust as West's Topic & Key Numbers for domestic case law research, it remains a useful tool for finding international decisions by topic. *The World Court Digest* offers a table of contents that may be browsed; however, researchers should be careful because the numbering of some of the chapters differs in the online version.[41] For those researchers without access to Westlaw or Lexis who are interested in finding the ICJ's most recent position on a topic, *The World Court Digest* can be useful.

B. International Criminal Court

Although negotiated through the UN, the International Criminal Court (ICC) was established through the Rome Statute as an independent body in

---

35. *See UN Documentation: International Court of Justice*, DAG HAMMARSKJOLD LIBRARY, http://research.un.org/en/docs/icj/judgments [https://perma.cc/775F-FGGK].

36. https://www.peacepalacelibrary.nl/research-guides/settlement-of-international-disputes/international-court-of-justice/ [https://perma.cc/JJT4-6KC6].

37. *See, e.g.,* Georgetown Law Library, Courts and Tribunals: International Court of Justice, http://guides.ll.georgetown.edu/c.php?g=365747&p=2471255 [https://perma.cc/5QQC-KXHF].

38. *See, e.g.,* Oxford LibGuides: International courts, cases & commentary: ICJ, http://libguides.bodleian.ox.ac.uk/c.php?g=423223&p=2889814 [https://perma.cc/WV9D-N3DK].

39. *See World Court Digest,* MAX PLANCK INST., http://www.mpil.de/en/pub/publications/archive/wcd.cfm?fuseaction_wcd=aktdat&aktdat=100000000006.cfm [https://perma.cc/WDL4-QDK8]. The World Court Digest is also available in print in most law libraries.

40. *See* Chapter 9 for a complete description of digest searching.

41. World Court Digest Synopsis of Chapters, http://www.mpil.de/de/pub/publikationen/archiv/world-court-digest.cfm?fuseaction_wcd=aktdat&aktdat=100000000007.cfm [https://perma.cc/ES5W-STZH].

2002.[42] The court is comprised of eighteen judges that are nominated by the member States, and is charged with resolving the most serious international criminal harms by individuals according to its Statute.[43]

The cases of the ICC are cited by case name, case number, type of ruling, paragraph number, and the date of the decision according to the Bluebook.[44] The reports of the ICC are indexed and available online at the official website of the ICC.[45] Similar to the ICJ website, the drawback of using the official site is that there is no feature to search full-text across all decisions. And, unfortunately, researchers are not able to search across all ICC materials on Westlaw or Lexis as they can for ICJ materials. They can, however, resort to using *International Legal Materials* on Westlaw or Lexis. However, only select decisions are included in that journal.

The International Criminal Courts section of the *Analytical Guide to the Work of the International Law Commission* offers background information on the area of international criminal law.[46] The *Annotated Digest of the International Criminal Court* is useful for searching by topic the work of the ICC. Additionally, the American Society of International Law (ASIL) offers a comprehensive guide by Gail Partin on international criminal law that is indispensable for the legal researcher handling an international criminal law matter.[47] It offers a section on specific crimes by topic.[48]

---

42. Rome Statute of the International Criminal Court, https://www.icc-cpi.int/nr/rdonlyres/ea9aeff7-5752-4f84-be94-0a655eb30e16/0/rome_statute_english.pdf [https://perma.cc/EY5S-TM55].

43. Hans-Peter Kaul, International Criminal Court, MPEPIL (Dec. 2010).

44. The Bluebook: A Uniform Manual for Citation 212–213 (20th ed. 2015).

45. *See* ICC, https://www.icc-cpi.int [https://perma.cc/W4ZN-5FFZ].

46. *See Analytical Guide of the International Law Commission*, http://legal.un.org/ilc/guide/gfra.shtml [https://perma.cc/X3H7-A9DQ].

47. *See*, Gail Partin, *International Criminal Law*, ASIL, https://www.asil.org/sites/default/files/ERG_CRIM.pdf?v=1 [https://perma.cc/J3G8-BQPR] (last updated Apr. 1, 2015); *see also UN Documentation: International Law*, Dag Hammarskjold Library, http://research.un.org/en/docs/icj/texts [https://perma.cc/EL3D-UDQZ] (introduction to courts and tribunals).

48. *Id.*, at 25.

C. International Criminal Tribunal for Yugoslavia / International Criminal Tribunal for Rwanda

The International Criminal Tribunal for Yugoslavia (ICTY) and International Criminal Tribunal for Rwanda (ICTR) were established in 1993 and 1994, respectively, prior to the ICC. They were established to handle crimes committed within a specific region and timeframe. While the ICTY is expected to close in December 2017, the ICTR closed in December 2015. A residual mechanism, the Mechanism for International Tribunals (MICT),[49] was put in place in December 2010 to operate in parallel to these two ad hoc courts and then to continue handling residual matters as these courts close. The Security Council reviews its work every two years. ICTY decisions can be found on its official website,[50] and both ICTY and ICTR decisions can be found on the MICT website.[51]

The MICT website offers two searchable databases: Judicial Records and Archives and the MICT/ICTR/ICTY Case Law Database. The Judicial Records and Archives database offers all public records including filing, exhibits, and transcripts.[52] While the database is currently in beta version, it does offer useful post-search filtering options for document type, language, file type and source. The MICT/ICTR/ICTY Case Law Database[53] offers intuitive basic and advance search options. As well, it offers a Notions List, an alphabetical list of topics that can be searched or browsed.[54]

The Annual Reports of the ICTY[55] and the ICTR[56] provide helpful chronological organization and summaries of the cases and associated documentation. There are also numerous research guides to their decisions and reports

---

49. *See* United Nations Mechanism for International Tribunals, http://www.unmict.org/en [https://perma.cc/36MF-N62Y].

50. ICTY, http://www.icty.org [https://perma.cc/V3M6-VAL6].

51. *See MICT/ICTR/ICTY Case Law Database*, MICT, http://www.unmict.org/en/cases/ictr-icty-case-law-database [https://perma.cc/M6H8-677D].

52. *See Judicial Records and Archive database*, ICTR, http://jrad.unmict.org [https://perma.cc/6PHU-98FD].

53. *See supra* note 49.

54. http://cld.unmict.org/notions/ [https://perma.cc/TF3Y-JSMH].

55. *See Annual Reports*, ICTY, http://www.icty.org/en/documents/annual-reports [https://perma.cc/96T3-J4U6]; *see also Digest*, ICTY, http://www.icty.org/en/documents/icty-digest [https://perma.cc/7NCR-XR2P].

56. *See Annual Reports*, ICTR, http://unictr.unmict.org/en/documents/annual-reports [https://perma.cc/94RL-TCHX].

for research including those by the United Nations and the PICT.[57] The decisions of International Criminal Hybrid Tribunals are also searchable on Westlaw (1995–present for press releases and basic legal documents).

D. European Court of Justice and European Court of Human Rights

Currently, the only supranational is the European Union (EU). The European Court of Justice (ECJ) is a court comprised of one judge from each EU country as well as 11 advocates general.[58] It is charged with ensuring that EU law is interpreted and applied consistently throughout the European Union. The ECJ claims final and exclusive authority to decide disputes related to controversies and disputes among the EU member states.[59]

ECJ decisions are available through EUR-Lex.[60] The EUR-Lex website provides a directory of EU case law by treaty classification scheme both before and after the 2010 Lisbon Treaty.[61] Similarly, a *Digest of EU Case Law* is available through the court's website for researchers searching by topic.[62] The *Digest of EU Case Law* also rests on a classification scheme arranged in nine parts since the changes brought about by the 2010 Lisbon Treaty. However, the prior arrangement is also offered with convenient cross-references.

In addition to the ECJ, researchers must also be aware of the human rights tribunal created under the purview of the Council of Europe which governs human rights issues in Europe.[63] According to the European Convention on

---

57. *See* UN Documentation: International Law, http://research.un.org/en/docs/law [https://perma.cc/YW6Y-MKV9]; *see also* the *Hybrid Courts*, PICT, http://www.pict-pcti.org/courts/hybrid.html [https://perma.cc/3YRL-5PGH].

58. Court of Justice of the European Union, https://europa.eu/european-union/about-eu/institutions-bodies/court-justice_en [https://perma.cc/DYP3-WXBD]; *see also*, https://europa.eu/european-union/about-eu/institutions-bodies/court-justice_en [https://perma.cc/DSN7-DJPW].

59. *See generally*, Matthew Parish, *International Courts of the European Legal Order*, 23(1) Eur. J. Int. L. 141–153 (2012).

60. *EU Case Law*, EUR-Lex, http://eur-lex.europa.eu/collection/eu-law/eu-case-law.html [https://perma.cc/6UVG-EV4N]. European decisions are published in the Official Journal of the European Union.

61. *See Directory of European Case Law*, EUR-Lex, http://eur-lex.europa.eu/browse/directories/new-case-law.html [https://perma.cc/7LXG-V232].

62. *See Digest of the Case-Law*, CURIA, http://curia.europa.eu/jcms/jcms/Jo2_7046/en/ [https://perma.cc/F8C3-NC2S].

63. *See* Council of Europe, http://www.coe.int/en/ [https://perma.cc/9DRP-PXKT].

Human Rights,[64] the European Court of Human Rights (ECHR) adjudicates human rights violations among members of the Council of Europe. The ECHR and the ECJ each have a specific charge according to their respective founding documents.

The ECHR decisions are accessible online through a portal called "HUDOC."[65] The judgments and decisions of the ECHR are full-text searchable through the HUDOC search template with post-search filtering by State, violation, keyword, and other helpful features.[66] The *Reports of Judgments and Decisions* is the official print publication of ECHR decisions. The *Reports* offer a detailed list of judgments by party name and an analytical index by article of the treaty to better locate European human rights decisions by subject matter.[67] Overall, these portals for EU case law are comprehensive and create official access to decisions without the need for consultation or full-text searching on a paid database.

E. Specialty International Tribunals

Specialty tribunals base their jurisdiction on subject matter, such as the law of the sea or intellectual property, and are usually created because expertise in the subject matter is required. Usually, specialty tribunals are established by international conventions. For example, the International Tribunal for the Law of Sea[68] (ITLOS) was established by the United Nations Convention on the Law of the Sea (UNCLOS).[69] Despite being established through the workings of the UN, ITLOS is an independent judicial body that handles disputes arising out of interpretation and application of the UNCLOS. A subsequent agreement, Agreement Relating to the Implementation of Part XI of the Convention, must be read together with UNCLOS.

---

64. *See* European Court of Human Rights (ECHR), http://www.echr.coe.int/Pages/home.aspx?p=home&c [https://perma.cc/4LPY-QULZ].

65. *See HUDOC Database*, ECHR, http://hudoc.echr.coe.int/eng#%7B%22document collectionid2%22:[%22GRANDCHAMBER%22,%22CHAMBER [https://perma.cc/7HA4-HAWM].

66. *See HUDOC Reports of judgments and decisions*, ECHR, http://www.echr.coe.int/Pages/home.aspx?p=caselaw&c=#n14597620384884950241259_pointer [https://perma.cc/45AA-6WK4].

67. *See id. See, e.g.,* http://www.echr.coe.int/sites/search_eng/pages/search.aspx#{"full-text":["analytical%20index"]} [https://perma.cc/T7JT-S46B].

68. *See, e.g., United Nations Convention on the International Law of the Sea*, http://www.un.org/depts/los/convention_agreements/convention_overview_convention.htm [https://perma.cc/46GD-3D9J].

69. https://treaties.un.org/doc/Publication/MTDSG/Volume%20II/Chapter%20XXI/XXI-6.en.pdf [https://perma.cc/8PW9-ZNL5].

The ITLOS website[70] offers a list of its cases, links to official judgments of the court, and a comprehensive docket.[71] The website also includes the basic texts, key terms, and ITLOS publications.[72] ITLOS decisions are not available on Westlaw or Lexis.

The American Society of International Law offers a comprehensive ITLOS research guide[73] that researchers should consult before carrying out ITLOS research. As well, there is a useful commentary, *The Rules of the International Tribunal for the Law of the Sea: A Commentary*,[74] that researchers will find invaluable.

F. Regional Courts — Africa/Americas/Asia

Researchers should also consider the possibility that a regional international court or tribunal may exist for various continents or regions of the world. While the African Union has made some progress toward a regional tribunal with a human rights mechanism via the African Court of Human Rights,[75] there is neither a regional Asian human rights court nor a regional trade or economic dispute settlement body.[76] The Inter-American Court of Human Rights is an important example of regional cooperation (OAS) regarding human rights in the Americas and prosecution of international human rights violations under the Inter-American conventions.[77]

---

70. International Tribunal for the Law of the Sea, https://www.itlos.org/en/top/home/ [https://perma.cc/WY47-PPH8].

71. *See* List of Cases, ITLOS, https://www.itlos.org/cases/list-of-cases/ [https://perma.cc/R9L8-TCSL].

72. *Id.*

73. *See, e.g.,* Barbara Bean, *Law of the Sea*, ASIL (Apr. 27, 2015), https://www.asil.org/sites/default/files/ERG_LOS.pdf [https://perma.cc/BUL6-K9KC].

74. Chandrasekhara & Gautier, eds., *The Rules of the International Tribunal for the Law of the Sea: A Commentary* (2006).

75. *See Judicial and Human Rights Institutions*, A.U.C., https://perma.cc/NNW2-BVVX; *see also African Court of Human and Peoples' Rights*, PICT, http://www.au.int/en/organs/cj [https://perma.cc/4XX9-YE63]; *Court of Justice of the Organization for the Harmonization of African Business Law*, AICT, http://www.aict-ctia.org/courts_subreg/ohada/ohada_home.html [https://perma.cc/U2R2-NSWZ].

76. *See* AsianLII for judicial decisions from the Asian national courts, http://www.asianlii.org/ [https://perma.cc/9VZQ-5BJC].

77. *See Decisions and Judgments*, Inter-Am. Court of Human Rights, http://www.corteidh.or.cr/cf/Jurisprudencia2/busqueda_casos_contenciosos.cfm?lang=en [https://perma.cc/JQJ7-7FSS].

While these regional courts offer a good portion of their work online, West-law offers only those case reports appearing in the Annual Report of the Inter-American Commission on Human Rights in its database. Researchers may find selected Inter-American decisions and other important regional decisions through *International Legal Materials*. There is a useful commentary for the Inter-American Court of Human Rights that researchers can consult to find case law related to various human rights.[78] Researchers can find research guides for these regional courts by searching online using the court's name and the phrase "research guide."

VII. Conclusion

The decentralized and autonomous nature of the courts and tribunals of the international legal system impacts not only the legal research process but also some of the types of finding aids and tools available to the researcher. Most notably, U.S. legal researchers do not need to search or cite to judicial decisions as they do in the national system. The decisions of international courts and tribunals can usually be found on their individual, official websites. Researchers should consider specialty, regional, and ad hoc courts and tribunals as potential forums in addition to the courts of general jurisdiction such as the ICJ, and ICC for criminal matters. Utilizing a research guide at the outset to gather a sense of the charge of the court or tribunal is essential. Digests may be used to narrow the scope of the research by topic. Much of the work of international courts and tribunals is available online for free but in some instances the subscription legal databases are useful for more advanced full-text searching. Finding and updating the decisions and opinions of international courts and tribunals must be considered notwithstanding the absence of the doctrine of *stare decisis* and the lack of an overarching hierarchical structure among international courts and tribunals.

---

78. Laurence Burgorgue-Larsen & Amaya Ubeda de Torres, The Inter-American Court of Human Rights: Case-Law and Commentary (2011).

Appendix—
Chart of International Judicial Decisions

Court	Availability	Full-Text Searchable?	Coverage
1. International Court of Justice (ICJ)	A) Westlaw/Lexis B) Court website—http://www.icj-cij.org/docket/index.php?p1=3&p2=2 [https://perma.cc/5476-QPWC]	A) Yes B) No	A) 1947–present B) 1947–present NOTE: this includes judgments, advisory opinions, and filings.
2. International Criminal Court (ICC)	A) Westlaw/Lexis: No B) Court website—https://www.icc-cpi.int [https://perma.cc/W4ZN-5FFZ]	A) N/A B) No, unless utilizing search engine function on court website	A) N/A B) 2002–present
3. European Court of Justice (ECJ)	A) Westlaw B) Court website—http://curia.europa.eu/jcms/jcms/Jo2_7045/en/ [https://perma.cc/V4N4-X4XQ]	A) Yes B) Yes = basic search of party names, full-text search, and digest of case law	A) 1954–present B) 1954–present
4. European Court of Human Rights (ECHR)	A) Westlaw B) Court website—http://hudoc.echr.coe.int/eng#%7B%22documentcollectionid2%22:[%22GRANDCHAMBER%22,%22CHAMBER [https://perma.cc/7HA4-HAWM]	A) Yes B) Yes	A) 1979–present (although some cases date back to 1960) B) 1999–present and in print—*European Human Rights Reports* (1979–present)
5. Inter-American Court of Human Rights (IACHR)	A) Westlaw/Lexis: No B) Court website—http://www.corteidh.or.cr/index.php/en [https://perma.cc/SJF5-KYAU]	A) No B) Yes = searchable and a digest of cases	A) N/A B) 1979–present

Appendix—
Chart of International Judicial Decisions

6. International Criminal Tribunal for the former Yugoslavia (ICTY)	A) Westlaw B) Court website—http://www.icty.org/en/documents/icty-digest [https://perma.cc/7NCR-XR2P]	A) Yes B) No—only a Google search of the site	A) 1995–present B) 1995–present
7. International Criminal Tribunal for Rwanda (ICTR)	A) Westlaw B) Court website—http://www.unmict.org/en/cases/ictr-icty-case-law-database [https://perma.cc/M6H8-677D]	A) Yes B) No—only a Google search of the site or search by the accused's name	A) 1995–2007 B) 1995–2007

Chapter 8

Secondary Sources

I. Introduction

Secondary sources are resources that explain, analyze, synthesize, critique, or comment on the law. They are written by legal commentators including judges, lawyers, and other policy makers as well as law students, members of NGOs, and newspaper reporters. Secondary sources are usually consulted to obtain background information and context for a research project. The citations found within them can be used to lead researchers to primary law and other relevant materials. While generally not cited in court documents, U.S. legal researchers will sometimes resort to citing secondary sources as persuasive authority where no primary authority exists or an argument is being made for a change in the law or for a new interpretation of the law.

There are a variety of types of secondary sources, some common to all disciplines and some unique to law. Those common to all disciplines include: dictionaries, encyclopedias (both international and national in scope), newspapers, blogs, books, and other journal articles. Those unique to law include: Words and Phrases, Restatements, American Law Reports (ALRs), commentaries, law reviews and bar journals, practice materials, and legal treatises.

U.S. legal researchers will not find the equivalent of all types of secondary sources in every foreign jurisdiction. For example, a foreign legal system that rests on a civil law tradition may not have a Restatement of the Law. To determine what is available, it is imperative to consult a legal research guide written by an expert in that field and jurisdiction. Foreign law research guides will list the types of secondary sources that are available in a jurisdiction and provide the titles as well as guidance on where to find them in print and online. A research guide will also provide information on other types of sources that might be unfamiliar to the U.S. researcher but are common in a foreign jurisdiction.

While reading secondary sources for background information, most researchers will also collect the citations to primary law and other secondary sources cited within. Utilizing secondary sources in this dual fashion expedites the legal research process by allowing the researcher to move seamlessly from secondary sources to relevant primary law sources. Over time, and with continued use, researchers will develop the ability to predict with relative certainty which type of secondary source will meet their particular research need. Until then, researchers should assess the depth and breadth of coverage of each of the sources they use. Additionally, they should consider the amount of time it takes for material to be published. For instance, if the legal researcher is handling a breaking legal issue, a legal blog may be selected over a law review article because a blog may be posted within days of an event (or more quickly) while a law review article may take a year to reach publication. Often, but not always, there is an inverse relationship between depth of coverage and time to publication.

Certain secondary sources may be used as a subsidiary means to determine primary law, either a rule of customary international law or general principles of law. Determining which secondary sources can be used as subsidiary sources is described in detail in Chapters 4, 5 and 6. These chapters should be read together with this chapter to ensure that the researcher does not overlook potentially useful secondary sources. As well, judicial decisions are considered persuasive authority in the international legal system and used in a manner similar to secondary sources. Many of the strategies used for finding secondary sources apply to finding international judicial decisions.

II. Types of Secondary Sources

A. Dictionaries

Dictionaries offer brief entries of numerous words or phrases. Most dictionaries are a single volume. There are two types of legal dictionaries that a researcher may encounter. The first is the standard legal dictionary that is used within any particular jurisdiction.[1] The second is a language translation dic-

---

1. *See, e.g.*, BLACK'S LAW DICTIONARY (Bryan A. Garner ed., 2014) (available on Westlaw) and Ballantine's Law Dictionary (available on Lexis).

tionary that renders the legal terminology from one language into another (or more than one other language).[2] Language translation dictionaries may or may not be bidirectional. Bidirectional dictionaries include an alphabetical listing in one language followed by an alphabetical listing in the other language.

Dictionaries also include a phonetic pronunciation for the word as well as information related to the parts of speech (i.e., noun, verb, adjective, and adverb). Legal dictionaries are different from lay dictionaries in that they often include a citation to legal authority in support of the definition. For this reason, legal researchers who are unfamiliar with an area of law may start their research with a dictionary not only to gather an understanding of the terms and phrases central to a subject and topic, but also to collect a citation to primary authority that defines the terms related to their research project.

Dictionaries are considered up to date through their publication date. All citations to primary law obtained from dictionaries must be run through a citator, either Shepard's or KeyCite. Legal researchers may find dictionaries by searching a library catalog using the following subject headings: **Law—Dictionaries—Spanish** (or substitute the jurisdiction of interest) or **Spanish Language—Dictionaries—English**.

Boczek's International Law: A Dictionary and *Parry & Grant's Encyclopaedic Dictionary of International Law (3d ed)* are examples of public international law dictionaries. Boczek's is arranged differently than other dictionaries, largely because it is a hybrid between a dictionary and a basic textbook. Because each chapter is arranged thematically with alphabetical subentries, it offers an alphabetical List of Entries for each chapter as part of the front matter of the book. It should be consulted before attempting to find a "definition" within.[3] There are other finding aids that are useful to the legal researcher, including Table of Cases, Chronology, Glossary and List of Acronyms, and Abbreviations. These types of finding aids are explained in Chapter 9.

Parry & Grant's is also a hybrid dictionary-encyclopedia. It is arranged alphabetically and contains terms as well as various types of phrases including proper names of individuals, legal doctrines, and tribunal opinions as they are commonly referred to. For example, *Parry & Grant's* contains entries for abuse of rights (doctrine); Ki-Moon, Ban (individual); and Right of Passage Case

---

2. *See, e.g.,* HENRY S. DAHL, DAHL'S LAW DICTIONARY SPANISH—ENGLISH/ENGLISH-SPANISH (2015).

3. This location is contrary to what a typical U.S. legal researcher would expect. Most would check the back of the book for an index once it was discovered that the dictionary is not arranged alphabetically but, rather, alphabetically within each chapter.

(ICJ opinion).[4] Entries that contain terms that are also defined in the dictionary are indicated by bold text.

B. Legal Encyclopedias

Legal encyclopedias contain brief, easy-to-read entries that provide an overview of a legal topic or concept. Due to this brevity, legal encyclopedias contain entries for several hundred topics usually in multi-volume sets that are arranged alphabetically by topic. Each entry includes footnotes which contain citations to the primary law that support the legal concepts covered. Unlike dictionaries, legal encyclopedias include a comprehensive index so that users can easily access the information in the main volumes. Researchers generally use legal encyclopedias toward the outset of the research project when they seek light to medium coverage of unfamiliar areas of law but may very well return to them later in the research project as new and unfamiliar information is encountered.

Scope and coverage of legal encyclopedias may vary by jurisdiction, subject matter or both. There are encyclopedias that cover a variety of subjects based on a particular jurisdiction. The two most popular jurisdiction-specific encyclopedias in the United States are American Jurisprudence, 2d (Am Jur 2d) and Corpus Juris Secundum (CJS). These encyclopedias are national in scope. They contain citations to federal as well as the state jurisdictions. There are also encyclopedias that cover a single subject area, such as public international law[5] or human rights law.[6] Researchers should consider the possibility of utilizing both types of encyclopedias at the outset of the research project.

Finding the equivalent of Am. Jur 2d or CJS in a foreign jurisdiction, where one exists, involves consulting a trusted legal research guide for that foreign jurisdiction to obtain the title to the national encyclopedia(s). Armed with the title to the encyclopedia, legal researchers may then search various catalogs to find which library holds the publication. For example, the *United States Library of Congress Foreign Law Research Guides*[7] offer a French Legal Research Guide that explains that the two major encyclopedias in France are

---

4. JOHN P. GRANT & J. CRAIG BARKER, PARRY & GRANT ENCYCLOPAEDIC DICTIONARY OF INTERNATIONAL LAW, (3d ed. 2009).

5. *See, e.g.*, RÜDIGER WOLFRUM, MAX PLANCK ENCYCLOPEDIA OF PUBLIC INTERNATIONAL LAW (2008), https://global.oup.com/academic/product/max-planck-encyclopedia-of-public-international-law-9780199231690?cc=us&lang=en&, [https://perma.cc/4TZ4-AGHM].

6. *See, e.g.*, THE HUMAN RIGHTS ENCYCLOPEDIA (James R. Lewis, Carl Skutsch eds 2001).

7. LIBRARY OF CONGRESS FOREIGN LAW RESEARCH GUIDES, http://www.loc.gov/law/help/foreign.php, [https://perma.cc/LY8Q-R4AL].

Les Répertoires Dalloz and Les Juris-Classeurs.[8] With a title in mind, legal researchers can search their home institution's library or worldcat.org to obtain a list of libraries that hold it.

While there are many U.S. law schools that offer legal research guides covering foreign jurisdictions, it is usually effective to search for a research guide created by a law library within a foreign jurisdiction. For example, the U.S. legal researcher conducting research into the laws of England, might consider consulting the research guides at Oxford University to discover that English legal researchers routinely begin their research with *Halsbury's Laws of England*.[9]

There are a handful of subject area encyclopedias in English including the widely-used *Max Planck Encyclopedia of Public International Law* (MPEPIL). Although it was originally issued in print, it has been offered online since 2008. It currently contains over 1600 entries.[10] Entries that reference other entries in the encyclopedia are hyperlinked and designated by an arrow (→) which is a remnant of how the encyclopedia alerted readers of the print version that there was another relevant entry within the encyclopedia. MPEPIL also contains a citator, Oxford Law Citator.[11] This citator references all Oxford University Press resources, including primary material.

Other subject specific encyclopedias can be uncovered by using a subject specific research guide. For example, a good human rights research guide should contain a reference to the *Encyclopedia of Human Rights*.[12] Other examples of encyclopedias based on subject area include: *Concise Encyclopedia of the United Nations*,[13] *International Encyclopedia for Labor Law and Industrial Relations*,[14] and the *Elgar Encyclopedia of Comparative Law*.[15]

Another strategy for finding encyclopedias based on subject area is to conduct a search in the catalog using a Library of Congress subject heading search.

---

8. LIBRARY OF CONGRESS *French Legal Research Guide*, https://www.loc.gov/law/help/guide/nations/france.php?loclr=bloglaw, [https://perma.cc/6AF3-4AZV].

9. *See* BODLEIAN LAW LIBRARY RESEARCH GUIDES, http://www.bodleian.ox.ac.uk/law/guides, [https://perma.cc/XL6A-CZHG].

10. *See* MAX PLANCK ENCYCLOPEDIA OF PUBLIC INTERNATIONAL LAW, *supra* note 6, https://global.oup.com/academic/product/max-planck-encyclopedia-of-public-international-law-9780199231690?cc=us&lang=en&, [https://perma.cc/4TZ4-AGHM].

11. *Id.*

12. *See* THE HUMAN RIGHTS ENCYCLOPEDIA, *supra* note 6.

13. CONCISE ENCYCLOPEDIA OF THE UNITED NATIONS (Helmut Volger ed., 2d ed. 2010).

14. INTERNATIONAL ENCYCLOPEDIA FOR LABOR LAW AND INDUSTRIAL RELATIONS (R. Blanpain ed. 1977–).

15. ELGAR ENCYCLOPEDIA OF COMPARATIVE LAW (JAN M. SMITS ED., 2006).

For example, **International Law—Encyclopedias** will produce a list of all encyclopedias covering international law.

C. Words and Phrases

Words and Phrases in print is a publication that is best described as a hybrid between a dictionary and an encyclopedia.[16] It offers light to medium coverage of over 350,000 terms that have been defined by the judiciary in legal opinions together with a citation to that opinion.[17] *Words and Phrases* is a multi-volume set that is similar to an encyclopedia in breadth of coverage and similar to a dictionary in depth of coverage. Citations within *Words and Phrases* are from the U.S. state, federal, or territorial jurisdictions. Apart from this national set, there are *Words and Phrases* volumes at the end of each of West's digest sets.[18] These *Words and Phrases* volumes include only those words and phrases that have been defined in the particular jurisdiction covered by the digest set.

The online version of *Words and Phrases* in Westlaw is not a separately searchable database that contains the print volumes. Rather, researchers must begin by selecting cases and then the advanced search link to obtain the template for words and phrases. Using this template, the algorithm searches the metadata field[19] for words and phrases. The search bar will reveal that an advanced search is being performed in the Words and Phrases field, as follows: advanced: WP (jus cogens). For platforms that don't have a *Words and Phrases* command, researchers can develop a Boolean search query that achieves a loose equivalent by including the following: (defin! OR interpret! OR explan! OR constru! OR mean!) /s "jus cogens".

Researchers should be careful when crafting Boolean searches so that they do not inadvertently exclude relevant results. For example, the above example will not capture every possible manner in which a court defines a term. For instance, in the Committee of U.S. Citizens Living *Nicaragua v. Reagan*, 859 F.2d 929 (1988), the court explained: "Jus Cogens, or the peremptory norms of international law, enjoy the highest status in international law...." In this sentence, the court has tucked the definition for Jus Cogens into a clause, using commas. The Boolean query would not capture this result. The same holds true for circumstances where the court merely defines the term by using the word "is." For example: Jus Cogens is a peremptory norm.

---

16. WORDS & PHRASES (1964–).
17. *Id.*
18. Digests are an index for case law and are discussed in Chapter 7.
19. Metadata fields are explained in Chapter 9.

D. American Law Reports

The American Law Reports (ALR) is a reporter series that offers annotations, sometimes called articles or entries, that cover an issue examined in a case.[20] There are eleven ALR series: ALR—ALR 7th, ALR Fed—ALR Fed 3d, and ALR-International. The ALR-International series is based on United States cases and cases from other global courts. First published in 2010, it is now discontinued.[21]

ALRs offer in-depth coverage of select topics. All topics have a basis in a case opinion or decision and tend to focus on emerging or controversial issues or issues that are fact-sensitive (case outcomes vary based on facts). In addition to exploring an issue, the ALR articles provide many references including: citations to cases based on jurisdiction; other ALR articles; legal encyclopedias, practice materials, forms and law review articles; West's Key Numbers and West databases; and an article index to aid the researcher in finding relevant portions of the annotation.

Unlike legal encyclopedias which are arranged by subject matter, ALRs are compiled in the order in which the articles are published. Consequently, legal researchers must rely on the index to find a relevant ALR annotation. The set of index volumes covers the entire ALR series, including the series for international law.[22]

Although Westlaw and Lexis offer the ALRs within the academic package, the ALR-International is not generally included in that package. However, by using a browse strategy and selecting Secondary Sources (from the All Content tab) > American Law Reports, the legal researcher will arrive at a screen that offers a link to the American Law Reports—International under the tools listing on the right-hand side of the page. This listing offers the titles to the ten most recent articles published in ALR—International. However, it does not offer the full text of the articles. A researcher must have a package that includes this publication or use the print version.

E. Bar Journals

Bar journals contain articles on various legal issues. They tend to focus on a single practice area and topic. Most often, bar journals offer a practitioner's

---

20. American Law Reports (1900s–).

21. American Law Reports International (2010–2017).

22. The ALR-International series was published after the current index set and so all references to the ALR-International volumes are found in the pocket parts of the Index.

perspective on a topic. Although they are shorter than law review articles and contain fewer footnotes, they are usually included in law journals databases. Legal researchers can use the strategies for identifying whether a journal is included in a database as described in Chapter 6.

To update, legal researchers will take note of the publication date of the article. All citations to primary law within a bar journal article must be run through a citator, KeyCite or Shepard's, to bring it up to date.

F. Practice Materials

Similar to bar journals, practice materials include publications geared toward the practitioner, including form books and continuing legal education materials. Often, there is a practice series that covers a single jurisdiction. Court and tribunal rules also fall under this category although often they are contained in databases along with other primary law materials from the legislature or judiciary. Researchers can find practice materials in foreign jurisdictions by using the strategies offered in Chapter 11 for foreign law sources. Additionally, the International Bar Association offers helpful materials on its website under the IBA Digital Content tab.[23]

For some practice materials, updating involves taking note of the date of publication, checking for pocket parts, if available, and taking note of the closing dates for the pocket parts. Of course, any citation to primary law from within the practice materials must be run through a citator, KeyCite, or Shepard's, for the most up-to-date treatment of that primary law.

G. Legal Blogs

The rise in online blogs has generated a relatively new type of resource available to legal researchers. Often, blogs offer current information from people or authors with "feet on the ground" experience or from people within a foreign jurisdiction who have the ability to offer translations in English of recent legal developments. The depth of coverage tends to be lighter than the coverage in a law review or bar journal article, but this may vary, depending on the blog writer. Some blog writers attempt to "break" the news and offer an early perspective. Legal blogs can be found online by typing in relevant keywords and including the word blog. Researchers should always assess the blog author's credibility and authority.

---

23. International Bar Association, http://www.ibanet.org/, [https://perma.cc/5CF9-NFFM].

H. Newspapers

Similar to blogs, legal researchers can consult current newspapers when dealing with an issue that is too current to be included in other publications. On the other end of the time spectrum, legal researchers can use newspapers for historical purposes that require a concurrent perspective from that time. Often, newspapers are used to gather background and context related to world events when researching state practice and *opinio juris*. Newspaper research entails locating a database that holds the newspaper of interest to the researcher. For historical research, the legal researcher is likely to use a microfiche or microform reader, although, increasingly newspaper archives are available online.

Bloomberg Law, Lexis and Westlaw offer a newspapers database within their subscriptions. Many newspapers now offer access to an archive of their newspapers for subscription. There are also stand-alone databases that include a variety of newspapers, both U.S. and foreign. For example, Newsbank—Access World News offers a number of foreign law newspapers in its database.[24] Newspapers published in a foreign language will typically need to be searched in the vernacular.

I. Secondary Sources used for Customary International Law Research: Commentaries, Government Gazettes, Yearbooks, Restatements, Law Reviews and Legal Treatises

Commentaries, government gazettes and yearbooks which are types of secondary sources that are frequently used for customary international law research are covered in Chapter 4. Restatements, law reviews and legal treatises which are types of secondary sources that sometimes contain the teachings of highly qualified publicists and are frequently used as subsidiary sources are covered in Chapters 6. Researchers should not overlook these options when considering which secondary sources to use.

---

24. NEWSBANK—ACCESS WORLD NEWS, http://www.newsbank.com/libraries/schools/solutions/us-international/access-world-news, [https://perma.cc/9C9T-KVGQ].

III. General Research Strategy for Secondary Sources

The United States national legal encyclopedias will be used as an example for explaining the legal research process. This process works across most types of secondary sources in print with minor variations. The two national encyclopedias in the United States are *American Jurisprudence (2d)* and *Corpus Juris Secundum*.

To begin, legal researchers will consult the index using the key words that were generated during the planning phase. Key word entries will refer the researcher to a relevant page, paragraph, or section in the main volume. The index to the national encyclopedic sets is found at the end of the main volumes and is itself a separate set of softbound volumes. For certain other secondary sources, the index may be at the back of the individual volume. An in-depth explanation of the various types of indexes and how to use them is included in Chapter 9.

Before turning to the page, paragraph or section of the main volume as identified from the index, the legal researcher should scan the table of contents or the outline to situate the specific page, paragraph or section in the larger arrangement of the article or chapter. By scanning the table of contents or outline, the researcher will find other relevant or related material. At a minimum, it allows the legal researcher to gather an understanding of the arrangement of the law by the publisher or author. Insights gained might later aid the researcher in finding information in other relevant resources.

The legal researcher then turns to the page, paragraph, or section identified as relevant (both from the index and the table of contents) to read them. While reading for background understanding of the legal topic, the researcher will encounter citations to primary law and other secondary sources. Taking note of these citations so that they can be consulted next is a productive research strategy.

After reading the main entry, the pocket part must be consulted.[25] Pocket parts might contain updated and revised text of the main entry or more re-

---

25. Some researchers prefer to consult the pocket part *before* the main text for certain secondary sources. Under certain circumstances this may be a time-saving technique, but most frequently it is preferable to begin with the text before proceeding to the pocket part. No matter the route, the legal research must understand how the main entry and pocket part function together. In all circumstances, both must be reviewed to obtain an overarching and complete understanding of the growth and development of the law in a subject area.

cent citations to supplement those in the main entry, or both. Researchers must take note of the current-through date for all sources consulted. The current-through date is the closing date listed on the pocket part cover. Even where no additional substantive information is gathered from the pocket part, the research is up-to-date through the current-through date on the pocket part. Taking note of the current-through date of the pocket part allows the researcher to return to the resource months later, and handily determine whether the pocket part was already consulted or whether a more recent pocket part has been published.

To bring the research further up to date, all relevant primary law must be run through a citator such as Lexis' Shepard's or Westlaw's KeyCite. Citators provide a list of subsequent documents that have cited to the source. Researchers check for validity and to understand the body of law as it relates to that source. By taking these additional steps, the researcher is effectively bringing the research up-to-date through the day that the research is conducted. Utilizing this route: index > outline for topic/chapter > main text > pocket parts > citator, ensures efficient and complete legal research.

When working with a secondary source online, researchers must guard against zeroing in on relevant information without also taking the time to explore where and how it fits into the broader arrangement of the publication in which it is included. Researchers must also determine whether related finding aids[26] are available. Tables of Authorities are routinely available at the document level. Most indexes are separately searchable databases. Tables of Contents tend to be somewhat hidden and researchers must make a concerted effort to find and browse them.

IV. Conclusion

It is vital to consult secondary sources for background information and context when beginning a research project. The use of secondary sources can also lead researchers to primary law and other relevant secondary sources. Many researchers handling complex international law issues find they return to secondary sources at point of need throughout the research process. Because certain secondary sources may be used as subsidiary sources, U.S. legal researchers should decide at the outset under which circumstances they intend to use a resource. It is entirely possible that a single resource is used in one instance for

---

26. The use of finding aids is discussed in detail in Chapter 9.

background understanding and in another as a subsidiary source to determine a rule of international law. During the planning phase of the research process, as described in Chapter 10, researchers should identify their intended use of secondary sources to ensure an orderly progression through the sources of law.

Chapter 9

Use of Finding Aids, Arrangement of the Law, and Search Techniques

I. Introduction

Given the availability of documents online and the development of sophisticated search and relevancy ranking algorithms, researchers usually find some information related to their research topic relatively quickly. However, *legal* research involves knowing how to use the information uncovered to further the legal research effort, including identifying mandatory and persuasive authority, understanding a body of law, and updating the law. Where a legal researcher finds too much information, it becomes vital to use narrowing strategies and various filters to obtain a relevant and more manageable set of documents. Where legal researchers find too little information, they must use strategies to broaden the effort. It may become necessary to verify that, in fact, nothing exists (as opposed to circumstances where the researcher has not exhausted every avenue of effort).

One of the fundamental differences in carrying out public international legal research, and which makes the effort considerably more laborious, is that no tool exists that can be used to search across all the international sources of law in one research pass. Whereas a U.S. legal researcher can search across all U.S. legislative, administrative, and case law documents with one search in a subscription database such as Westlaw or Lexis, there is no similar tool that will search across all treaties, customary international law, and general principles of law. Indeed, the very nature of customary international law and general principles of law precludes such a database.

This chapter begins with a brief overview of retrieving sources with known citation information, one of the most basic research efforts. Consulting print resources remains an essential step in most legal research projects. With the increased need to use finding aids when handling unfamiliar international legal research sources, this chapter describes the types of finding aids that a researcher can expect to encounter and explains how best to use them, both in print and online. Often, the strategies outlined can be used in concert to increase efficiency.

This chapter then describes strategies for searching by subject and topic. Because individual States collect and publish international law according to their own organizational arrangement of the law and in the vernacular, searching by subject and topic is considerably more difficult when handling a public international law research project. By offering a survey of several arrangements of international law in English, the legal researcher can begin to gain an appreciation for the challenges involved with legal research of public international law. The chapter then offers a brief explanation of both natural language and terms and connectors searching. It closes with an explanation for the need to utilize control strategies to ensure that nothing is overlooked.

II. Retrieval of a Source with a Known Citation

With complete citation information, retrieving a source becomes a relatively easy task. At most, it requires searching for and identifying a library or a database, whether free or subscription, which contains the desired source. To determine whether a library contains a resource, searches may be conducted through individual library catalogs or by using worldcat.org.[1] While WorldCat does not provide a listing of participating libraries,[2] it does offer the opportunity to search across multiple worldwide catalogs with a single query. Should the legal researcher's home institution's library not offer the publication, it may be requested from another library via an interlibrary loan program. Researchers who anticipate they will need foreign law materials should allocate time for requesting these materials through the interlibrary loan program.

---

1. *See* OCLC Worldcat, www.worldcat.org [https://perma.cc/3NQX-8VSU].
2. Worldcat offers that it "... is growing every day" but lists no specific number of participating libraries. See www.oclc.org/worldcat.en.html [https://perma.cc/DN2X-QJYA].

One strategy for finding websites that offer a database or collection of legal materials relevant to the researcher entails including the term "database" or "collection" or "series," together with the subject area key words, into an online search query. This will return websites that hold collections of documents that the researcher can then search with specific citation information. For example, a search for Ethiopia's labor law related to occupational hazards is better handled by searching for a database that contains foreign labor laws first and then searching within that database for laws governing occupational hazards by country. Including the term "database" along with "international" and "labor laws" in a search query using Google will yield a result for NATLEX, a database maintained by the International Labour Organization that contains records from over 196 countries, including Ethiopia.[3]

Often the legal researcher has access to subscription databases that offer a comprehensive set of legal materials that includes primary sources of law and numerous other publications and documents. Under these circumstances, researchers should begin by checking whether the online database offers an option for search by citation. This is either accomplished by entering the citation directly into the search bar (where the algorithm recognizes citations) or by entering the details of the citation into an advance search template offered specifically for searching by citation. These templates will often supply the correct format, including abbreviations for the publications.

While many databases are quite forgiving when it comes to recognizing citation formats, some do require specific abbreviation, spacing, and punctuation to search by citation. While it can be efficient to search by citation without checking the search syntax[4] first, if the citation entered does not return the desired document, the legal researcher cannot be certain whether it is because the database does not contain the document or because the information entered does not conform to the required syntax. At this point, the researcher would take the time to gather an understanding of the search syntax and run the search again as a control strategy to make the final determination that the database does not hold the desired document.

If neither of these two quick searches produces the desired document, it becomes necessary to take the time to search the database directory to determine if the desired document is included in the database. Researchers using Westlaw or Lexis may search for a particular resource in two different manners. First,

---

3. *See* INTERNATIONAL LABOUR ORGANIZATION, http://www.ilo.org/dyn/natlex/natlex4. home?p_lang=en, [https://perma.cc/9DS5-LPY6].

4. Search syntax is the required abbreviations, punctuation, and spacing as well as the connectors.

the researcher may search by title by simply typing the title into the search bar. Options will appear under a "Looking For This?" (Westlaw) or "Add sources filter" (Lexis) directly below the search bar. Alternatively, researchers using Westlaw may use the "My Content" list from the tools tab on the home page to obtain an alphabetical listing of all material included in the subscription. Researchers using Lexis may use the "Browse" link at the top of the page to "find a source." In the event the researcher is unable to find the desired document in a database that would otherwise appear to contain the information, the information (or simply "i") link will offer details related to the scope for the publication. Failure to retrieve the desired result may simply be a matter of the database not containing the publication for the year required by the researcher.

While many would instruct a legal researcher to check the "i" link first, it is more efficient when searching with a known citation to carry out the search first, because if the desired result appears, the researcher can continue with the next step in the research process. If the results list does not yield the desired information, the researcher should check the "i" link for scope as a control strategy and to confirm that nothing was inadvertently overlooked. This strategy only applies to searches with a known citation, not general-topic, legal research. For unfamiliar citation abbreviations, legal researchers should consult citation manuals[5] and other abbreviation-deciphering tools such as the *Cardiff Index to Legal Abbreviations*.[6]

III. Search Using Finding Aids

Where the legal researcher begins the effort without citations, there are a variety of finding aids that must be used. Often, a combination of finding aids may be used to expedite the research effort.

A. Spine of Book

When working in print, one of the most basic finding aids is the information printed or affixed on the spine of a book, which may include: title, au-

---

5. *See, e.g.*, *The Bluebook: A Uniform System of Citation* (20th ed. 2015); *Guide to Foreign and International Legal Citation*, (2d ed. 2009); Donald Raistrick, *Index to Legal Citations and Abbreviations* (4th ed. 2013). Other titles can be found with a subject heading search in a catalog using: law-abbreviations or citation of legal authority.

6. *Cardiff Index to Legal Abbreviations*, http://www.legalabbrevs.cardiff.ac.uk/ [https://perma.cc/2QL4-TBN5].

thor, publisher and call number. Sets of volumes may include volume numbers, dates, alphabetical listings, or other helpful location information.

B. Indexes

An index is an alphabetical list of key words that direct the legal researcher to the relevant substantive material in a publication. Generally, there are two types of indexes. The first type lists the words and concepts contained within a single book or set of books and is called a "back of book" index. The second type comprehensively compiles words and concepts across many books and is called a bibliographic index. Bibliographic indexes are stand-alone publications not associated with the main volumes of a set.

i. Back of Book Index

Back of book indexes are a list of key words arranged in alphabetical order. Each page of the index offers a heading in bold at the top of the page to aid the legal researcher in locating the desired key word. For example, a legal researcher looking for references to *jus cogens* in an index may find the entry on the page with the headings for *judicial bodies* and *justiciability*. Scanning the key words included on that page allows the legal researcher to find the entry for *jus cogens*.

Directly following the entries, the index will list a locator. The locator may be to a page number within that book (where the index is at the back of the book), to the relevant volume and section or paragraph number (where the index is at the end of a set of volumes), or to another word within the index. Where headings would otherwise have a number of locators, sub-entries are typically used to further refine or specify locations within the main volume. Locators are then listed following each of these individual sub-entries.

A cross-reference occurs where one entry directs to another entry. Sometimes, after proceeding to the cross-referenced word, a legal researcher will find the original key word listed as a sub-entry. This will not always be the case and is dependent on the indexing standards used. Some publishers include "see," "see also," and "see under" as cross-referencing directions. It is advisable to make a mental note or keep track of the additional key words discovered within the index because they can be used to refine future search efforts.

Not all key words generated during the planning phase of the research project will be found in every index. Simply because a particular key word is not found does not necessarily mean that the word or concept is not covered within that volume or set of volumes. Rather, it means that the person or computer program that indexed the publication did not choose that word as a heading or key word. Legal researchers must understand that consulting an index as a finding aid takes persistence. In circumstances where the key word is not included as a heading, a legal researcher's ability to generate synonyms and understand the arrangement of the law comes into play.

Understanding the arrangement of the law allows the legal researcher to consider that a particular key word not found as a heading may be found as a sub-entry under a broader heading. For example, an index may not have a heading for *denunciation* but may include it as a sub-entry under *treaties*. Over time, legal researchers begin to build a structure in their minds for the arrangement of the law based on subject > topic > issue > concept > point of law > key words, and they can move up and down this hierarchical arrangement depending on their need to search more broadly or narrowly with their key words. It takes a concerted effort to understand the general arrangement of the law. This may be accomplished by paying attention to whether certain finding aids are available as separately searchable databases and, where available, by employing a browse strategy rather than a search strategy. Often, when using a browse strategy to view the arrangement of the law, the legal researcher must click on a plus symbol (+) or check a box to reveal the complete list of sub-entries. If there is an option to 'open all' it should be used to view the entire architecture of the arrangement of the law.

ii. Bibliographic Index

The second type of index is a bibliographic index which is a compilation of citation information related to resources by more than one publisher. These are the types of indexes that were used before the existence of online databases. Usually, bibliographic indexes are a separately bound title or database, and not included at the back of a book or at the end of a set of volumes. As such, they are ripe for inclusion in databases as a separate file that should be searched, independently from full-text database, because often they contain many more entries than are included in the full-text database. Examples include: *The Index to Legal Periodicals, the Index to Foreign Legal Periodicals, and LegalTrac.*

Bibliographic indexes offer complete bibliographic information related to the stated scope of the index. They commonly offer multiple alphabetical arrangements: by author, by title, and by subject, or some combination of the three. Using this type of index allows the researcher to search through an enormous amount of material and narrow to only those items that appear relevant. When searching an index by subject, researchers can find articles about a relevant topic; whereas a full-text search with key words will return all documents that contain those key words, many of which may be lacking in 'aboutness' or relevancy. Although consulting an index adds a step to the research effort, it typically returns only documents about the topic and not those that might include only one reference to the key words.

Use of the information collected from a bibliographic index allows the legal researcher to find the desired materials elsewhere, either in a library or a comprehensive legal database. The information contained in the bibliographic index is equivalent to the concept of a "locator" in a standard "back of book" index. However, because the bibliographic index crosses many publications, more complete citation information, as opposed to merely a page or volume number, is included.

For example, a legal researcher can use the *Index to Legal Periodicals* to find a relevant article on state sovereignty. After identifying an article, the legal researcher takes note of the title to the journal that has published the article as well as the article title itself. The researcher then proceeds to a catalog or a database to determine if the library or database holds that journal title. If so, after accessing the journal, the researcher can search for the desired article. It is important to note both the journal title and the article title when using a bibliographic index. Those accustomed to searching full-text databases frequently overlook the intermediate step of finding the journal that contains the article before searching for the article itself. In these circumstances, they can avoid the inefficiencies of having to retrace their steps by jotting down or copying and pasting *all* of the citation information included in the bibliographic index.

C. Specialty Indexes

Comprehensive treaty indexes are used to find the authoritative texts of treaties. Treaty indexes include additional details that aid in the treaty research effort including parties, subject matter, entry-into-force date, depositary, and citation information. These types of indexes can span volumes or be a standalone volume. An example of a treaty index is the *United States Treaties in Force* (*TIF*) which is available in print and online in pdf at the U.S. Department of State website.[7] In 2016, *TIF* rearranged its categories to enhance finding treaties by topic. A detailed explanation of *TIF* and other comprehensive treaty indexes is included in Chapter 2.

---

7. *Treaties in Force (TIF)*, Dep't of State, http://www.state.gov/s/l/treaty/tif/index.htm [https://perma.cc/K79W-XGPJ].

D. Table of Contents

The table of contents is another finding aid that helps the researcher gather a sense of where to find information within a book or set of books. While indexes are typically found at the end of a book or set of books, the table of contents is typically located at the front of the book. It is arranged in the order in which the material has been presented in the book, by page number, rather than alphabetically.

It is worthwhile to scan the table of contents even when a reference to a page number within the book has already been obtained through the index. Scanning the table of contents allows the legal researcher to ascertain the depth and breadth of coverage in the book as well as a sense for how the author arranged the material in the book. Because authors customarily arrange material by subject and topic, information located in adjacent sections or chapters is often also relevant and easily discoverable by scanning the table of contents.

E. List of Acronyms

Legal researchers of international law encounter a variety of acronyms for documents as well as international organizations. Frequently, international law materials will contain a list of the acronyms used within the text of the document. This list is usually included at the beginning of the source but can also be included at the end. Typically, the list is arranged alphabetically by acronym.

F. Table of Authorities

A Table of Authorities is a list of every citation included within a document. Usually, it is arranged by headings for the types of authority cited, both primary and secondary, and will include references to the page or pages on which the citation appears within the document. Many court filings, such as briefs, memoranda, or memorials in support of a motion or other filing, will contain a Table of Authorities.

When working online, many databases offer a Table of Authorities for legal opinions that also includes the treatment for those cited authorities. This allows the legal researcher to immediately see whether the court's reasoning from the original legal opinion rests on authority that was subsequently treated negatively. If so, the legal researcher can more quickly assess whether the original legal opinion and reasoning have stood the test of time. Simply because a cited authority rests on authority with negative treatment does not suggest that the original legal opinion has been weakened. Rather, it should prompt the legal researcher to make an assessment as to why the cited authority has been treated negatively. It is entirely possible that it has nothing to do with the reason for which the researcher intends to cite to the case. If it does, however, then the strength of the original legal opinion has indeed eroded and the legal researcher must continue to update to understand the body of law on that particular issue.

G. Table of Cases

A Table of Cases is frequently included in treatises, reporter volumes, and digests. It is an alphabetical list of all cases referred to within the volume together with the full citation and the page on which the case appears. It appears at the back of the book or the set of volumes. This tool is useful in three circumstances. First, the Table of Cases may be used when the legal researcher is working in print and has a case name, but not a full citation. The Table of Cases can be consulted quickly to obtain complete citation information. Second, the Table of Cases may be used where the legal researcher has already identified a leading case elsewhere and wants to check whether this particular secondary source offers commentary on it. In this circumstance, the legal researcher consults the Table of Cases included in a treatise to find the pages on which the case is discussed within the treatise. And third, a legal researcher can tap into the Table of Cases to gather a list of all the case law that the author of a treatise or other secondary source has determined important as it relates to a topic.

H. Conversion Tables and Translation Tables

Conversion Tables allow the legal researcher with only a slip law or session law number to convert it to the applicable code section. For example, the legal researcher with a Public Law number may use a conversion table to find the applicable U.S. Code section.

Publishers may also use conversion tables where the law has been renamed and renumbered. The conversion table will list the current law number and a reference to the prior law number so that the legal researcher may trace the development of the law despite the renumbering.

Translation Tables allow legal researchers to find topic and key numbers that have been renamed or renumbered in West publications. Sometimes the body of law grows and develops in a way that it becomes necessary for the publisher to create new topic and key numbers or rename and renumber old ones. For example, in 1990, Westlaw added "RICO" as a topic. In 2000, "Sentencing" was added. In 2013, West broke out "Extortion and Threats" into two separate topics: "Extortion" and "Threats, Stalking & Harassment." At other times, societal influences dictate that a topic should be renamed and numbered. For example, the topic "insane persons" was renamed "mental health." In 1978, the topic "drunkards" was renamed and numbered under "chemical dependents." When an old topic and key number is replaced with a new one, the publisher offers a translation table so that researchers can update the old topic and key number with the equivalent new topic and key number. Translation tables are bidirectional, which means that researchers may use them whether they have the old or new topic and key number.

In print, these translation tables are included in digests and their associated pocket parts. Online, translation tables are incorporated within the search algorithm so that a search using the current topic and key number will bring up results that include the replaced topic and key number as well and vice versa. Those who prefer to conduct terms and connectors searches should include topic and key numbers in their search query (connected by an OR and within parentheses) to ensure thoroughness.

I. Popular Name Table

A Popular Name Table is offered to help the researcher find documents where only the common or colloquial title is used. The popular name table lists laws and acts by their popular name and includes references to the citations. Where the legal researcher has the popular name of a law, such as the Case Zablocki Act or the Foreign Sovereign Immunities Act, but has no citation, consulting the Popular Name Table refers the legal researcher to the full title and relevant citation. This tool is particularly useful in circumstances where an Act is not contained in a single code section. It is also very useful when researchers have the title to a treaty that has been implemented into U.S. law. Usually, the Popular Name Table is included at the end of an index set as a separate finding aid. Online, it may be a separately searchable database. Chapter 2 offers examples that demonstrate the use of this tool in connection with finding U.S. implementing legislation of international conventions.

J. Catalogs

Researchers accustomed to full-text searching may have little patience for catalog searching, which tends to be considerably less forgiving in that more precision is required. Titles and authors must match exactly to how they were entered into the catalog database by the cataloger. Most catalogs typically offer title, author, subject, and call number searches. Some catalogs offer key word searches. However, users should be reminded that the key words are those found within the cataloging information (title, author, and sometimes table of contents), not full-text.

Despite these challenges, catalog searches must be included in the research effort. Legal researchers should conduct searches in the catalog of their home institution, or that which they are affiliated, and in worldcat.org. By utilizing the subject heading links from within a relevant title, the legal researcher can expand the original search (which was perhaps by title or author) to a broader search (by subject) to uncover all the books classified similarly in a collection. It is loosely akin to carrying out a topic and key number search from within a single case opinion. In both instances, the legal researcher is taking advantage of the classification scheme to find additional, relevant material.

K. Abstracts

Abstracts of articles (and other documents) are comprised of a paragraph summary of the content. They are used to help readers identify the article's purpose. Searching abstracts using key words will generate a result set that is both smaller and more relevant than searching full-text within a database. Additionally, the researcher can be certain that the entire document is about the key words, as opposed to a result set that contains documents with the key words appearing anywhere in the document. Searching abstracts may require the researcher to review the key words that were brainstormed at the outset and that were collected during the research process up to that point, to select the ones that would most likely be included in an abstract. It may be more effective to use general key words and terms when searching abstracts, and then re-query to include more specific terms after considering the original results set.

Researchers should be cautioned, however, that where abstract fields exist in databases, abstracts are not necessarily included for every document. As such, this approach should always be used in conjunction with other approaches to ensure thorough research. Searching the abstracts first and then conducting a full-text search is discussed more fully below under Part VI: Control Strategies.

IV. Search by Subject and Topic

Typically, a legal researcher approaches most open-ended research projects by employing a strategy of searching by topic. This strategy requires the researcher to identify the field of law, the subject area within that field, and then the topic at the center of the research matter. The difficulty encountered with international legal research is that individual jurisdictions classify and arrange the law in accordance with their national needs. There is no overarching organizational scheme for international legal publications and materials similar to the arrangement in the U.S. that rests on West's topic and key numbers.

One strategy for gathering a sense of subject and topics in public international law is to use the organizational scheme, or the arrangement of the law, of various reputable organizations in the field of public international law. An examination of The American Society of International Lawyers' (ASIL) research tool, Electronic Information System for International Law (EISIL), and the Multilateral Treaties Deposited with the Secretary General (MTDSG) of the United Nations, offers a glimpse of how public international law organizations structure and arrange international legal materials. These can be considered against the various U.S. arrangements that include the U.S. Treaties in Force, the Library of Congress Subject Heading, and West's Topic and Key Numbers.

A. Arrangement of ASIL's Electronic Information System for International Law

ASIL is a scholarly association comprised of lawyers, judges, academics, students, and others interested in public international law. EISIL is an ASIL project meant to support researchers by helping them "locate the highest quality primary materials, authoritative web sites and helpful research guides."[8] EISIL arranges international law by subject and topic. It currently offers fourteen broad subject areas from General International Law to Use of Force:

General International Law	Private International Law
States & Groups of States	International Environmental Law
Individuals & Groups	International Air, Space & Water
International Organizations	International Criminal Law
International Dispute Settlement	International Human Rights Law

---

8. *See* http://www.eisil.org/index.php?sid=788301076&t=about [https://perma.cc/CMV 9-74RN]. The Electronic Information System for International Law (EISIL) has not been updated since 2012. Efforts to revive the project are ongoing as of this writing. Nevertheless, the EISIL tool remains a valuable insight into the arrangement of international law.

International Economic Law	International Humanitarian Law
Communications & Transport	Use of Force

Within each broad subject area, EISIL has broken down the law into topics. For example, under the subject Use of Force, EISIL offers the following topics: Collective Security, Law of Armed Conflict, Arms Control & Disarmament, Peace and Neutrality, and Armed Non-State Actors. Each subject area also contains the topic subsection "Basic Sources," which offers links to the primary law in the subject from the most authoritative sources as well as vetted websites and research resources.

B. Arrangement of the United Nations Multilateral Treaties Deposited with the Secretary General

The United Nations collection of multilateral treaties, the MTDSG, is also arranged by topics designated as chapters.[9] The chapter designations are simply the chapter titles from the print version and are not associated with an official document arrangement (and are not in alphabetical order):

Charter of the U.N. and Statute of the ICJ	Narcotic Drugs & Psychotropic Substances
Pacific Settlement of International Disputes	Traffic in Persons
Privileges & Immunities, Diplomatic & Consular Relations	Obscene Publications
Human Rights	Health
Refugees and Stateless Persons	International Trade and Development
Educational and Cultural Matters	Transport and Communications

---

9. *See* UNITED NATIONS TREATY COLLECTION, MULTILATERALS DEPOSITED WITH THE SECRETARY-GENERAL, https://treaties.un.org/pages/participationstatus.aspx [https://perma.cc/SW9C-LRPS].

Declaration of Death of Missing Persons	Navigation
Status of Women	Economic Statistics
Freedom of Information	Commercial Arbitration
Penal Matters	Law of Treaties
Commodities	Outer Space
Maintenance Obligations	Telecommunications
Law of the Sea	Disarmament
Environment	Fiscal Matters

While the MTDSG scheme offers an example of an arrangement geared toward treaties, EISIL offers a more broadly applicable arrangement.

After examining these organizations' arrangements of the law, the challenges of searching by topic become apparent. The public international legal researcher must employ search strategies over many platforms and websites, using different subjects, topics, and terminology, to ensure thorough and complete research. For example, using EISIL, the *Convention on Consent to Marriage, Minimum Age for Marriage and Registration of Marriage* is found under the subject "International Human Rights" with Marriage as the topic. This same convention in MTDSG is found under the subject (designated as Chapter XVI) "Status of Women." Yet, the conventions related to eliminating discrimination against women are found in Chapter IV on Human Rights.

While most attempts to arrange the law are based on a logical framework, legal researchers fast discover the inevitable subjectiveness that is inherent in the effort. Over time, researchers develop the sense for identifying which legal principles may appear in one place in an arrangement as well as consider other equally logical locations in the arrangement. This can only be achieved if a deliberate and concerted effort is made to take note of the arrangement of the law during each research project. Unfortunately, current online, full-text searching hinders legal researchers from developing this skill because the arrangement of the law is difficult to view as a whole, or it has been incorporated into the search algorithms which work behind the scenes. Legal researchers must actively make an effort to uncover and consider the arrangement of the information, or law, they are researching.

Naturally, the U.S. legal researcher will begin with the various subject and topic arrangements that are available and familiar on the domestic front. This entails understanding the Library of Congress subject headings as a classification scheme for the arrangement of items in a library collection. As well, it involves exploring West's Topic and Key Numbers to gather a sense of the arrangement of U.S. law. Additionally, if the research project entails treaty research, Treaties in Force may be examined for a U.S. perspective of the arrangement of treaty law.

C. Arrangement of United States Treaties in Force

Treaties in Force (TIF) includes a subject arrangement of U.S. treaties. Divided into a bilateral and a multilateral lists, TIF arranges by jurisdiction with which the U.S. has entered into a treaty and topics. For example, scanning the TIF topics, beginning with the letter A, reveals jurisdictions, such as Africa and Austria, as well as topics such as Agriculture and Aviation:

- Africa
- African Development Bank
- Agricultural Develop Fund
- Agriculture
- Aircraft
- Aliens
- Antarctica
- Anzus Pact
- Arbitration
- Armistice Agreements
- Arms Control
- Arms Limitation
- Artistic Exhibitions
- Asian Development Bank
- Astronauts
- Atlantic Charter
- Atomic Energy
- Austria
- Automotive Traffic
- Aviation

Examining several arrangements of the law reveals some of the difficulties of searching international law by topic. Taking the time to understand the arrangement of the law will lend to the researcher's ability to consider a more broad or narrow abstraction of an issue or topic which will help when attempting to expand or narrow a result set. As well, scanning the arrangement of the law at the outset of the research effort may help the legal researcher find additional and potentially useful key words.

D. The Library of Congress Subject Headings

Using the Library of Congress subject headings can be a productive approach to searching by topic. The list of subject headings has been in use since 1898 and is continually updated with approximately 8,000 new headings and subdivisions added each year.[10] Garnering a basic understanding of the subject headings will increase a legal researcher's efficiency when searching by topic.

Various people, institutions, and governments are considered capable of authorship (among others including corporate bodies, jurisdictions, and uniform titles). Each of these "authors" are given a subject heading. By way of example, the Library of Congress' subject authority file currently contains over 22,000 personal name headings, over 8,000 corporate headings, and ten meeting or conference headings.[11] There are 234,000 topical subject headings and over 58,000 geographic subject headings.[12] Fortunately, it is not necessary to memorize all potentially relevant subject headings.

Instead, the researcher who has already found a relevant title can tap into the subject headings assigned to it. For instance, suppose the legal researcher identified a relevant title while carrying out secondary sources research. After proceeding to a catalog to pull up that title, the legal researcher will take note of the subject headings assigned to it in the catalog record. These subject headings will link to a full list of books in the collection that are classified under that same subject heading. Because the subject headings work across all libraries that adhere to the Library of Congress system of classification (as opposed to those using a different classification scheme such as the Dewey Decimal System), researchers who identify a relevant subject heading in one catalog may use it in others, increasing their efficiency in finding relevant titles within a collection.

For certain research projects, it may be worthwhile to become familiar with the top level Library of Congress subject headings. Subclass K is meant for items related to international law. Below are the broad subclasses related to law:

---

10. *Introduction to the Library of Congress Subject Headings*, Library of Cong., p. vii (Mar., 2012), https://www.loc.gov/aba/publications/Archived-LCSH34/lcshintro.pdf [https://perma.cc/JF92-8VXQ].

11. *Id.*

12. *Id.*

- Subclass K—Law in general. Comparative and uniform law. Jurisprudence
- Subclass KB—Religious law in general. Comparative religious law. Jurisprudence
- Subclass KBM—Jewish law
- Subclass KBP—Islamic law
- Subclass KBR—History of canon law
- Subclass KBS—Canon law of Eastern churches
- Subclass KBT—Canon law of Eastern Rite Churches in Communion with the Holy See of Rome
- Subclass KBU—Law of the Roman Catholic Church. The Holy See
- Subclasses—KD/KDK—United Kingdom and Ireland
- Subclass KDZ—America. North America
- Subclass KE—Canada
- Subclass KF—United States
- Subclass KG—Latin America—Mexico and Central America—West Indies. Caribbean area
- Subclass KH—South America
- Subclasses KJ-KKZ—Europe
- Subclasses KL-KWX—Asia and Eurasia, Africa, Pacific Area, and Antarctica
- Subclass KZ—Law of nations

Review of the subclasses reveals that the Library of Congress classifications for law are further divided not only by geographical location but also on various religious legal traditions, including Islamic law and religious canon law. In addition to selecting the subject heading link from within a relevant catalog record, another strategy involves carrying out a subject heading search following a key word search of the catalog, especially where the legal researcher is using key words that do not generally relate to topics, author names, or geographical areas.

E. West's Topic & Key Number Arrangement

West's topic and key numbers[13] may be used to understand the arrangement of the U.S. treatment of public international law. West has assigned "Interna-

---

13. *See* A Guide to Electronic Key Word Searching on Westlaw.com, https://lawschool. westlaw.com/marketing/display/RE/29 [https://perma.cc/9EML-4KT3]. *See also,* Westlaw Quick Reference Guide, http://lscontent.westlaw.com/images/content/kns-quick-ref-guide-

tional Law" the topic number 221. Working with the online listing in Westlaw, under this topic there are 13 key numbers, of which only five are broken down further into sub-keynumbers. The researcher can scan to see that international organizations and tribunals is a separate topic with a sub-keynumber for privileges and immunities. This gives the legal researcher a sense of arrangement of the law in the United States.

The ability to search across all key numbers, rather than browse them, is a useful way to find relevant key numbers. For example, a search for "international law" across all Topic and Key Numbers will yield a results list that includes: Courts (topic 106), Sentencing and Punishment (topic 350), and Treaties (topic 385). Indeed, much of what would otherwise be classified under public international law is included under domestic U.S. law based on the application and relation of international law in the U.S. system, including the treaty implementation process discussed in Chapter 2. This is demonstrated by the fact that international law appears not only as a topic but also as a subtopic under other topics. For example, International Law appears as a sub-keynumber under Statutes.

- 361 STATUTES (Up to 10,000)
  - 361III Construction (Up to 10,000)
    - 361III(G) Other Law, Construction with Reference to (Up to 10,000)
      - 361 ⌐ 1209 International law.(36)

A legal researcher does well to recognize that all attempts to arrange public international law are influenced by the domestic jurisdiction's legal tradition and history. Bearing this simple fact in mind helps the legal researcher to remain open-minded and creative when searching in foreign jurisdictions.

F. Digests

Digests are a set of volumes that contain short summaries of the legal points of law considered by the courts followed by citation information. In essence, digests are an indexing tool for case law. As such, researchers use digests to find case law by topic. Digest sets generally cover a specific jurisdiction. The digest set itself will have a descriptive word index that is used as an entry point for finding information.

Originally a print finding aid, some digests can now be found online. West's Topic and Key Number System is one example of an online digest and the World

---

1-361255.pdf [https://perma.cc/Q3RR-D4H5] at 1 (contains a listing of topic and key numbers).

Court Digest is another.[14] Researchers will find digests for some but not all international courts and tribunals. Some IGOs capture their work or practice in digests called repertories.[15] Digests are covered in greater detail in Chapter 7.

IV. Natural Language Search and Boolean Search

At the start of any project, researchers should compile a list of potentially useful key words[16] and add to that list as the research unfolds. It is essential to select appropriate key words to achieve a relevant results list. There are two options for searching full-text using key words: (1) natural language and (2) terms and connectors, which is also known as Boolean search.

i. Natural Language Search

Many researchers use natural language search based on their positive experiences with search engines like Google. It involves typing key words or phrases into a search bar and relying on the relevancy ranking algorithm to include the most relevant results toward the top of the list. A natural language search will offer a results list that contains documents that use not only the key words that were entered into the search bar, but also associated words based on the algorithm working behind the scenes. For example, if a researcher types in the key word *labor*, the algorithm may also search labour. Similarly, if a researcher types in the key word *convention*, the algorithm may also search treaty. While this is beneficial to those who do not have familiarity with an area of law, it may frustrate others who want a precise results list. At a minimum, it prevents a legal researcher from knowing exactly how and with which particular search terms the algorithm created the results set.

Generally, relevancy ranking algorithms incorporate a number of factors in making a determination of relevancy. On a very basic level, relevancy ranking algorithms include how frequently key words are used in a document as well as the location in which the key words appear in the document. Those documents that contain the key words more frequently and those that contain the key words in the title or the headings (as opposed to a footnote, for example)

---

14. World Court Digest (1986–2000), http://www.mpil.de/en/pub/publications/archive/wcd.cfm?fuseaction_wcd=aktdat&aktdat=100000000006.cfm [https://perma.cc/WDL4-QDK8].

15. *See Repertory of Practice of United Nations Organs*, http://legal.un.org/repertory/ [https://perma.cc/6AH2-YXUC].

16. Developing key words is discussed in Chapter 10.

will be considered more relevant. Of course, strong relevancy ranking algorithms take into consideration many other factors, as well, including court hierarchy and citation information. Additionally, as mentioned above, the algorithm usually incorporates synonyms to the key words and will assign a differing weight for each synonym and search for those words as well as the entered key words. The relevancy ranking algorithm is but one of the "value-added" features to any subscription database and as such is a closely-guarded trade secret. In addition, relevancy ranking algorithms are routinely updated or refined which makes comparisons between them difficult.

It is best to use a natural language search and rely on the relevancy ranking algorithm when dealing with an unfamiliar area of law or if one's Boolean search skills are not yet well-developed. After reviewing a number of results and gathering a stronger understanding of the area of law, the researcher may elect to follow-up with Boolean searching, as discussed below. A Boolean search at the end of the process, places one in a better position to evaluate the results set to decide whether the Boolean search was properly constructed. Also, because well-constructed Boolean searches are more precise, they will reveal anything inadvertently overlooked from the larger natural language result set. Eventually, when a legal researcher's ability to construct effective Boolean search queries is sufficiently developed, the Boolean query is generally considered the preferable and superior approach.

Sometimes search engines will offer options when a researcher is typing key words into the search bar. For example, researchers may observe a synonym list or "did you mean" or clustering results (depending on the search engine). These are opportunities to peek behind the relevancy ranking algorithm to gather a sense of the factors used for ranking relevancy.

ii. Boolean Search

Boolean search involves generating key words and connectors to direct how the key words should appear in relation to each other. A Boolean result set offers all documents that satisfy the query. This means that every document in the results set is relevant. There is no need for an associated relevancy ranking algorithm. Researchers must evaluate the entire results set, not only those entries that are listed at the top of the list.

When constructing a Boolean search, researchers may connect their terms or phrases using the search syntax provided by the subscription database or platform. Most researchers are familiar with the basic AND, OR, and NOT connectors. Legal subscription databases offer a variety of other connectors that allow the legal researcher to be much more precise. Key words may be connected by paragraph (/p), sentence (/s), or within a given numeric proximity to another word (/15). The legal researcher may direct the algorithm to search for a word preceding another word (pre/s) or restricting the search to exclude a particular term (and not). Each database provider tends to have its own search syntax (examples provided in preceding parentheses are merely illustrative). Although many legal databases use similar syntax, researchers should seek the syntax legend or use the help features to learn the terms and connectors search syntax.

When crafting a Boolean search, terms and phrases of a related concept should be connected first and enclosed in parenthesis; then, that concept should be connected to other concepts, which themselves have been connected according to terms and phrases enclosed in parenthesis, using the appropriate search syntax. This is represented abstractly below and more concretely by example:

> ((concept one term OR concept one term) OR (concept one phrase)) /p (concept two phrase) AND (concept three phrase OR concept three phrase)) /s (procedural concept)

> ((jus cogens OR ius cogens) OR (peremptory /5 norm!)) /p "sovereign immunity" AND ("international law" OR "human rights") /s jurisdiction

This can be an especially efficient and economical way to search when the subscription databases offer the option to search within (or locate or find within) a result set at no additional cost. In essence, these 'search within' features are merely a way to **reorder** the results set so that only those documents with the desired terms are included in the list, cutting down on the time it takes to review the complete results set.

iii. Multiple Language Synonyms

When searching online, researchers should determine whether the search algorithm incorporates U.S./U.K. spelling differences. If not, and certainly when conducting Boolean search, it is necessary to account for differences in spelling for certain words. A short sampling is included below:

Analyse/analyze
Centre/center
Colonise/colonize
Encyclopeadia/encyclopedia
Favourite/favorite
Harbour/harbor
Honour/honor

Kilometre/kilometer
Labour/Labor
Licence/license
Offence/offense
Practise/practice

Generally, these can be reduced to the differences listed below, with U.K. usage on the left and U.S. usage on the right. Thinking in terms of these differences can help the legal researcher identify certain less-frequently used words:

-our/-or
-re/-er
-ce/-se
-ise/-ize
-yse/-yze
-ogue/-og
-ae/-e

iv. Search by Field in Online Subscription Databases

Databases are nothing more than a collection of documents, whether articles, treaties, case law, statutes, or otherwise (possibly images or audio files). Each of the documents contained within a database are tagged with metadata. Metadata is data about the data within a document. For example, in a case law database, each case opinion is tagged with descriptive metadata related to the parties' names, the judge(s) who authored the opinion, the date of the opinion, the attorneys of record, the court's holding, the disposition, and the full-text of the opinion. The metadata for different types of documents will vary according to the document. For example, while there may be judge metadata for a case opinion, there would not be judge metadata for legislation. Including metadata increases discoverability and retrievability of the documents within a database. On the front end of systems, researchers tap into this metadata when they search using the advanced search template. Typically, a case law database will have individual fields for each of the discrete pieces of descriptive metadata collected for the cases.

To demonstrate the value of metadata and field searching, consider the example of a researcher attempting to find all opinions written by Judge Hamilton. An inexperienced legal researcher might type *Judge Hamilton* into a natural language search bar. This query would return all documents that contained the word judge (this term alone would return virtually every document in a case law database) and that contained the word Hamilton. All cases that contained the word Hamilton whether a party name, the name of a company, the name of a product, or a location would be included in the results list, along with the desired cases authored by Judge Hamilton. Because a natural language search is searching the database full-text, it will return many more irrelevant results than an inexperienced researcher might otherwise expect.

A more advanced legal researcher might develop the Boolean search *judge +5 Hamilton* to obtain a more precise result set. By connecting *Judge* and *Hamilton* so they appear within five words of each other, the legal researcher is accounting for those circumstances where Judge Hamilton's full name may be used. Results will include all those documents that contain Judge Hamilton as well as Judge David F. Hamilton. This search results list will include all opinions by Judge Hamilton as well as all cases authored by another judge who referenced Judge Hamilton. These additional results would be considered irrelevant and not what the legal researcher intended by searching *judge +5 Hamilton*.

For this reason, an experienced legal researcher will seek to search by field. By restricting the research to the field for Judge and searching by the term *Hamilton* within that field, the legal researcher will obtain a result list of only those documents authored by Judge Hamilton. This field-restricted search offers a complete results set of all documents authored by Hamilton. The legal researcher must review all of the documents in the list because all of the documents satisfy the query. The results set will not contain any of the irrelevant documents that a natural language search for *judge Hamilton* or a Boolean search for *judge +5 Hamilton* would return.

Combining, or searching more than one field at a time, is another strategy that provides the legal researcher with a smaller and more relevant results set. This decreases the amount of time researchers must spend ruling out irrelevant results. Legal researchers may create a Boolean search to combine the judge field with a date field to obtain only those opinions authored by Judge Hamilton within the past ten years, for instance. Certain fields lend themselves to being searched together. For example, before appearing in court, an attorney may search judge and date fields or judge and holding fields to gather a sense of how that judge may have decided similar types of motions or cases during a specific time frame. Similarly, by searching the attorney and holding field, a researcher may gather a sense of how many cases an attorney has handled, as well as the outcome of those cases.

Because the nature of a document will determine the types of metadata collected and fields offered, researchers must determine which fields are associated with any particular document to utilize this strategy effectively. For example, legal researchers can select the advanced search link from the home page on either Lexis or Westlaw to obtain a list of field options. This advanced search home page allows the legal researcher to search full-text using AND, OR, NOT, and date, citation, and title fields. However, by first selecting cases from the home page under Browse > All Content listing (Westlaw) or Explore Content (Lexis), and then clicking on the advanced search link, the legal researcher will obtain a different listing of fields specifically tailored to case law documents. This advanced search page, specifically for case law, offers more fields (e.g., judges, synopsis, attorney, docket number) than the advanced search home page. Similarly, by selecting statutes from the Browse All Content (Westlaw) or Explore Content (Lexis) listing, and then advanced search, the legal researcher obtains a template that offers options related to statutes, including restricting a search to the caption, historical notes, or annotations.

v. Search by Field Online

For researchers accustomed to using field searches on Westlaw or Lexis, searching the open web becomes an exercise in frustration due to a lack of precision. The ability to mimic some of the enhanced search functionality that researchers have come to expect with the legal subscription databases may be achieved on the open web using some search engines, like Google.

For instance, a loose equivalent of field searching online may be achieved by using the extensions from URLs. Many legal researchers are aware that *.int* is the extension for international organizations. By including *inurl:.int* into the search query, the legal researcher restricts the results list to only those websites that contain the *.int* in their URLs. It is recommended that when using the *inurl* command, the legal researcher add this command to the beginning of the search query rather than the end. This is because *inurl:.int* "human rights" and "human rights" *inurl:.int* will return a different results list. By including *inurl:.int* command first followed by the search terms 'human' and 'rights,' only those results with *.int* in the URL that also contain human rights in the documents will be included on the results list. Whereas "human rights" *inurl:.int* returns those sites that contain *.int* as well as *.org* in the URLs with human rights in the documents. This is because the relevancy ranking algorithm takes into consideration the order in which the legal researcher lists the search terms in the search bar. Those entered first are either given greater weight or are processed first, or a combination of both.[17] Indeed, entering 'rights human' will provide a different results list than 'human rights.' As mentioned previously, legal researchers who know how relevancy ranking algorithms generally

---

17. Because the relevancy ranking algorithms are proprietary it is impossible to know the details.

work understand the need for carrying out a few searches to serve as a control strategy.

vi. Search by Command

Searching by command, where available, allows a legal researcher to tap into field searching without having to resort to a template or advanced search feature. The command abbreviations followed by a colon and the search terms is the standard format for search by command.

The Westlaw and Lexis platforms offer the ability to search by command. However, at the point of publication, most of these commands are not listed on homepage. Researchers familiar with these platforms proceed to the advanced search link and fill in the templates to discover the commands that are being utilized behind the scenes and then use those commands directly. For example, if a legal researcher is interested in finding a case where one of the parties was Colorado Coal, the following command could be used: advanced: TI("colorado coal"). It is important to remember that the commands are part of the Boolean search functions for the search engine. As such, if a legal researcher knows both parties names rather than type in *Roe v. Wade* in order to use the command, the legal researcher would connect *Roe* and *Wade* with a narrow connector, either /s or /15. Or, simply type into the search bar: TI(roe /s wade).

The same approach holds true for dates. Once the legal researcher knows the date command it may be used at the outset of query development. For all documents after January 1, 1995, the following date command could be used: DA(aft 01-01-1995). Other alternatives for dates include the 'between' restriction: DA(aft 12-31-1959 & bef 01-01-2017). However, on some level, it may be just as efficient to fill out the advanced search template as it is to ensure that the command format is correct. These advanced strategies are for the legal researcher who uses a particular subscription database exclusively and frequently.

Another way to investigate the commands for any particular database is to check whether, after conducting an advanced search using a template, the database supplies the search query (either in the search box or at the top of the results list). In circumstances where it does, the commands may be apparent. For example, suppose the legal researcher was interested in finding an article by an author with the last name Smith related to law reform. After conducting an author search in the HeinOnline Law Journals database, using the template, the resultant search query shows: ("law reform" AND creator:(smith)). The HeinOnline database, by making this information transparent, allows the user to see the syntax that was generated through the template. When researchers can see the syntax generated, they can incorporate it directly into their subsequent searches. Legal researches are cautioned to avoid adding a space following the colon when conducting command searches.

V. Comparing Search Approaches and Tools

By utilizing a natural language search, a legal researcher will obtain a re-sults list that includes all documents that contain the key word or phrase, whereas searching the index or table of contents will offer only those docu-ments where the text contains a discussion related to the key word or phrase. What makes searching full-text less efficient is the need to spend additional time evaluating a lengthy list that may very well contain a number of irrele-vant documents. While reliance on the relevancy ranking algorithms may allow the legal researcher to focus only on those documents near the top of the list, at some point the legal researcher must make a judgment call on when to stop checking additional results on the list. It is at this point that the legal researcher is declaring that the rest of the list probably offers results that con-tain the key words used only once or in a manner irrelevant to the particular research needs. This may result in a nagging feeling that something has been overlooked.

Carrying out a search of the indexes and table of contents first, to find only those documents that contain a discussion related to the key words or phrase, is usually productive. An index or table of contents search will deliver a result set that includes only those documents that are about the key words. Whereas, a full-text search will contain all documents that contain the key words, whether the document is about those words. Online indexes and tables of contents in-crease efficiency even though they require the legal researcher to carry out an additional search.

For example, a researcher may have a fact pattern related to lights being used to torture an individual. If this researcher were to enter the query: *light /s torture* into the search bar, the results list should contain all documents where the word *light* is within the same sentence of *torture*. The legal researcher is expecting to find documents that describe the torture suffered by a plaintiff. The legal researcher can envision the following types of sentences: "plaintiff was tortured by the use of flashing extremely bright lights." Or, "strobe lights were used to torture the plaintiff." And indeed, the results list contains a num-ber of documents that contain the words *torture* and *light*. However, by scan-ning the results set, the legal researcher discovers that the word *torture* is sometimes used in a sentence containing the phrase "... in light of the fact that...." As it turns out, this full-text search yields a results list that contains a number of irrelevant results. This could be avoided by searching an index for *torture* and then scanning for a subentry for *lights*, the legal researcher obtains only those results that cover using lights as a method of torture.[18]

It is the nature of the English language, where words have multiple meanings and can be used in phrases or contexts that do not immediately occur to the researcher while generating a search query, that requires researchers to carefully evaluate the results list. The legal researcher must develop a sense for when to re-query rather than to begin with a search of the index or table of contents. A re-query to eliminate the phrase "… in light of …" may be used; however, it might inadvertently exclude a highly relevant result—one where the terms are used as originally anticipated but that same document also uses the phrase '… in light of …'. The legal researcher who understands the strengths and weaknesses of the various approaches does not hesitate to run multiple and pointed searches, despite the cost, when comprehensive research is required.

VI. Control Strategies for Various Search Techniques

Experienced legal researchers employ at least one of the previous strategies and usually a combination of these strategies. At times, the legal researcher may be utilizing an additional strategy or approach to confirm what is already uncovered. This is considered utilizing a control strategy. It allows the legal researcher to verify that the original search achieved the desired objective.

For instance, a legal researcher may first conduct a search of abstracts and then follow it with a full-text search. Starting with abstracts followed by full-text allows the researcher to evaluate the full-text results set more efficiently because all of the relevant results from searching the abstracts should appear in the full-text search (although not necessarily near the top of the results list depending on the strength of the relevancy ranking algorithm). The full-text results that are unfamiliar to the researcher who has already carried out an abstracts search may then be skimmed for relevancy. This lends to efficiency because the searcher, when skimming, understands that the result may not be

---

18. Additionally, it should be pointed out that by searching an index for *torture* and then scanning for *lights* as a subentry, the researcher can readily find other means of torture that are listed as subentries. Such an approach encourages a legal researcher to develop arguments by analogy.

about the search terms but rather may only contain references to the search terms. This allows the legal researcher to more confidently focus on the portion of the document that might be relevant. This approach also accounts for any articles or documents that do not have an associated abstract, or that would be overlooked if the researcher had carried out only the abstract search.

Control strategies may also be used to help the legal researcher understand how a particular database functions. If there are no associated costs with a database, the legal researcher may elect to run a few searches to assess the strength of the relevancy ranking algorithm (presuming the researcher has a sense of what should appear toward the top of the results list) or to better understand the search syntax.

VII. Conclusion

The international legal system has no single over-arching architecture or arrangement of the law. However, by surveying several available arrangements, legal researchers can begin to develop a framework for carrying out international legal research by topic. Researchers should remain flexible yet persistent and utilize the variety of finding aids available to them. Due to the complexity of international legal research, researchers should develop and practice their natural language and Boolean search skills while employing control strategies to ensure nothing is inadvertently overlooked.

Chapter 10

Planning and Recording Research

I. Introduction

A research plan serves as a road map for the legal research process. A good research plan includes all the sources of law that the researcher must consult together with a comment about how to find and use each source. The complexity of international legal issues, the nuances related to handling the sources of law, and the abundance of databases and legal publishers worldwide contribute to the need for a detailed research plan. Ultimately, taking time to generate a research plan at the outset of a project will save the researcher time and frustration.

When crafting a plan it is important to recognize that there is typically more than one good route for gathering all relevant material. The route taken will depend on the availability of resources as well as what that researcher already knows about the subject area. However, the methods for handling the international law sources, described in detail in earlier chapters, must be included in every good research plan. By adhering to a planned and methodical approach, the legal researcher can be sure that nothing is inadvertently overlooked.

When handling public international law sources, researchers must account for the fact that certain publications may express the law itself as well as serve as evidence of customary international law or general principles of law. For example, a researcher may cite to the *Vienna Convention on the Law of Treaties* as treaty law in one instance and as evidence of customary international law in another.[1] In both instances, the researcher is citing primary authority. In the former, the primary authority is the treaty and in the latter the primary authority is customary law. However, in the latter instance, the researcher is using the treaty to show evidence of the custom. This approach of using various sources of law to show evidence of other sources of law (either customary international law or general principles of law) complicates the research process and underscores the need for the researcher to create and adhere to a clear plan.

While on paper the plan may appear linear, the research process is anything but. While all legal research is inherently iterative in nature in that it requires re-searching and circling back around as knowledge and understanding are gained through the process itself, public international legal research is even more so given the particular attributes of some of the sources of law. Adhering to a plan allows the researcher to make forward progress through the sources of law in a systematic and orderly fashion despite these challenges.

When generating a plan, most legal researchers tend to focus on the nuts and bolts of developing an issue statement and identifying which resources to consult and in which order. While these elements are the crux of all good plans, there are a number of other administrative and brainstorming details that must be addressed as well. The elements of the below plan include administrative details (elements 1–3), brainstorming details (elements 4–6), and issues, jurisdiction, and resources for handling those issues (elements 7–10). Taking the time to actively include this information in a plan is essential for building a mental framework against which new information may be organized and made into knowledge.

Elements of an Effective Research Plan for Public International Law

1. Time constraints & deadlines
2. Format of the end product
3. Cost considerations
4. Relevant facts
5. Search terms; including the field of international law
6. Assessment of what is known
7. Preliminary issue statements & jurisdiction considerations
8. Use of a reputable research guide & tools to identify sources by proper names and uncover where they may be available.

---

1. *See* Chapters 2 and 4, *supra,* for a complete discussion.

9. Identification of the sources of law including the publications and on-line databases that contain those sources of law and how to use them
10. Updating

II. Elements of a Plan

A. Time Constraints & Deadlines

Identify deadlines, either for filings or for reporting back to someone else: a client, a colleague, a supervisor. Work backwards from that day, bearing in mind other obligations, and generate a schedule for your research sessions. Sometimes, public international legal research involves collaborating with others, and experienced legal researchers build in time for that. Other nuances related to international legal research that often go overlooked at the outset are differences in time zones which influence the speed with which a researcher will get a response if dealing with resources involving other people. These details must be accounted for in the planning phase of the research project.

To develop a sense for how much time a research project may take, researchers should track the actual time spent on each research project. When handling a research project where time runs short, it is important to always acknowledge, either in the final written product or when reporting back orally, which sources were not yet consulted, what they may contain, and why they may be important. This allows those relying on the research to assess the return on investment of additional research. It also allows the researcher to follow up efficiently should additional time or money become available for further research.

B. Format of the End Product

The format of the end product often informs how, where, and to what depth to perform legal research. Identifying the format of the end product at the outset and understanding the requirements ensures that all necessary details are captured during the research process. By taking this step, the researcher avoids having to retrace steps to gather additional information. The legal researcher should consider how best to present the legal research produced. Is the end product of a document that will be filed with the court or is it personal notes to refer to in counseling a client? Does the end product require citation to the sources in a particular format? Not all jurisdictions require *Bluebook* format. If using other than *Bluebook* format, what citation information is required? It is best to ascertain citation requirements, if any, at the outset, to avoid re-tracing steps to obtain details for the citation while in the midst of the writing phase of the project.

C. Cost Considerations

Most researchers have a sense of the content included in the subscription databases available to them as well as the costs incurred in their use. When they do not, they can usually contact an office manager, a librarian, or the vendor to make this determination. When researchers require material outside of their subscription databases, and they have identified a specialized subscription database that includes relevant content, they must consider the costs involved. Databases that offer hard-to-find international materials are generally quite expensive.

Other than circumstances where there are no alternatives, it is essential to assess time-saved against cost-incurred when determining whether to use a subscription database. Researchers must ask themselves: Are the materials findable in print or online elsewhere for free? If available online or in print for free, as well as in a subscription database, are the increased costs for the subscription database offset by a time savings? Both time consideration and monetary constraints inform research choices. Researchers must carefully assess the options at the outset, during the planning phase, to remain within budget.

D. Relevant Facts

Before any research is undertaken, the legal researcher should summarize the facts provided by the client or as gleaned from the client file. Typically, a legal researcher will find that they either have too much information or too little information. When dealing with too much information, the legal researcher must extract only the legally relevant facts. On the other hand, when dealing with insufficient information or circumstances where the researcher is not yet aware that there is the need for more information, the researcher must keep detailed notes of the specific information required so that it may be obtained from the client, supervising attorney, or opposing counsel.

There are three strategies for determining which facts are relevant and which facts may be missing at the outset of any research project. First, the legal researcher can set forth all of the facts supplied in chronological order in an effort to shed light on where there are gaps in information. Second, the legal researcher can identify all of the people, States, and organizations involved and explain their role, place, or relationship in the controversy to reveal whether the facts related to that person, State, or organization are legally relevant. Third, the legal researcher can prepare a written summary of the facts and evaluate what value or function is served by each fact included. If no value or function can be identified, then it is likely not a relevant fact.

If the researcher is not in a position to gather additional information prior to the beginning of the research project, then the research project will increase in size. In this circumstance, the legal researcher will have to resort to an if/ then approach for handling the project. If the missing information is A, then the result will be X. If the missing information is B, then the result will be Y. Obviously, it is always most efficient to have as much information as possible at the outset of the research project.

E. Search Terms

To generate the search terms that will be used with online and print sources (i.e., indexes), a legal researcher must scour the file or "work the problem" to identify terms or phrases that relate to the controversy. Classifying terms into the following seven categories, will reveal to the researcher whether any additional terms are needed.

- Field of international law
- Subject and topic of issue
- Parties involved and their descriptive relationships
- Types of places
- Things, objects, or actions
- Potential claims and defenses
- Relief sought

Researchers should make a point of proactively expanding upon their initial search terms by increasing the depth and breadth of the most promising terms. Increasing breadth involves generating synonyms. Increasing depth involves understanding the arrangement of the law, as discussed in Chapter 9, and tapping into terms that are of greater abstraction or greater detail.

For instance, suppose a fact pattern revolved around the use of force against insurgents who had seized an abandoned house in connection with their attempt to reform the government. The term "house" may be actively expanded in breadth by using the synonyms "home" and "residence" or even "shelter," as it relates contextually to this particular fact pattern. These terms are then at the forefront of the researcher's mind when consulting indexes or in generating an online query, whether natural language or Boolean.

Increasing depth involves understanding how the law is arranged as well as understanding levels of abstraction related to various terms. This is made particularly difficult in public international law, as discussed in depth in Chapter 9, because there is no global, uniform, organizational structure. For those in the United States, there is a fairly static arrangement of the law as a result of the work of the West editors classifying all legal points of law by topic and key number. Using this same fact pattern, the legal researcher can consult a secondary source or West's topic and key numbers to understand that the facts involve revolutionaries or a de facto government. The legal researcher can work with the phrase 'de facto government' to uncover that the law is arranged so that this point of law falls under the topic of international law and a subtopic, 'change in sovereignty.' It might look like this in the research plan:

international law
↓
change in sovereignty
↓
revolutionary and de facto governments

Understanding this arrangement allows the legal researcher to generate terms that may be useful in tailoring search queries or in handling a search in an index. If the researcher determines 'de facto government' does not yield enough results, additional results may be gained by re-querying with the phrase 'change in sovereignty.' Clearly, it is necessary to have an understanding of how any particular jurisdiction's law is arranged in order to tap into this strategy.

Sometimes legal researchers will encounter differences in terms or phrases when dealing with international law issues. For example, trademarks are considered marks elsewhere. Other times, researchers will encounter differences in concepts between U.S. and foreign jurisdictions. For example, the E.U. states' concepts of unfair competition may more closely align with consumer law than pure unfair competition law as it is understood in the United States. The experienced legal research will account for these differences in generating search terms and again later when crafting Boolean search queries.

In the event these differences in phraseology or concepts are unknown at the outset of the process, the legal researcher must adapt as the research unfolds and knowledge of such differences is gained. Having a plan to refer back to and a list of search terms allows the researcher to associate these new terms and concepts seamlessly.

F. Assessment of What Is Known

A legal researcher should proactively consider what is known about the subject area of the law before beginning a research project. Assessing what is known at the outset of a research project primes the mind to be able to assimilate new information more easily and rapidly into knowledge. With each research project, knowledge is acquired about the substantive issues as well as about how to conduct international legal research itself. Researchers should separate what is known about the substantive issues from what is known about the research process because development on these two fronts may proceed at varying rates. Often, gaining an understanding of how to research will progress more rapidly because the strategies and skills involved apply across a variety of substantive legal issues.

Assessing what is known also involves considering what has been supplied at the outset of the project. A supervisor, a client, or a colleague may provide a citation to a particular source of law. This information can be worked into the initial research plan in order to expedite the effort. For example, if a citation to a judicial decision from an international tribunal is supplied, a researcher would begin by reading that decision before consulting secondary sources and the primary sources of international law. Indeed, by using the strategies related to finding aids, the legal researcher might easily find secondary sources that cite to this judicial decision, thus narrowing more quickly to relevant secondary sources. Other examples involve a researcher's accumulated knowledge. As explained in greater detail in Chapter 2, where a researcher is already familiar with the legal, political, and foreign relationships of the States involved in a treaty research matter, consulting the RUDs before earlier steps of the treaty research process can confirm the researcher's knowledge and should be worked into the research plan.

G. Preliminary Issue Statements & Jurisdiction Considerations

Formulation of a research issue statement helps to define the scope and direction of the research project. It serves to set the outside parameter of what is to be researched. The act of generating an issue statement sometimes requires knowing something about the law. As such, researchers should expect that issue statements will be revised and refined as the research unfolds and an understanding of an area of law is gained.

It is important to remember that "research" issue statements are different than "Question Presented" issue statements, which are typically included in the final written documents, or memorials, filed with a court. Research issue statements are less refined and less tightly-written. They are meant to break down the research project into more manageable pieces. At the outset and during the planning phase, if there is a gap in the researcher's knowledge, then the first details to be researched will focus on filling those gaps. Once filled, the legal researcher should be able to craft a more refined research issue statement related to the project at hand.

Most research projects will involve one or two central issues. Usually, these issues can be categorized as related to: the substantive law, procedural law, or relief sought. Generating issue statements and classifying them in this manner helps the legal researcher to allocate time and ensure complete and thorough research. Not all projects contain all three types of issue statements but it is worthwhile to use the three as a checklist when planning. After the issue statements have been developed, the legal researcher should compare them with the list of search terms to ensure a sufficient number of terms have been generated for each issue.

As discussed in greater detail in Chapter 7, given the existence of concurrent jurisdiction which results from the horizontal structure of the international legal system, the matter of selecting a court or tribunal to decide a controversy is rather complex, especially for cases involving human rights violations. A solid understanding of international law doctrines and principles, including sovereignty and immunity, must be considered in a way that U.S. legal researchers might not anticipate based on their domestic experiences with *in rem* and *in personam* jurisdiction. Frequently, as a preliminary matter, there is considerable research and strategy involved in selecting an international court or tribunal.

H. Research Guides & Tools to Consult during the Planning Phase

Most legal researchers will use a variety of research guides and reference tools in preparing the research plan itself. They will use these guides and tools to identify legal traditions, obtain proper names for publications, decipher legal abbreviations, and translate words. Sometimes this preliminary research will bleed into the substantive research effort. Researchers should guard against this tendency during the planning phase of the process. The preliminary research is meant to be used to complete a useful research plan. It is limited in scope to identifying the titles to resources and where they may be located. A legal researcher may certainly circle back around to use some of these same tools later in the process, especially if something unexpected arises. However, generally, these tools should be used most heavily during the planning phase.

i. Research Guides

Legal researchers should consult at least one research guide and preferably two or three while actively generating a research plan. Before relying on the information in any guide, however, it should be evaluated for authority, accuracy, objectivity, currency, and coverage. While consulting two or more guides will result in obtaining overlapping information, this also allows the legal researcher to assess the quality of the guides against each other. One may be substantively good, but with less up-to-date links than another, for example. Or, two guides may simply serve to reinforce that the information contained in them is accurate and reliable. Using at least two guides in tandem should allow the legal researcher to obtain a more complete picture of the landscape of what needs to be researched and the publications and tools available for doing so.

Most general subject or topical research guides will contain a chapter or section on the international law related to that topic. For example, a research guide on labor law will often contain a section on international labor laws. Certain international topics are so widely researched that there are research guides devoted exclusively to those topics. These guides can be found by carrying out an online search using the topic and the phrase "research guide." The benefit of consulting a topical research guide is that the author of the guide has already identified the sources of law and where they may be found. Often, the guide will contain citation to the relevant primary law by pin cite. As such, finding a reputable, topical research guide will save the legal researcher considerable time as the research effort becomes more a matter of pulling or retrieving the law with known citation than searching by topic.

There are a number of collections of research guides including the Foreign Law Guide,[2] Globalex[3] and the Law Library of Congress.[4] Often, law school websites will offer research guides.[5] Another strategy that may be used to find

---

2. *See* FOREIGN LAW GUIDE, (Hoffman ed., 2012), http://www.brill.com/publications/online-resources/foreign-law-guide [https://perma.cc/EF94-8VRM] (available through HeinOnline).

3. *See* GLOBALEX, http://www.nyulawglobal.org/Globalex/ [https://perma.cc/8ZBV-FXQL].

4. *See* LAW LIBRARY OF CONGRESS FOREIGN LAW RESEARCH GUIDES, http://www.loc.gov/law/help/foreign.php [https://perma.cc/SU5F-J2SE].

5. *See, e.g.,* BODLEIAN LAW LIBRARY RESEARCH GUIDES, http://www.bodleian.ox.ac.uk/law/guides https://perma.cc/L9Q3-9YGG.

reputable research guides is to search a catalog, or WorldCat, using the phrase "research guide."

One of the main purposes for consulting a research guide is to find the titles to the publications that contain the primary law. Often, for U.S. legal researchers, it is productive to consult *The Bluebook: A Uniform System of Citation* for titles to publications from foreign jurisdictions and public international law sources as a preliminary step.

ii. Tools to Identify Legal Traditions

While most jurisdiction-specific research guides will offer basic information on a the legal tradition underlying a State's legal system, there are some useful tools that are available to make a preliminary determination while preparing the research plan. Identifying the legal tradition upon which a legal system rests allows the legal researcher to gather a sense of the types of sources of law that must be found and the relative weight of authority that will be ascribed to them in that foreign jurisdiction.

Tools to identify the legal tradition include Juriglobe,[6] CIA World Factbook,[7] and encyclopedias. The University of Ottawa offers Juriglobe, a tool that may be used to identify the legal tradition upon which the foreign jurisdiction rests. Juriglobe expressly acknowledges the difficulties in classifying legal traditions and offers an explanation for why it classifies only civil law, common law, Muslim law, customary law, and mixed legal traditions.[8] It is a useful starting point as it allows the legal researcher to gather a framework within which to identify sources and plan for the order of carrying out the research in those sources of law.

Information gleaned from Juriglobe must be verified through the use of other research and reference tools such as CIA World Factbook and encyclopedias. The CIA World Factbook is a reference tool that has been offered by the CIA for U.S. government officials since 1981 and made available on its website since 1997.[9] It is updated weekly. Those unfamiliar with this resource should consult the *World Factbook Users Guide* to obtain a sense of the breadth

---

6. *See* Juriglobe World Legal Systems, http://www.juriglobe.ca/eng/index.php [https://perma.cc/X6J3-TY54].

7. *See* Central Intelligence Agency, The World Fact Book, https://www.cia.gov/library/publications/the-world-factbook/ [https://perma.cc/A922-NW2J].

8. *See* http://www.juriglobe.ca/eng/sys-juri/intro.php [https://perma.cc/SXG2-LMHT] (tab for legal system classification introductory remarks).

9. *See* Juriglobe, *supra* note 6, at https://www.cia.gov/library/publications/the-world-factbook/docs/history.html [https://perma.cc/Y9C2-TNQ8].

of what is available and for a description of the various online tools including the *Guide to Country Profiles* and *Guide to Country Comparisons*.[10]

Encyclopedias should be consulted during the planning phase to verify the information included in the plan as well as to gain valuable background information in the legal, social, cultural, political, and historical system at the center of the research project. Legal encyclopedias related to identifying legal traditions and foreign jurisdictions may be found by searching a catalog. A relevant subject heading is: **international law — encyclopedias**. A particularly useful encyclopedia for this purpose is the *Legal Systems of the World: A Political, Social and Cultural Encyclopedia*. Other encyclopedias that are useful, more generally, include the *Max Planck Encyclopedia of Public International Law* and Parry & Grant's *Encyclopaedic Dictionary of International Law*.

iii. Tools to Handle Citations and Abbreviation Decoding Strategies

Researchers must identify and include in their research plan the title to the official publications that contain the law. Often, these publications are abbreviated or in citation format in the scholarly literature or within comprehensive databases. Deciphering citation abbreviations at the outset of the process allows the researcher to evaluate results sets obtained online more quickly. For example, U.S. legal researchers quickly learn to decipher a results list of: U.S., F.3d., and F. Supp. 3d, as case law citations for cases from the three levels of the federal court system. They can choose to read the mandatory authority first and expedite their research effort. Understanding citation abbreviations allows the legal researcher to make informed choices about which result to view first and why.

Similarly, a U.S. legal researcher can use abbreviation tools and citators to gather an understanding of citation abbreviations in a foreign jurisdiction. For example, a legal researcher, carrying out French legal research, who came across the following citations, N.C.P.C. and J.O., could readily determine from *The Bluebook: A Uniform System of Citation* that the results list contained materials from the French code of civil procedure, *Nouveau Code de Procedure Civile*, and a statute or decree (*loi* in French) published in the official journal of France which is cited as J.O. Not only will researchers be able to read and understand a results list more easily, but they can also use these abbreviations as search

---

10. *See supra* note 7, at *The World Factbook Users Guide*, https://www.cia.gov/library/publications/the-world-factbook/docs/guidetowfbook.html [https://perma.cc/XBK5-RUM6].

terms. One caveat is that often a foreign jurisdiction will utilize a citation manual other than the *Bluebook* and the abbreviations within that jurisdiction's vernacular material may be different than the English translations. For example, the U.S.S.R. (the English abbreviation) is also referred to as C.C.C.P. (the Russian abbreviation).

Other than the *Bluebook* which U.S. legal researchers are generally familiar, the *Guide to Foreign and International Legal Citations*[11] and *The World Dictionary of Legal Abbreviations*[12] are particularly useful. Researchers working online can consult the *Cardiff Index to Legal Abbreviations*[13] which is a bidirectional tool for finding titles and abbreviations. Other citation manuals can be found using a subject heading search in the catalog: **citation of legal authorities—[insert country]**.

iv. Translation Tools

Translation tools must also be considered at the outset. Relying on Google Translate or Yahoo's Babelfish may be useful during the research phase; however, no researcher should rely solely on these translation services. Rather, researchers must find an official translation in English (or other language in which there is proficiency).

The primary source is the document in the vernacular. Anyone who has studied languages understands that translation involves making subjective evaluations with respect to how phrases should be interpreted into another language. For this reason, translations, unless dealing with an official translation, are considered secondary sources.

I. Identification of the Titles of the Sources of Law & the Publications or Online Databases That Contain Those Sources of Law

In addition to developing strong issue statements, the meat of any research plan is clear identification of the sources of law, where they are available, and how to find them. To be useful as a tool, the plan must include a list of the sources of law by their titles together with a comment about availability on-

11. *Guide to Foreign and International Legal Citations* (2d ed. 2009).

12. Igor I Kavass & Mary Miles Prince, eds., *The World Dictionary of Legal Abbreviations* (1991–).

13. *See* Cardiff Index to Legal Abbreviations, http://www.legalabbrevs.cardiff.ac.uk [https://perma.cc/45SW-DF8T].

line or in print. Consulting a research guide is essential for identifying proper names for the titles of the publications that contain the law. Usually, the research guide will advise of the databases that hold the publications or whether they are available in print only.

If a research guide does not provide information for where to find the official publications, armed with a title, the legal researcher may then actively check online databases (whether subscription or free) to determine whether a title is included by using a directory, the "information" link, or other "publications-included" listing. Alternatively, the legal researcher may search library catalogs to determine print availability. Where the researcher's home institution's law library does not have a title, an interlibrary loan request may be placed in order to obtain it from another library.

The plan must contain not only the sources of law, where those sources might be found, but also, the order in which the legal researcher intends to carry out the research. Earlier chapters covered the sources of law for public international law in detail.

J. Updating

The process of updating is listed as a separate element because it is essential to update not only while carrying out the research initially; but again, before filing anything with a court, conferring with clients, or interacting with opposing counsel. Each time the legal researcher intends to rely on the research, it must be updated to close the gap in time between when the research was first completed and the current date. Updating while carrying out the initial research generally entails obtaining a current-through date. Specifics for updating the individual international sources of law has been handled in the earlier chapters. In short, closing this gap requires checking to make sure that there is no recent change in circumstances related to the source that would negatively impact the basis for the citation.

K. Summary

After considering these ten elements of a legal research plan for public international law, it becomes self-evident that preparing a plan at the outset encourages efficiency, accuracy, thoroughness, and accountability. A well-thought out plan helps to avoid repetition of steps and search queries. It allows the researcher to take up and put down the research project as other work and obligations demand without backtracking. A plan promotes accuracy by requiring identification of sources by title and ascertaining whether they are included in a particular database. Such planning encourages a professional vocabulary. Plans promote thorough research in that the legal researcher is able to periodically refer back to the plan to ensure that all potentially relevant sources of law have been consulted. Finally, having a written plan allows the researcher to be accountable. The legal researcher will be able to hold a conversation with others to report on their conclusions and advice in an organized and detailed manner.

III. Research Logs—Implementing the Plan

A. Order for Carrying Out the Research Plan

The most efficient approach for handling any legal research project is to identify the hierarchy of legal authority and research in the order of that authority. For instance, on the domestic front, a U.S. legal researcher would typically proceed in the following order: constitutional law > statutes > administrative rules and regulations > case law > legislative histories. This tends to be the most efficient approach. When dealing with public international law sources, Article 38 of the Statute of the International Court of Justice sets forth the sources of law but is silent on whether the list is hierarchical.[14] Nevertheless, there is an orderly progression that makes sense from a research perspective. Typically, public international legal researchers will proceed in the following order when handling a research project by topic and without any known citations to begin with:

> Research guides and tools > secondary sources > jus cogens > treaties governing the parties involved > customary international law (which may involve additional and expanded treaty research as well as research using the teachings of highly qualified scholars and judicial decisions) > general principles of law (which may involve research using the teachings of highly qualified scholars and judicial opinions as well as foreign law research) > soft law.

---

14. STATUTE OF THE INTERNATIONAL COURT OF JUSTICE, June 26, 1945, art. 38(1), 59 Stat. 1031. 59 Stat. 1031, T.S. 993, http://www.icj-cij.org/documents/?p1=4&p2=2 [https://perma.cc/NY98-29PP]. While there is some scholarly writing on this topic which suggests that the sources listed in Article 38 are set forth in hierarchical order, most acknowledge that the language of Article 38 is silent with respect to hierarchy of authority and that it

Due to the iterative nature of international legal research, legal researchers sometimes attempt to collapse treaty research and customary law research into one step. This approach should be avoided. Too frequently, by attempting to handle treaty research at the same time as customary international law research, the legal researcher becomes confused and fails to find and cite to relevant treaty sources as evidence of customary international law. This generally demonstrates a fundamental lack of understanding of how to research customary international law. For this reason, it is recommended that the legal researcher approach all research projects by compartmentalizing the effort as it pertains to each of the sources of law as listed in Article 38 of the Statute of the ICJ. Additionally, U.S. legal researchers should guard against considering judicial decisions as primary authority, as is discussed in greater depth in Chapter 7.

B. Keeping Track of Research in a Log

While carrying out the research, it is best to keep track in a research log. Research logs may take a variety of formats. They tend to be unique to each individual researcher. No matter the format, however, the legal researcher must keep a record of all sources consulted. At a minimum, this record should include the source consulted by title, how the source was accessed, what was found, and the current-through date. For resources that may be used in the final product, it is important to capture all information that comprises the citation. Researchers should check the court rules and procedures of the particular international tribunal for details. For *Bluebook* format this generally includes: author, title, edition, volume, page, and date. For circumstances where the researcher is required to use another country's citation guide, it is advisable to check at the outset of the research process what is required. This will eliminate having to return to each resource if a portion of the citation information was not captured and recorded in the research log at point of use.

In limited circumstances, U.S. legal researchers will be using Lexis or Westlaw for a portion of their research. Although these platforms provide research histories or trails, it is advisable to keep personal notes as well for two reasons. First, these tools do not capture every step of the process. For example, the History generated by the system on Westlaw includes a reference to KeyCite when that tool is used. However, each time the researcher filters within KeyCite,

---

does not represent a hierarchical list. *See* JAMES CRAWFORD, *Brownlie's Principles of Public International Law* (8th ed. 2012).

the History does not capture this level of detail. In particular, the History does not include how citing references were filtered by headnote.

Second, the History is not available online indefinitely. Depending on the database, the research record may only exist during a single research session; that is, until the legal researcher logs off or signs out. Or, it may be available for a limited number of months. In all events, the History should be saved and stored on the legal researcher's own computer so that it may be accessed in the future should the need arise. Often, legal research must be updated months, and sometimes years, later as controversies are negotiated, litigated, or otherwise disposed of.

C. Level of Detail Included in Log

Legal researchers should use the same format for tracking their research each time they carry out a research project. Doing so ensures that they develop strong habits and that the process becomes rote. Logs may take any format that works for the legal researcher. Many researchers use a table format or keep notes in a narrative format. Once legal researchers become competent with the process, they may resort to keeping track with a simple checklist or an outline. At a minimum, useful logs should include the following:

   i. Source
   ii. How the source was accessed
   iii. Results
   iv. Notes/Thoughts
   v. Current-through/date information

i. Source Field of the Research Log

The Source Field requires legal researchers to adjust their thinking with respect to the concept of a source. 'Source' for purposes of a research log is defined expansively to include primary source of law, secondary sources, and finding aids. Additionally, general search engines like Google, Bing, Yahoo, are considered a source in a vein similar to an index or other finding aid in print. As well, because all search engines have their own proprietary relevancy ranking algorithm, it is necessary to keep track of the search engine used as well as the date searched.

ii. How Accessed Field of the Research Log

This field requires legal researchers to capture their entry point into a source. For online searches, researchers should copy and paste their exact query into the log. Sometimes, the Accessed Field may simply be that a link was selected from the prior search results list. When working with print materials, it is easy to collapse two steps into one by placing the finding aid (e.g., Index) in the 'How Accessed' field and the main volume consulted in the 'Source' field. This should be avoided because the finding aids often have their own currency date. If the finding aid is replaced with a more recent volume in the future, the legal researcher must decide whether to re-consult it.

For example, the below log entry collapses the finding aid step and the main volume step into one entry, which can be confusing. Because some online finding aids, including indexes and table of contents, may be separate databases, it is important to establish the habit of capturing this research effort as two discrete steps in the process.

Source: Am. Jur. 2d Costs to Credit Cards, for Courts

Accessed: From Index under F.

Results: Forum non conveniens

Thoughts: found good analysis and citations.

Date: Main volume dated 2015 and pocket parts dated May 2016.

iii. Results Field of the Research Log

Researchers should offer a description of the results set and include citations for the next resources they plan to consult. When the research process is at the point of examining the destination documents, researchers can include a rule of law or the language of a code or a brief description of a point of law as a result. This field does not include the researcher's thinking.

iv. Notes/Thoughts Field of the Research Log

The Notes/Thoughts information is one of the few pieces of information that may be left blank when capturing the research effort in a log. Where appropriate, it should be used by the legal researcher to capture thoughts as they arise or as connections are made. This is the field that legal researchers use to track additional information that must be gathered when they realize they have insufficient factual information from the client or client file. At times, a step is so straight forward that there is no need to capture any detail in this field. When legal researchers revisit their plans and logs at the end of the research process, it is often this column that helps them to make strides in developing research skills.

Generally, metacognition rather than cognition should be included in this field. Metacognition is a higher order of thinking. It typically involves the legal researcher asking the following types of questions:

Planning:
- Can I identify the issues and select appropriate strategies to be able to resolve them?
- Have I considered how much time this research project may take and plan accordingly?
- Have I predicted useful secondary sources to consult?
- Can I describe how to carry out research using these secondary sources?
- Have I predicted which type of primary law will govern?
- Have I considered all potential sources of primary law?
- Am I able to describe how I will use that primary law including the use of finding aids?
- Have I described the process for updating the law?

Monitoring:
- Can I summarize what I just learned from reading this secondary source or primary law?
- Am I able to assess how well I learned something new? Do I need to review additional materials that explain this same topic or idea?
- Am I able to change strategies when my result sets do not make sense? Do I know the questions to ask to determine why results do not make sense?
- Once a result is obtained, do I remember to check to see that it agrees with what I expected?
- Am I aware and do I understand why I am deviating from my legal research plan?
- Do I know which steps to skip if time is running short or clients have a tight budget?

Evaluating:
- Did I make a point of verifying everything: my understanding of the problem, citations to primary law and other documents I intend to use?
- Did I break down the problem into smaller research steps and was I able to put it all back together at the end?

- Did I recognize when I had a gap in knowledge as the research was unfolding and was I able to fill it?
- Can I identify what I learned from this research project to use in future similar projects?
- Can I identify which research strategies were effective and understand why?

v. Current-Through Field of the Research Log

Often, legal researchers keep sloppy information related to the "Current-Through" Field of a log. It is important to keep track of the current-through date for all materials. Even where the researcher is working with primary law material and the determination is made that the material is not germane to the research issue, it is useful to jot down the current-through date. This allows the researcher to be able to report back that this primary law material was consulted as of a particular date and deemed irrelevant. Often, finding applicable law entails a process of elimination and keeping track of what is considered to be "not relevant" is valuable. Clearly, others may raise the possibility of the applicability of a particular law and having captured this information in the log allows the legal researcher to respond, "yes, I checked that and as of (DA/MO/YEAR) date, the law was not relevant because...."

When referring to a pocket part, researchers should include the date on the pocket part and include how frequently it is updated. When carrying out a Google search, researchers should include the date of the research session itself. However, after a link from the Google results list is selected, the current through field should include the date that page was "last updated" or the date of the destination document.

IV. Conclusion

Planning and logging the research process are essential components of the research project. And while some may view them as time wasters; more experienced researchers realize that the contrary is true. While they require time at the outset and during the implementation phase, planning and logging increase efficiency and thoroughness. As well, they contribute to the legal researcher's ability to report back in a detailed and professional manner, including referring to publications by their proper names and titles. They are also particularly valuable when dealing with circumstances where despite hours of research, no definitive answer may be supplied or in circumstances where the legal researcher has been asked to prove the non-existence of a particular rule or norm (e.g., that a particular custom does not exist). In these circumstances, the legal researcher is in a position to describe the steps taken and the resources consulted to reach that conclusion.

Naturally, when planning at the outset, the legal researcher is invariably operating under conditions of incomplete understanding. As the researcher implements the plan and new insights are gained, adjustments to the original plan can be incorporated into the effort on the fly. This is to be expected. However, it is only when the legal researcher takes the time to review the plan against the log after the project is completed that the next research project will benefit from these gains. Having a written plan allows the legal researcher to revisit that plan at the end of the research project and examine it for ways to approach the next research project more efficiently.

Chapter 11

Cultural Competencies

I. Introduction

Examining the history and various definitions of cultural competency will broaden the U.S. legal researcher's ability to handle an international legal research project. The United Nations has articulated an approach to cultural competency within the context of peacekeeping and espoused the core values of integrity, diversity, and professionalism.[1] In addition, work with other cultures may often require multilingual competencies.[2] The roots of cultural study and observation of culture are often traced back to the discourse of American cultural anthropology.[3] Numerous scholars have pointed to Barna's "stumbling blocks" to achieving effective cultural communication: 1) assumption of similarities; 2) language differences; 3) nonverbal misinterpretation; 4) preconditions and stereotypes; 5) tendency to evaluate; and 6) high anxiety or tension.[4] This provides a starting point for achieving a preliminary understanding of

---

1. *See, e.g.,* Nana Odoi, Cultural Diversity in Peace Operations: Training Challenges, KAIPTC Paper, No. 4 (March 2005), http://www.kaiptc.org/Publications/Occasional-Papers/Documents/no_4.aspx [https://perma.cc/744J-AA7S].

2. *See, e.g.,* Raquel Aldana, Teaching Inter-Cultural and Bilingual Legal Competence: The Role of U.S. Law Schools, University of the Pacific McGeorge School of Law (2015), http://www.ialsnet.org/wordpress/wp-content/uploads/2015/08/Aldana.pdf [https://perma.cc/PZ9D-LC8C].

3. *See, e.g.,* George D. Spindler and Louise Spindler, Anthropologists View American Culture, 12 Ann. Rev. 49–78 (1983) (noting that Franz Boaz was one of the first anthropologists to have written about American culture).

4. *See* LaRay M. Barna and Milton J. Bennett, Association of American Colleges and Universities Summer Institute, Basic Concepts of Intercultural Communication,

cultural differences, but it is by no means exhaustive for purposes of carrying out legal research in a multicultural context. More generally, cultural competency might be defined as recognition and overall awareness of the implications of individualist, moderate, and collectivist cultures.[5]

Culturally diverse work, such as international lawyering or working with foreign laws and legal systems as an attorney, may be very demanding and require establishment of professional relationships built on mutual trust.[6] One example that illuminates this issue of cultural understanding and trust would be the separate doors at the United Nations for negotiating with States. The United Nations has three doors leading into mediation rooms because, in some cultures, just walking through the door first has negative connotations that would prevent success during the dispute resolution process.[7] As a result, each State party enters from their own respective doors and the United Nations mediator enters from a third door.

The U.S. legal researcher should work to gain a thorough understanding of international ethics and codes of conduct, a basic understanding of a foreign legal system and legal traditions, and should strive to achieve a baseline level of knowledge of the essential legal resources in the jurisdiction or cross-border transaction before embarking on an international legal research project.

---

http://archive.aacu.org/summerinstitutes/igea/documents/Allresources_000.pdf [https://perma.cc/UXC6-XHZV]. See also Bennett, Milton, Intercultural communication: A current perspective. In Milton J. Bennett (Ed.), Basic concepts of intercultural communication: Selected readings. (1998 Intercultural Press), http://www.mairstudents.info/intercultural_communication.pdf [https://perma.cc/6MNW-CUYW].

5. See DAVID LIVERMORE, LEADING WITH CULTURAL INTELLIGENCE: THE REAL SECRET TO SUCCESS 33 (2d ed. 2015); See generally DAVID LIVERMORE, EXPAND YOUR BORDERS: DISCOVER TEN CULTURAL CLUSTERS (2013) (identifying ten cultural clusters of the world and associated characteristics within the broad individualism/collectivism framework as Anglo, Arab, Confucian Asia, Eastern European, Germanic Europe, Latin America, Latin Europe, Nordic Europe, Southern Asia, and Sub-Saharan Africa).

6. See, e.g., Paul Lomio, Henrik Spang-Hanssen, and George Wilson, LEGAL RESEARCH METHODS IN A MODERN WORLD: A COURSEBOOK (3rd ed. 2011).

7. See, e.g., United Nations Office on Drugs and Crime, Training Manual on Alternative Dispute Resolution and Restorative Justice 60 (Oct., 2007), http://www.unodc.org/documents/nigeria//publications/Otherpublications/Training_manual_on_alternative_dispute_resolution_and_restorative_justice.pdf [https://perma.cc/M3NE-8KHK].

II. Codes of Conduct, Ethical Rules, and Bar Admission Requirements

To gain a grounding in cultural competency it is imperative to gather an understanding of the codes of conduct, ethical rules, and the bar admissions requirements in foreign jurisdictions. As noted by the American Society of International Law, there are many professional standards and codes of conduct plus specialty ethical rules for counsel who appear before international tribunals.[8] There are also international, European, and other national rules regarding choice of law ("double deontology") principles and emerging regional international standards to resolve choice of law issues.[9] The ABA publishes a comprehensive and current guide to the international bar admission requirements.[10] Cross-border transactions may intersect areas of criminal law, domestic and family law, employment law, and they may require corporate lawyers as in-house counsel, and non-traditional legal occupations. Overarching rules governing ethical obligations and transactions govern any international legal research project in conjunction with the local or municipal laws and legal system in the particular countries that are affected by the issue(s).

The ABA has model rules that anticipate international or transnational practice and adherence to the U.S. ethical rules as well as the ethical norms of other nations through choice of law provisions.[11] Other jurisdictions, such as the European Union and International Criminal Court, have similar codes of conduct for international practice and appearing before international tribunals.[12] These international ethical rules and international/regional rules for interna-

---

8. *See, e.g.,* A.S.I.L., Professor Laurel S. Terry, Codes of Conduct for International Tribunals and Arbitration, A.S.I.L. 103rd Annual Meeting (March 27, 2009, rev. May 11, 2009), http://www.personal.psu.edu/faculty/l/s/lst3/presentations%20for%20webpage/ASIL_Terry_Codes_International_Tribunals.pdf [https://perma.cc/9CCC-BDNZ].

9. *Id.;* see also Catherine Rogers, Regulating International Arbitrators: A Functional Approach to Developing Standards of Conduct, 41 STANFORD J. INT'L L. 53 (2005).

10. *See* Nancy A. Matos and Russell W. Dombrow, THE ABA GUIDE TO INTERNATIONAL BAR ADMISSIONS (2012).

11. *See, e.g.,* MODEL RULES OF PROF'L CONDUCT r. 8.5 cmt. 7 (AM. BAR. ASS'N 2016) (Choice of Law comment).

12. *See* CODE OF CONDUCT FOR THE EUROPEAN LAWYERS, CCBE (May 19, 2006), https://www.sav-fsa.ch/de/documents/dynamiccontent/2-1_berufsregeln_e_08-09-06.pdf [https://perma.cc/25WT-325N]; see also CODE OF PROFESSIONAL CONDUCT FOR COUNSEL, ICC (Dec. 2, 2005), https://www.icc-cpi.int/NR/rdonlyres/BD397ECF-8CA8-44EF-92C6-AB4BEBD55BE2/140121/ICCASP432Res1_English.pdf [https://perma.cc/8WRF-SZBV].

tional procedure and associated explanations are often very detailed for specialty areas of international practice; thus, they must be consulted and reviewed by international attorneys or U.S. attorneys with a transnational practice. The U.S. norms and ethical rules may deviate significantly from other traditions, so it is important to carefully consult the ethical and civil/commercial/criminal rules of procedure in foreign jurisdictions.

Even when making every effort, it is virtually impossible to gain full cultural competency in another legal system. An apt analogy involves considering two States whose values, beliefs, attitudes, culture and legal system are represented by glasses with different colored lenses. The person who grows up in State A where everyone wears glasses with a yellow lens sees and understands the world through that lens. The person who grows up in State B where everyone wears eyeglasses with a blue lens sees and understands the world through that lens. When a person from State A travels to State B, the State A person views State B by superimposing the blue lens over their yellow lens. The best that a State A person can do by way gaining cultural competence in State B is to view and understand it through a green lens.[13] Even where U.S. legal researchers work hard to understand another State's legal system, it is virtually impossible to remove every bias that exists from being raised, educated, and schooled in law in a home jurisdiction. Acknowledging these challenges, the next section provides the resources that can be used to begin to gather an understanding of other legal systems and cultures.

III. Researching and Understanding Selected Legal Systems and Traditions

Determining whether a foreign legal system is rooted in a common law, civil law, customary law, religious law, or mixed legal tradition is essential to understanding it. This process informs the legal researcher of the types of sources that will be used for researching and allows the researcher to make an assessment of the difficulty level of the research project. Juriglobe offers a useful interactive map of the prevalent legal traditions of the world.[14]

---

13. *A Dialogue about Measuring Intercultural Competence*, Marquette's Office of International Education and Center for Teaching and Learning (April 2, 2013) (hosted by Dr. Darla Deardorff).

14. See the University of Ottawa, Juriglobe, http://www.juriglobe.ca/eng/ [https://perma.cc/9JM7-3M84] for a world visualization of the types of prevalent legal systems for international legal research.

IV. Sources of Law in Common Law Legal Traditions

U.S. legal researchers are familiar with the federal sources of law for common law legal traditions. The overarching legal document is the constitution, where one exists.[15] The remainder of the sources are generated through the three branches of government: statutes from the legislature or parliament; administrative rules and regulations, or delegated legislation from the agencies of the executive branch; and opinions and decisions from the judiciary. Research involves determining whether an issue is governed by the U.S. Constitution, U.S. Code, agency's rules and regulations, or case law. Often, issues are governed by a combination of these sources and the legal researcher must understand the hierarchy of authority and how they interrelate in order to carry out efficient and effective research.

These primary sources of law must be distinguished from secondary resources. Secondary sources contain explanations and commentary or criticism of the primary law. In simplest terms, secondary resources are all writings other than the law itself. After gaining a background understanding through the use of secondary sources, most legal researchers find that carrying out the research process by consulting the sources of primary law in the order listed above, by descending hierarchy of authority, tends to be the most efficient.[16]

V. Sources of Law in Civil Law Legal Traditions

In contrast, under a civil law tradition, the constitution, code, and administrative rules and regulations are primary law. Judicial decisions and scholarly commentary, on the other hand, are considered secondary resources. Although both judicial decisions and scholarly commentary are considered

---

15. Although the U.S. and England rest on common law legal traditions, England's Constitution is not a single, written document, similar to our U.S. Constitution. Rather, there are a series of documents and laws that comprise the basis for sovereignty and England's legal structures.

16. Where a common law issue is at the center of the research, legal researchers typically move from a secondary source directly to case law research.

secondary resources, scholarly commentary is typically researched and consulted before case law. Civil law legal traditions do not follow the doctrine of *stare decisis* like common law traditions.[17] The legal research process in civil law traditions involves looking first to the code or statutes before determining whether to research case law, as its weight of authority is only persuasive. Indeed, researchers in civil law traditions are more likely to turn to scholarly interpretation and explanation of a particular code section before considering what judges might have to say about it.

The concept of finding the rule of law as stated in judicial decisions is an unusual concept for legal researchers who have been educated and licensed as lawyers in civil legal traditions. It is one of the major features that distinguishes legal research in common law legal traditions from civil law legal traditions. Because there is no need to search case law to uncover the rule of law in civil law systems, it follows that the publication process and the need for some of the finding aids, searchable databases, and research tools that are available in common law traditions are not replicated in civil law systems. For example, the U.S. legal researcher should not expect to find large, comprehensive, searchable databases of case law in civil law systems, nor will the U.S. legal researcher find the equivalent of the West's Topic and Key Number System replicated in civil law systems. There simply is not a need because of the manner in which the rule of law is created in legal systems that rest on civil law traditions.

A caveat must be offered for the legal researcher whose home jurisdiction is of common law legal tradition when researching in a civil law tradition. It is not merely the order in which to carry out the research or the weight of authority afforded to the various sources that distinguishes common law jurisdictions from civil law jurisdictions. The very nature of the legal system itself, how lawyers practice including the impact of procedural laws, as well as other historical influences, affects how a legal researcher approaches the research. At a minimum, a U.S. legal researcher carrying out the research process in a civil law tradition must consult a legal research guide.[18] Even then, the U.S. legal researcher should remain mindful of what cannot be known and understood having been schooled in the U.S. legal education system. Lawyers,

---

17. Although it has been demonstrated that civil law traditions and courts within that system are reluctant to hand down conflicting opinions on the same legal issue. See GUIDO ACQUAVIVA & FAUSTO POCAR, Stare Decisis, MAX PLANCK ENCYCLOPEDIA OF PUBLIC INTERNATIONAL LAW (Oxford University Press 2016).

18. *See, e.g.,* GLOBALEX, http://www.nyulawglobal.org/globalex/ [https://perma.cc/5XR9-6CKG] (research guides at New York University School of Law). Research guides are covered in Chapter 10.

therefore, sometimes retain local counsel when researching and practicing in foreign jurisdictions.

VI. Sources of Law in Religious-Based Legal Systems

Today, there are few pure, religious-based traditions. Rather, religious-based traditions tend to be "mixed" in the sense that they have their roots in a religious document as well as in either a civil, common, or custom based legal tradition. Generally, the process for religious-based legal research follows the common law, civil law, or customary law approach with the added step of identifying and finding the relevant religious document. Researchers must understand how the religious-based document interacts with the other primary sources of law within a jurisdiction. Determining its level in the hierarchy of authority is vital. Sometimes it serves as a supplement to national law. Other times, it governs only a certain subject area of the law, for example, family law. Consulting a reputable legal research guide at the outset of the process will help the researcher to place the religious-based document in context.[19] In addition, research into the historical background of the legal tradition will lead to a more robust understanding of the system and how the sources of law operate within it.

The Islamist legal system is the most widespread and prevailing religious-based legal tradition. The religious component of the Islamist legal system rests on Shari'a law. Shari'a law is comprised of two primary sources, the Quran and Sunna. Where there is conflict between the two, the Quran preempts the Sunna.[20] There are two schools of thought in Islamic law related to secondary sources. The Sunni school subscribes to interpretation by consensus (Ijma) and reasoning by analogy (Qiyas) whereas the Shi'a school subscribes to consensus (Ijma) and reason (Aql).[21] Islamist jurisprudence developed from these approaches is called Fiqh.[22] Garnering a basic understanding of the similarities and differences in various religion-based legal traditions helps the legal re-

---

19. *See, e.g.,* Marylin J. Raisch, Update: Religious Legal Systems in Comparative Law: A Guide to Introductory Research, GLOBALEX (Apr. 2017), http://www.nyulawglobal.org/ globalex/Religious_Legal_Systems1.html [https://perma.cc/8H2V-ZDN4].

20. *Id.*

21. See Said Mahmoudi, *Islamic Approach to International Law,* MPEPIL (April 2011).

22. *Id.*

searcher to develop an approach for tackling a legal research problem involving one of these religious-based traditions or involving a mixed, religious-based tradition.

VII. Sources of Law in Custom-Based Legal Systems

Today, there are few pure custom-based legal systems. Rather, like religious-based systems, they tend to be mixed. Customary law systems are based on respect for the traditions of a community's ancestors. Practices are handed down over time and become obligatory. Adherence stems from pressure of the group or community.[23]

The same approach and strategies described above for religious-based traditions work well with custom-based traditions: researchers should identify the custom and ensure they understand where it fits in the hierarchy of authority or how it is related to other customs and sources. Researchers should be mindful that legal systems rooted in customary law traditions tend to be focused on restoring the community to a whole by addressing imbalances and restoring damaged relationships.[24]

VIII. Source of Law in Mixed Legal Traditions or Pluralistic Legal Traditions

There are a number of combinations for mixed and pluralistic legal traditions: common law/civil law, such as it exists in Louisiana in the United States and as is seen in Quebec in Canada; civil law/customary law as exists in Japan and North and South Korea; and civil law/Muslim law as exists in Syria, Iran, and Iraq. In some sub-Saharan African States, multiple legal traditions operate simultaneously. For example, the legal system in Djibouti rests on a pluralistic tradition of civil, Islamist, and customary law.[25]

---

23. Dana Zartner, *Courts, Codes and Custom: Legal Tradition and State Policy Toward International Human Rights and Environmental Law* (2014).

24. *Id.*, at 193.

25. *See, e.g.*, Mustafe Mohamed H. Dahir, *Researching the Legal System of Dijibouti*, GlobaLex (Nov/Dec 2015), http://www.nyulawglobal.org/globalex/Djibouti.html.

As with religious traditions, it is important when researching in mixed or pluralistic legal traditions to ascertain at the outset how the sources of law in the system interrelate. Is there a distinct hierarchy? Is the mixed system truly intermixed or does one legal tradition dominate certain subject areas while another in different subject areas? For example, in Hong Kong, a common law/customary law mixed tradition, Chinese customary law governs matters of family and land tenure while English common law governs the remainder of subject areas.[26] The importance of consulting a research guide early in the process and possibly obtaining local counsel in these mixed jurisdictions cannot be overstated.[27] A good research guide will describe primary and secondary sources of law and offer titles to the publications that contain the law.[28] Overall, the comprehensive research guide should offer some grounding in the hierarchy of authority and an efficient approach for handling the research process.

IX. Resources and Research Process for Selected Jurisdictions

This section does not attempt to comprehensively review all legal systems or address every obstacle to cultural competency when confronting international legal research issues. Rather, it provides an overview of the research process in selected jurisdictions: Argentina, Brazil, China and Japan to highlight the differences that researchers can expect to encounter. By exploring these various systems which are rooted in civil, religious and pluralistic legal traditions, researchers can begin to understand the strategies and sources available for attempting to gain a greater level of cultural competency. For each jurisdiction an exploration as it relates to human rights is included because these are overwhelmingly popular areas of public international legal research that an attorney with a global practice encounters.

---

26. See Hong Kong Department of Justice, Legal System in Hong Kong, http://www.doj.gov.hk/eng/legal/ [https://perma.cc/WBD2-2JTN].

27. See Anna Stolley Persky, *Despite Globalization, Lawyers Find New Barriers to Practicing Abroad*, ABA JOURNAL (Nov. 1, 2011), http://www.abajournal.com/magazine/article/the_new_world_despite_globalization_lawyers_find_new_barriers_to_practicing/ [https://perma.cc/R5NV-7NDH].

28. *See, e.g.*, Thomas Reynolds & Arturo Flores, Foreign Law Guide, BRILLONLINE (Marci Hoffman ed. 2015), http://referenceworks.brillonline.com/browse/foreign-law-guide (https://perma.cc/A5VH-9N5Q).

A. Argentinian Law Research

The Argentinian legal system is derived from the French and German civil code traditions and the Brazilian civil code and is a jurisdiction with a Roman civil law tradition with a Federal model.[29] Argentina (like Mexico) is one of the few Latin American countries with a developed and fairly consistently applied judicial and legislative structure.[30] There is a federal and provincial system of legislatures and associated judicial branches.[31] There are numerous helpful online resources and databases for learning about Argentina's legal system. Researchers traditionally begin with an authoritative reference work like Reynolds and Flores' Foreign Law Guide, which most academic law libraries subscribe to online or in print.[32] Additionally, foreign law research often begins with basic country information and economic data, such as the country overviews provided in the CIA World Factbook.[33] One challenge for most U.S. researchers when researching Argentinian law is finding English-language materials because most legal information is provided in the vernacular.[34]

i. Human Rights: Argentina

There are myriad helpful websites for beginning to understand the Argentinian legal profession, but the Reynolds and Flores Foreign Law Guide[35] and the GlobaLex article with an overview of the legal resources in Argentina by

---

29. *See* Thomas Reynolds & Arturo Flores, Foreign Law Guide, Argentina—Legislation and the Judicial System, BrillOnline (2012), http://referenceworks.brillonline.com/browse/foreign-law-guide [https://perma.cc/A5VH-9N5Q].

30. *Id.*

31. *See* Gloria Orrego Hoyos, Update: A Research Guide to the Argentine Legal System GLOBALEX (Sept. 2015), http://www.nyulawglobal.org/globalex/Argentina1.html [https://perma.cc/E9CA-WUYJ].

32. *See* Reynolds and Flores, *supra* note 28 (Argentina).

33. The World Factbook, CIA, https://www.cia.gov/library/publications/the-world-factbook/ [https://perma.cc/6PCV-W956] (provides country overviews for every foreign jurisdiction's geography, people and society, government, economy, energy, communications, transportation, military and security, and a summary of transnational issues).

34. *See, e.g.,* Global Legal Monitor, LAW LIBRARY OF CONG. (Apr. 25, 2014), https://www.loc.gov/law/foreign-news/article/argentina-proposal-to-reform-the-criminal-code/ [https://perma.cc/KEG9-XRAX], reports on Argentina, which directs researcher to websites in Spanish for the Penal Code); Other jurisdictions can be located on the Global Legal Monitor at the Law Library of Congress as well. Global Legal Monitor, LAW LIBRARY OF CONG., https://www.loc.gov/law/foreign-news/jurisdiction/ [https://perma.cc/KM2D-W4TX].

35. *See* Reynolds, *supra* note 29 and accompanying text.

Gloria Orrego Hoyos[36] are authoritative sources that should be consulted first. Researchers may also consult the Law Library of Congress Guide to Law Online: Nations of the World that includes Argentina as a jurisdiction for foreign law research.[37] Although a bit outdated, there is also an LLRX article that provides a guide to the Argentinian Executive, Legislative, and Judicial System authored by several members of the judiciary in Argentina.[38] The BBC offers a great country overview for Argentina and its political structure through a recent country profile.[39]

For human rights issues, attorneys are well-served to look at the recent Universal Periodic Review for Argentina by the United Nations Office of the High Commissioner on Human Rights to glean recent human rights monitoring and trends.[40] Additionally, Human Rights Watch[41] and Amnesty International[42] have annual country reports, including those specific to Argentina, for national monitoring of human rights conditions and abuses while monitoring human rights violations on an international scale as NGOs. The International Committee of the Red Cross ("ICRC") monitors country-specific abuses of human rights in conjunction with the Geneva Conventions and provides a detailed national implementation database for international humanitarian law that includes Argentina.[43] These online, free databases can assist researchers with specific Argentinian research and finding Argentinian legislation or reports on international human rights issues. Finally, Argentina is a member of

---

36. *See* Hoyos, *supra* note 31 and accompanying text.

37. *See* Guide to Law Online: Nations of the World, LAW LIBRARY OF CONG., http://www.loc.gov/law/help/guide/nations.php [https://perma.cc/87UH-N5XQ] (Argentina).

38. *See* C.P. Ernesto Nicolás Kozameh Jr. et al., http://www.llrx.com/2001/07/features-guide-to-the-argentine-executive-legislative-and-judicial-system/ [https://perma.cc/KG9D-73PR], LLRX (July 15, 2001).

39. *See* Argentina Country Profile, BBC (Mar. 22, 2016), http://www.bbc.com/news/world-latin-america-18707514 [https://perma.cc/DS7Y-VMFQ].

40. *See* Universal Periodic Review—Argentina, U.N. HUMAN RIGHTS OFFICE OF THE HIGH COMM'R (Apr. 16, 2008), http://www.ohchr.org/EN/Pages/Home.aspx [https://perma.cc/A4JP-LGCN]; *see also* Argentina, U.N. HUMAN RIGHTS OFFICE OF THE HIGH COMM'R, http://www.ohchr.org [https://perma.cc/A4JP-LGCN] (the U.N. human rights country profile page for human rights treaties and other documentation for Argentina).

41. *See* World Report: Argentina, HUMAN RIGHTS WATCH, https://www.hrw.org/world-report/2015/country-chapters/argentina [https://perma.cc/95CT-6YFB].

42. *See* Annual Report: Argentina 2015/2016, AMNESTY INT'L, https://www.amnesty.org/en/countries/americas/argentina/report-argentina/ [https://perma.cc/UB6D-NQG2].

43. *See* National Implementation Database, ICRC, https://ihl-databases.icrc.org/applic/ihl/ihl-nat.nsf/vwLawsByCategorySelected.xsp?xp_countrySelected=AR [https://perma.cc/89H7-MG28] (search for Argentina under the by state search option).

the Organization of American States,[44] and is involved with the Inter-American Court of Human Rights[45] for human rights disputes between member States and the Inter-American Commission on Human Rights.[46] It is important to research those vital portals of information for country-specific human rights information concerning Argentina.

B. Brazilian Law and Research

Brazil is the second largest nation in the Western hemisphere and has roots in the Spanish/Portuguese legal traditions and the Napoleonic civil code traditions.[47] The Organization of American States also includes Brazil as a member state[48] and the World Legal Information Institute (WorldLII) also includes information for Brazil in its classification of foreign legal resources.[49] It is challenging for U.S. researchers to find Brazilian legal information in English. They often resort to using basic web translation tools such as Google translate and Google Chrome's webpage translator for purposes of research,[50] or for more formal needs, they might consider hiring a legal translator. The Law Library of Congress's Guide to Law Online: Nations of the World provides a thorough list of links for governmental and legal information concerning Brazil that are useful when beginning foreign legal research.[51] The CIA Factbook[52] and BBC Country Profile[53] for Brazil provide comprehensive background information for the country's economic, political, and social facts. GlobaLex (NYU) also

44. *See* Member States, OAS, http://www.oas.org/en/member_states/default.asp [https://perma.cc/8N4Y-X82A].

45. *See* INTER-AM. COURT OF HUMAN RIGHTS, http://www.corteidh.or.cr/index.php/en [https://perma.cc/E3N4-9NUG].

46. *See* INTER-AM. COMM'N ON HUMAN RIGHTS, OAS, http://www.oas.org/en/iachr/ [https://perma.cc/T8G5-2PFW].

47. *See* Reynolds, *supra* note 28 (Brazil).

48. *See, e.g.,* Member States: Brazil, OAS, http://www.oas.org/en/member_states/member_state.asp?sCode=BRA [https://perma.cc/GWF7-444L].

49. *See* WORLDLII, http://www.worldlii.org [https://perma.cc/9G53-9Q9B].

50. *See, e.g.,* Google Translate, https://translate.google.com/m/translate [https://perma.cc/MND4-Q7EN] (an operating system that provides a list of languages, including Portuguese, in which a researcher can translate foreign material into English).

51. *See* Guide to Law Online, *supra* note 32 (Brazil).

52. The World Factbook, *supra* note 37 (Brazil).

53. Brazil Country Profile, BBC, http://news.bbc.co.uk/2/hi/americas/country_profiles/1227110.stm [https://perma.cc/Y2CD-WGSK].

offers a research guide for beginning legal research in Brazil and discovering authoritative websites or databases for research.[54]

i. Human Rights: Brazil

For human rights issues, lawyers should consult the recent Universal Periodic Review for Brazil by the U.N. Office of the High Commissioner on Human Rights and its Special Rapporteur to learn and gather information about recent human rights monitoring and trends.[55] Additionally, Human Rights Watch[56] and Amnesty International[57] have annual country reports, including those specific to Brazil, for national monitoring of human rights conditions and abuses while monitoring human rights violations on an international scale. The International Committee of the Red Cross ("ICRC") monitors country-specific abuses of human rights in conjunction with the Geneva Conventions and provides a detailed national implementation database for international humanitarian law that includes Brazil.[58] These online, free databases can assist researchers with specific Brazilian legal research and finding Brazilian legislation or reports on international human rights issues. Finally, Brazil is a member of the Organization of American States,[59] including the Inter-American Court of Human Rights[60] for human rights disputes between member states and Inter-American Commission on Human Rights.[61] It is important to research those vital portals of information for country-specific human rights information for Brazil.

---

54. *See* Monaliza Da Silva, Update: *Doing Legal Research in Brazil*, GLOBALEX (June 2015), http://www.nyulawglobal.org/globalex/Brazil1.html [https://perma.cc/6PYK-YK9D].

55. *See Universal Periodic Review—Brazil*, U.N. HUMAN RIGHTS OFFICE OF THE HIGH COMM'R (Apr. 11, 2008), http://www.ohchr.org/EN/HRBodies/UPR/Pages/brsession1.aspx [https://perma.cc/F7U7-XDWZ]; *see also Brazil*, U.N. HUMAN RIGHTS OFFICE OF THE HIGH COMM'R, http://www.ohchr.org/EN/countries/LACRegion/Pages/BRIndex.aspx [https://perma.cc/8F4X-44TT] (the U.N. human rights country profile page for human rights treaties and other documentation for Brazil).

56. *See World Report 2015: Brazil*, HUMAN RIGHTS WATCH, https://www.hrw.org/world-report/2015/country-chapters/brazil [https://perma.cc/E8T5-J4RA].

57. *See* Amnesty International, *Annual Report: Brazil 2015/2016*, AMNESTY INT'L, https://www.amnesty.org/en/countries/americas/brazil/report-brazil/ [https://perma.cc/2CSQ-MVX9].

58. *See National Implementation Database*, ICRC, https://www.icrc.org/en/war-and-law/ihl-domestic-law [https://perma.cc/M43F-TWTR] (search for Brazil under the *by state* search option).

59. *See* OAS, *supra* note 44.

60. *See* INTER-AM. COURT OF HUMAN RIGHTS, *supra* note 45.

61. *See* INTER-AM. COMM'N ON HUMAN RIGHTS, *supra* note 46.

C. Chinese Law and Research

China has a rich history of dynasties in its legal traditions and is derived from Confucian principles. There are numerous helpful online sources, such as Asian Legal Information Institute (AsianLII),[62] which provides a free on-line repository of legal information. Although there was great resistance in the twentieth century to develop a more formalized legal system, there are now general legal codes that govern Chinese law in the Republic.[63] The CIA Factbook has a good general overview of the Chinese demographics, political system, and transnational issues.[64] GlobaLex provides a research guide for beginning exploration of the Chinese laws and the Hong Kong legal system.[65] Researchers should also consult the website for the Ministry of Foreign Affairs in China which provides a good overview of China and its trade history for beginning research.[66]

i. Human Rights: China

China has adopted some domestic human rights legislation. Its legislation is available online at LawInfoChina or through Westlaw China (formerly IsinoLaw by subscription).[67] The BBC country profile for China is also informative for a general overview of country conditions and economic data.[68] International lawyers should also peruse the recent Universal Periodic Review

---

62. AsianLII, http://www.asianlii.org [https://perma.cc/R7ZR-GC89].

63. *See* Reynolds, *supra* note 28 (China).

64. *See* The World Factbook, *supra* note 33 (China),

65. Roy Sturgeon & Sergio Stone, Update: One Country, Two Systems of Legal Research: A Brief Guide to Finding the Law of China's Hong Kong Special Administrative Region, GlobaLex, http://www.nyulawglobal.org/globalex/Hong_Kong1.html [https://perma.cc/QCQ3-P2L8] (last updated March, 2011); *see also* Guide to Law Online, *supra* note 32 (China).

66. *See* Ministry of Foreign Affairs of the People's Republic of China, http://www.fmprc.gov.cn/mfa_eng/wjb_663304/zzjg_663340/tyfls_665260/ [https://perma.cc/8JZX-53Y4], *see also* Michael J. Meagher & Lucia Lian, Chinese Law for Lao Wai: A Survey of Chinese Law for American Business Lawyers, 51-Feb. B. B.J. 17 (2007) (summarizing Chinese Law for American business lawyers).

67. *See, e.g.*, LawInfoChina, http://www.lawinfochina.com [https://perma.cc/TN4B-K3XJ] (translating Chinese domestic legislation into English); *see also* Westlaw China, http://www.westlawchina.com/index_en.html [https://perma.cc/CS3E-Z6E7].

68. *See China Country Profile*, BBC (Aug. 31, 2016), http://www.bbc.com/news/world-asia-pacific-13017877 [https://perma.cc/MJY2-3WQC] (noting that China is the world's most populous country).

for China by the United Nations Office of the High Commissioner on Human Rights to ascertain recent human rights monitoring and trends.[69] Human Rights Watch[70] and Amnesty International[71] have annual country reports, including those covering China, for national monitoring of human rights conditions and abuses. The International Committee of the Red Cross ("ICRC") monitors country-specific abuses of human rights in conjunction with the Geneva Conventions and provides a detailed national implementation database for international humanitarian law that includes China.[72] These free online databases can assist researchers with specific Chinese human rights legislation and finding reports on international human rights issues. The Chinese Ministry of Foreign Affairs provides a comprehensive website for researching Chinese trade policy.[73] Overall, China has a strong and active presence within the international community and the United Nations.[74]

D. Japanese Law and Research

Japan has a unique tradition of a constitution, acts of the Diet, treaties, judicial precedent, and scholarly opinion; there are several helpful websites, such as Asian Legal Information Institute (AsianLII),[75] that provide an online repository of legal information. The Japanese legal system is modeled on a parliamentary system and several historic Asian legal traditions, including Chinese law. It has both a parliamentary structure for promulgating acts and a so-

---

69. *See Universal Periodic Review—China*, U.N. HUMAN RIGHTS OFFICE OF THE HIGH COMM'R, http://www.ohchr.org/EN/HRBodies/UPR/Pages/UPRCNStakeholdersInfoS4.aspx https://perma.cc/LD9E-2V46; *see also* China, U.N. HUMAN RIGHTS OFFICE OF THE HIGH COMM'R, http://www.ohchr.org/EN/HRBodies/UPR/Pages/UPRCNStakeholdersInfoS4.aspx [https://perma.cc/LD9E-2V46] (the U.N. human rights country profile page for human rights treaties and other documentation for China).

70. *See World Report 2015: China*, HUMAN RIGHTS WATCH, https://www.hrw.org/world-report/2015/country-chapters/china-and-tibet [https://perma.cc/BDJ6-VEP6].

71. *See China*, AMNESTY INT'L, https://www.amnesty.org/en/countries/asia-and-the-pacific/china/ [https://perma.cc/E5YM-H86X].

72. *See National Implementation Database*, ICRC, https://www.icrc.org/en/war-and-law/ihl-domestic-law [https://perma.cc/M43F-TWTR] (search for China under the *by state* search option).

73. MINISTRY OF FOREIGN AFFAIRS OF THE PEOPLE'S REPUBLIC OF CHINA, http://www.fmprc.gov.cn/mfa_eng/ [https://perma.cc/U2AY-785N].

74. *See* PERMANENT MISSION OF THE PEOPLE'S REPUBLIC OF CHINA TO THE U.N., http://www.china-un.org/eng/ [https://perma.cc/A99A-9HK3].

75. AsianLII, *supra* note 62.

phisticated judiciary.[76] The CIA World Fact Book offers an overview of the Japanese demographics, political system, and transnational issues.[77] GlobaLex (NYU) has a guide for beginning Japanese legal research.[78] Researchers might also consult the Japanese Ministry of Justice website which compiles an overview of Japan and its history for beginning research.[79]

i. Human Rights: Japan

Japan has adopted some domestic human rights legislation and is also a party to international human rights conventions.[80] The BBC country profile for Japan is informative for a general overview of country conditions and economic data.[81] International lawyers are also advised to look at the recent Universal Periodic Review for Japan by the U.N. Office of the High Commissioner on Human Rights to ascertain recent human rights monitoring and trends.[82] Human Rights Watch[83] and Amnesty International[84] have annual country reports, including those for Japan, for national monitoring of human rights conditions and abuses. The International Committee of the Red Cross ("ICRC") also monitors any country-specific abuses of human rights within the frame-

---

76. *See* Reynolds, *supra* note 28 (Japan).

77. *See* The World Factbook, *supra* note 33 (Japan).

78. Keiko Okuhara, UPDATE: Japanese Law Research Guide, GLOBALEX (March, 2015), http://www.nyulawglobal.org/globalex/Japan1.html [https://perma.cc/3ZYW-LT7J]; see also Guide to Law Online, *supra* note 37 (Japan).

79. *See* MINISTRY OF JUSTICE, http://www.moj.go.jp/ENGLISH/ [https://perma.cc/ UXC2-WSMR] (website for Japan's Ministry of Justice).

80. *See, e.g.,* Japanese Judicial System, JAPAN FED'N OF BAR ASS'NS, http://www.nichiben-ren.or.jp/en/about/judicial_system/judicial_system.html [https://perma.cc/XDZ6-XHDH] (description of the Japanese legal system).

81. *See* Japan Country Profile, BBC (Feb. 17, 2016), http://www.bbc.com/news/world-asia-pacific-14918801 [https://perma.cc/96RW-KYJT].

82. *See* Universal Periodic Review—Japan, U.N. HUMAN RIGHTS OFFICE OF THE HIGH COMM'R (May 9, 2008), http://www.ohchr.org/EN/HRBodies/UPR/PAGES/JPSession2.aspx [https://perma.cc/8NYY-LMHJ]; see also Japan, U.N. HUMAN RIGHTS OFFICE OF THE HIGH COMM'R, http://www.ohchr.org/EN/HRBodies/UPR/PAGES/JPSession2.aspx [https://perma. cc/8NYY-LMHJ] (the U.N. human rights country profile page for human rights treaties and other documentation for Japan).

83. *See* Japan, HUMAN RIGHTS WATCH (Aug. 30, 2016), https://www.hrw.org/asia/japan [https://perma.cc/BM5F-K7TV].

84. *See* Annual Report: Japan 2015/2016, AMNESTY INT'L, https://www.amnesty.org/en/ countries/asia-and-the-pacific/japan/ [https://perma.cc/TV47-6BBV].

work of the Geneva Conventions for Japan.[85] Overall, Japan has a history of recently supporting good human rights practices and an active presence within the United Nations.[86]

X. Conclusion

Although it is difficult to become fully culturally competent, simply acknowledging the inherent biases that prevent U.S. researchers from achieving full competency is a strong first step. Researchers should make every effort to understand the legal codes of conduct of foreign jurisdictions or that govern practice in international courts and tribunals; appreciate the cultural norms, legal history and customs of those from other jurisdictions; and utilize the available foreign law resources. Increasingly, researching and practicing law in a global community requires working with others who have been raised, educated, practice law in foreign jurisdictions. Naturally, these others lack full U.S. cultural competency in the same way we do in their cultures. U.S. legal researchers can develop their skills and understanding by recognizing the bidirectional challenges that arise when researching and interacting in the international system.

---

85. *See* National Implementation Database, ICRC, https://www.icrc.org/en/war-and-law/ihl-domestic-law [https://perma.cc/M43F-TWTR] (search for Japan under the by state search option).

86. *See* PERMANENT MISSION OF JAPAN TO THE U.N., https://perma.cc/BR4S-5G82.

Index